D1561743

POISON WIDOWS

ALSO BY GEORGE COOPER

*Lost Love: A True Story of Passion, Murder,
and Justice in Old New York*

*A Voluntary Tax? New Perspectives on
Sophisticated Estate Tax Avoidance*

POISON

WIDOWS

A TRUE STORY OF WITCHCRAFT, ARSENIC, AND MURDER

GEORGE COOPER

ST. MARTIN'S PRESS ❧ NEW YORK

A THOMAS DUNNE BOOK.
An imprint of St. Martin's Press.

Photo Credits (references to pages of photo inserts): p. 1:
Alfonsi, LaVecchio, HSP; Cerrone, Romualdo, UA; pp. 2, 10,
and 11: HSP; pp. 3, 4, 5, and 15: UA; p. 6: Arena, Rodio, UA;
Carina, Cassetti, HSP; p. 7: McDevitt, Exhumation, Guide, HSP;
Romualdo, UA; p. 8: Alfonsi, Display, UA; Myer, HSP; Spirits,
Collection of Milton Liedner; p. 9: Favato, UA; Valenti/Polselli,
Favato Home, HSP; p. 12: Stella and Lawyers, HSP; Alexander,
D'Alonzo, UA; p. 13: Rose to jail, Cacopardo, UA; New Rose,
Rose and Rita, HSP; p. 14: McDevitt, UA; Petrillo, Sortino,
Scoreboard, HSP; p. 16: Stella and sons, U of P; Rose and
family, Collection of Grace Buttacavoli and Joseph Buttacavoli.
HSP—Historical Society of Pennsylvania; UA—Urban
Archives, Temple University, Philadelphia, Pennsylvania; U of
P—The University Archives and Records Center, University of
Pennsylvania.

Design by Victoria Kuskowski

Library of Congress Cataloging-in-Publication Data

Cooper George.
    Poison widows : A true story of witchcraft, arsenic, and
    murder / by George Cooper
        p. cm.
    ISBN 0-312-19947-3
    1. Bolber, Morris, d. 1954. 2. Petrillo, Herman, d.
1941. 3. Petrillo,Paul,d.1939. 4. Murder—Pennsylvania—
Philadelphia—Case studies.
    5. Insurance, Life—Corrupt practices—Pennsylvania—
Philadelphia—Case studies. I. Title.
HV6534.P5C66   1999
364.15'23'0974811—dc21   98-43796
                                                        CIP

First Edition: March 1999

10   9   8   7   6   5   4   3   2   1

TO MY WIFE, JUDY,
WITH WHOM I SHARE EVERYTHING
IN JOY AND GOOD HEALTH,
INCLUDING PASTA

CONTENTS

INTRODUCTION

Passyunk Avenue cuts across the regular grid of South Philadelphia streets, an old Indian trail proudly asserting its historic right to go where it wants, rather than where city planners might have put it. At one time it marked the southern edge of the city, the point below which civilization gave way to less raucous rural entertainments. By the 1930s, however, the city had spread miles farther, to its current boundaries, and Passyunk had a new role, as a commercial and entertainment spine of the growing "South Philly" Italian immigrant population.

Numbering only three hundred in 1870 and only a few thousand in 1890, the Italian-born population of the city had exploded to 76,734 in 1910 and more than 155,000 by 1930. They formed a community, a Little Italy, that centered on this street they called "Pass-shunk," particularly the East 1600 to 1900 blocks. Passyunk was not a grand boulevard, only wide enough for one lane of traffic in each direction. Horses still being used to pull delivery wagons clogged its narrow course, and children felt safe shooting marbles against the curb. But for a population that came largely from bucolic villages of southern Italy, it was enough of a thoroughfare. Right in the middle of the 1800 block, where Passyunk intercepted Thirteenth and Mifflin Streets, making a triangular island, horses paused to drink at a fountain, leaving a mushy residue the formerly rural population found reminiscent.

Passyunk's character came not from its size but from its irregular orientation, and from the merchants who clustered along it. The shops offered everything the immigrants might desire, whether from the traditions they understood (Anthony Mazzeo's barbershop at number 1602, Phil Santomaria's tailor shop at number 1716, Michele Brancato's fruit stand at number 1902) or the modern world they wished to join (the Alahambra movie theater at number 1628, Katten's gas and electric fixtures at number 1800, the Amoco station run by Tony "Cadillac" at number 1824). In the evening after work, the sidewalk was crowded with shoppers taking advantage of late store hours, and strollers who found their primary entertainment in taking the air and mingling with their neighbors.

The streets that radiated out from this commercial center, both the main ones like Mifflin and Tasker and the side streets like Sigel and McClellan, were tightly packed with tiny row houses, one after another, unadorned boxes only fourteen feet wide, with party walls and their fronts smack up against the cement sidewalk. They were not built as separate houses, but as huge blocks of twenty-five, extending from corner to corner, all identical except the end units, made slightly larger to provide for the inevitable corner grocery or confectionery. No trees or shrubs softened the landscape. The only street plantings were utility poles carrying cables for the newly popular telephones and now-customary electrical service. The ugly web of lines was worst on the primary streets, for every one had tracks and overhead wires for the electric-powered trolleys that provided the community's essential transportation.

The harsh landscape was more homely than homey. But the houses were solid two-story structures, all made of brick or stone under Philadelphia's Franklin-inspired building code. Most had a

rear yard where the occupants could have a little garden, a miti-
gating patch of green, to summon memories of the land across the
sea, and, for many, to provide a place for the family's only privy.
A surprising percentage of these houses were owner-occupied, a
common occurrence in this "city of homes" where half the population made payments on mortgages rather than for rent. Back in
southern Italy, many families had owned a home, too, but it was
commonly a single-room affair without windows, maybe without
even a covered floor, often shared with livestock that was too valuable to let roam. To have a second floor (known as the piano
nobile), where you could sleep in security and privacy, was a sign
of wealth. So these new South Philadelphia homeowners, remembering or being told of their past, were well satisfied with their
American dwellings.

These immigrants brought many traditions and traditional
attitudes with them. They believed in hard work in unforgiving
conditions, a lesson learned from generations of eking an agricultural living from the parched, eroded soil of Calabria, Apulia, or
Sicily. They came from a social structure that was almost feudal,
with strict class, even caste, lines. Their ancestors were the peasant population that depended on agricultural lands rented from
absentee owners. They were a people whose traditional proverbs
instructed, "The poor sow that the rich may reap," and warned,
"Do not make your children better than you." Theirs was a society
of rules, strictures, and beliefs, deeply held beliefs.

They believed in a religion, of course. It was Catholicism, but
their own brand of it. Though they were adherents of the Church
of Rome, they were also the direct descendants of pagans who
occupied the area millennia before. An eighteenth-century French
traveler commented, "Europe ends at Naples," or as Carlo Levi
put it, "Christ Stopped at Eboli." Modern Europe certainly did.

The southern religion emphasized a worship of statues of Madonnas and saints that harkened back to pagan ritual. And it was riven with superstitions and devotions to odd customs.

For many, the powers of witchcraft and the supernatural were as great as those of a Christian God. They had a name for it, *la fattura*—the use of magic potions used to cast spells, accompanied by occult practices. More than anything, they believed in *il mal'occhio,* the evil eye. Whatever misfortune befell one, from the loss of a job to an infant's sudden death, could be blamed on *il mal'occhio.* Only a chosen person could neutralize the evil eye or rid someone of its effects. Usually, it was a special family member, maybe an aunt, who would come over whenever the curse appeared. She would sprinkle drops of olive oil in a bowl of water while blessing the afflicted person with a pious benediction, *"In nome del Padre, del Figlio, e dello Spirito Santo,"* or maybe a sorcerous chant, *"Schiatta mall' occhio, e non più vanti"* (Burst evil eye and go no further). If the oil stayed in drops, all was well, but if it spread out, sometimes with animated sputtering, the evil eye was at work. And she would repeat the process, dozens of times, hour after hour, hoping the drops stayed stable.

Passyunk, which catered to all the needs of its clientele, naturally had *fattucchieri,* masters of witchcraft, who claimed to have power over *il mal'occhio* It also was home to those who carried on another southern Italian tradition, that of men who, in the midst of an endlessly toiling population, survived without visible effort. Many of these in Italy had been priests, who were present there in numbers far exceeding any spiritual need. Others had no ostensible occupation, or none that they could admit to authorities.

This is the story of a macabre criminal conspiracy concocted in the back room of a Passyunk tailor shop by a group of finagling *fattucchieri* who figured out a way to make their magic produce some easy money. For six years, from 1932 to 1938, these *cospiratori* sent men (and a few women) to their graves, for no reason other than to collect the proceeds of small life-insurance policies. These were not gangland killings. The victims were, for the most part, simple Italian immigrant laborers or factory workers. The dreadful deeds were not done by mafiosi hit men, but by the men's wives, who acceded to the advice of the spiritualists and witch doctors who devised the plan and preyed on their clients' superstitions.

In the press, these women would all be lumped together as *poison widows,* a suitably sinister term that evoked spiders devouring their mates. But they were a mixed lot. Some were simple peasants who barely spoke English and whose minds and hearts were still in the closed, tradition-bound villages of their childhoods. Others, some born and raised in this country, had fully adapted to the open, aggressive "make your own way and get out of mine" America that was their true home. Rather than being victimized by the evil scheme, these modern women seemed more to be *cospiratori* themselves.

When the scheme was eventually exposed in the winter of 1938–1939, the plotters and the widows, one and all, found themselves enmeshed in a new-world system of criminal justice that did not respond to the old magic formulae. In this world, *avvocati,* not *fattucchieri,* knew the incantations. But the results they produced were no less bizarre.

PART I

La Fattura

PROFESSORE P. PATRIL

Consigliere e guaritore spirituale

RISOLVE PROBLEMI DAMORE, MATRI-
MONIO, AFFARI, FORTUNA. UNO VERO
PSICHICO CON L'ABILITÀ DI AIUTARVI A
LIBERARVI DAI VOSTRI NEMICI E IN-
FLUENZE MALEFICHE CHE INFLUISCONO
SULLA VOSTRA SALUTE, SUCCESSO, MA-
TRIMONIO. CONSULTATE SUBITO.

1
PROFESSOR P. PATRIL

Paul Petrillo emigrated from his native Naples to Philadelphia in 1910, when he was seventeen, and immediately started pursuing the American dream. He married his sweetheart, Angelina, a fellow Italian immigrant, and began raising a family. Capitalizing on his boyhood training as a tailor, he took up that trade here, and after not too many years, he managed to develop a large and satisfied clientele. Paul was a charming man who knew how to turn a complimentary phrase and win the confidence of his customers. The short and somewhat rotund young tailor dressed himself impeccably and with style, always tucking a silk handkerchief in the breast pocket of a handsome suit and wearing a fine snap-brimmed Stetson fedora. He was a walking advertisement of his own craft.

It was not long before Paul was successful enough to open his own shop, "Paul Petrillo, Custom Tailor to the Classy Dressers," at number 1822 East Passyunk Avenue, in the heart of his *compatriote*'s community. The business prospered. By 1929, he had accumulated enough savings to pay $2,200 cash for a house at 1306 Sigel Street, a good investment, or perhaps a place to house his growing family. It was only a block away from the shop, enabling Paul to dash home for lunch, and the kids to drop in on their father after school. It seemed to be an admirable and upright life. But there were problems. Angelina was sickly, in bed more often than not. At least that is what Paul told people. She was rarely seen about in the community, leading some people to say there was more wrong with her than just poor physical health. And as the dismal 1930s progressed, business fell off. Reality began to diverge from the dream.

Paul looked beyond tailoring for the solution to his problems. For years, he had been speculating in life insurance, a racket that had been brought to his attention by insurance agents who patronized his tailor shop. These agents sold cheap life policies to struggling immigrants. They worked their "debits," territories where they peddled industrial policies with weekly premiums of fifty cents or a dollar, and went around collecting the installments. One agent, Gaetano Cicinato, who hung out at Paul's shop, using the back room as a part-time office, educated the tailor about a shadowy side of the insurance business. The inexpensive policies that these agents sold were a source of reassurance to many families, as they rightly were meant to be. But they were also a source of speculation. There was something about making the weekly payment of fifty cents that was akin to playing the lottery. If the insured was a beloved husband, you were just protecting against the loss of a breadwinner. But if love had begun to fade, the possibility of hitting this lottery began to become more and more appealing.

Paul gossiped about this aspect of the policies with Gaetano

Cicinato and the other insurance agents who frequented his shop. Although it was technically illegal, they assured him that the companies really did not mind if one wanted to use them as a lottery. Why else would they be willing to write policies with no medical examination? They made enough money to cover the risk. Now, if you were aware of a really bad risk, someone whose health you knew for sure was ebbing as you talked, you could beat the odds and make a killing. Many Italian men in their thirties, men who should have been young and healthy, had fought in the Great War and been gassed, suffering irreparable damage to their lungs. Paul always asked about this when he met a newcomer to the community. It was useful information.

Over time Paul accumulated a portfolio of these insurance speculations, a stack of small policies that he kept stashed in a tin box—his *cassaforte*—in his lower-right desk drawer. Sometimes the policies were obtained by the man's wife or children and assigned to Paul. In other instances, Paul took out the policies directly, listing himself as "cousin" or "brother" of the insured. All these insured men and women were, in Paul's words, "anointed for death." But that was wishful thinking. He dearly wanted to improve the odds in his favor.

His hope was *la fattura*. Paul believed deeply in this old-world magic. He feared witches and devils and was said to carry eleven rabbits' feet in his hip pocket as protection against them. He even tried to practice witchcraft, distributing business cards proclaiming himself "Professor P. Patril—Divine Healing, Private Readings." The address given, 1817 South Thirteenth Street, was the back door of his tailor shop.

2
HERMAN THE HUSTLER

Paul's closest confidant was his younger cousin Herman Petrillo. A fellow son of Italy, born in the Neapolitan province of Campania in 1899, Herman had emigrated to America in the same year as Paul, 1910. He first worked here as a barber, but he soon found a profession more suitable to his skills. The short, slick Herman was a conniver and a persuasive talker. He claimed to be a spaghetti and olive oil salesman, and Herman might have been a success at that if he had pursued it with diligence. But he liked the quicker buck, so he came up with criminal schemes. He was the sort of guy who, with no education and no consistent means of support, always had money in his pocket, wore sharply tailored suits, and drove a new car. Herman had never met a crime he didn't like.

Arson was one. A self-educated bomb maker, Herman knew how to employ high technology to blow up the well-insured property of his choice. When he decided to go out of the barbering business, police, called to investigate a suspicious smell, found a large bottle of gasoline in the basement of his shop. The bottle was connected by a soaked cord to the tubes of a radio, ready to ignite when the radio got hot. A few years later, fire marshals, investigating a burned-down house at 2434 West Clearfield Street in North Philadelphia, discovered it had been bought by Herman only a year before. They also found a homemade bomb packed with three pounds of dynamite in the cellar. It was powerful enough, said the marshals, "to shatter the whole block." The bomb had been rigged to go off when someone rang the doorbell, and it could have sent the unlucky caller up in smoke along with the property. But Herman was not the kind to worry about such details. He just moved on to his next endeavor, pleased as usual that the police, despite their suspicions, never seemed to find enough evidence to pin a crime on him.

Counterfeiting was another of Herman's diversions. He would make weekly trips up to New York, to the corner of 112th Street and First Avenue in East Harlem, where he knew he could score fake five- and ten-dollar bills. Agents of the United States Secret Service, the so-called T-men, who investigated counterfeiting, knew about it. They tried for years to catch Herman in the act, stopping his shiny green Plymouth for surprise searches and seducing him to sell bogus bills in sting operations. But they never could catch the crafty counterfeiter with the goods.

Agent Landvoight of the Secret Service had a file on Herman, full of tips about his counterfeiting exploits. The Philadelphia fire marshal knew of Herman's incendiary proclivities. It would be only a matter of time before someone caught up to him. That moment seemed to come in 1937, when police investigated a blaze that destroyed a house at 6876 North Twentieth Street in North Philadelphia. They found a stash of homemade dynamite in the garage, then discovered that the owner of the house, a woman named Margaret Vasano, was Herman's wife. The fire marshal finally thought he had his man. Herman was arrested and tried for the first time in his long and variegated criminal career.

But Herman was acquitted. On the way out of court, the freed man taunted the fire marshal: "What d'ya think now, flatfoot?"

"Okay, Petrillo," the marshal replied, "you beat that one, but you'll land in the hot seat yet."

Herman smiled. He collected three thousand dollars'* worth of insurance on the burned-down house, and he moved up from his Plymouth to a slick new Dodge sedan. The marshal was not off the mark in talking of the "hot seat," however, for murder was within Herman's repertoire. He frequently proposed it to his cousin Paul as the way to take care of Paul's accumulating insurance portfolio. Just "send the guy to California" was the way Herman like to put it, but he didn't have in mind a berth on the Santa Fe Super Chief. Paul, however, was wary—not necessarily scrupled, just wary of Herman's reckless ways.

Herman would eventually proceed on his own. He found the perfect victim in Ralph Caruso, a fifty-year-old vagrant. Caruso was a semi-invalid from injuries suffered in a trolley accident. Able to walk only by leaning heavily on a cane, he eked out a living on the small sum he had been given as compensation. Herman befriended the piteous Ralph, who was being evicted from his rooming house. "I'll find you a place to live," Herman told his new buddy. He took the crippled man to Christine Cerrone, an old woman who rented rooms at her house at 1305 Porter Street

---

*For a rough sense of current values, multiply all dollar amounts by twelve, the increase in the consumer price index from the 1930s to 1998. By that measure, Herman's insurance booty was the approximate equivalent of $36,000 in 1998.

in South Philadelphia. Herman agreed to pay the six-dollar-a-week room-and-board bill.

Christine fussed over Caruso. She liked him. She bought a couch for him so he could lie down in the living room rather than climb the stairs to his room during the day. She treated his injured leg, rubbing alcohol on it. "He was a nice man," she said. "He would go down and light the fire for me in the morning. He would go out and buy things for me. My children liked him, too. Everybody around the house liked him."

"Did he make any proposals of marriage to you?" a lawyer asked her.

"Seventy years old? Talking about marriage? He never said that," Christine scoffed. But she enjoyed his company. No wonder. It was rumored that most of the tenants to whom she rented rooms stayed only for a very short time. They were men who needed a place for a few hours alone with a woman. That's how Christine Cerrone made her living, quietly, without disturbing the neighbors.

A week or two later, Metropolitan and Home Life agents, buddies whom Herman had met while hanging out at Paul's tailor shop, began coming to the house to sell life insurance to Caruso. Herman accompanied them to help answer questions. The illiterate Caruso put his "X" on the first few applications, which made the landlady Christine beneficiary. But as Herman became bolder, he brazenly forged Ralph's signature on the applications and had the policies made payable directly to "Herman Caruso," as "brother" of Ralph. Over several months, Herman built up an insurance portfolio on Caruso worth more than three thousand dollars in case of accidental death. Herman paid all the premiums. It cost him another two dollars a week.

Caruso loved to go fishing. "Stop going," Christine told him.

"You make me sick, going fishing every day." But his friend Herman encouraged it. Fishing was always a little adventure. You never knew what was going to happen. Herman was, of course, scheming, trying to figure out how he might best boost the adventure along. He wanted a helping hand, but not from anyone who would want too big a share of the benefits.

Herman finally found his man in Salvatore Sortino, a simpleminded itinerant huckster who fell for whatever line "Herman the Hustler" wanted to spin. "How would you like to go fishing?" he asked Sortino one day. "Meet me next Sunday in Fairmount Park. Right after supper. Look for my car on the West River Drive near the Girard Avenue Bridge." The Schuykill River flowed through the park.

Sortino arrived about seven o'clock on the July evening. Herman and the crippled Caruso were down by the edge of the river, fishing without rods, tossing lines over the sheer concrete embankment that dropped several feet straight down to the water below. Herman walked over to Sortino. He had a simple task to propose. Putting his hand on his comrade's shoulder in a gesture of solidarity, Herman laid out the plan. Gesturing toward Caruso at the riverbank, he said, "I want you to give that man a 'cold bath.' You know, knock him into the river."

To Sortino, the request presented a moral dilemma. "Herman Petrillo had done me a favor and lent me ten dollars to pay my rent a few weeks ahead of time, so I didn't know what to do," he later told authorities. But Herman was not a man to be denied. So Sortino sneaked up behind Caruso in the gathering twilight and shoved him with both hands. As soon as he heard the body splash, he took off. Caruso did not give up easily. Herman, disgusted at his henchman's quick flight, was forced to jump in the shallow water himself and hold the flailing victim's head under until he stopped kicking.

Officer John McLain of the Fairmount Park police discovered the body the next morning, stuck on a mudflat between the Girard Avenue Bridge and the Pennsylvania Railroad Bridge. "It was only partly floating," he told investigators. "He was facedown. It was pretty shallow and the toes of the body seemed to be touching the mud bank. The head—the back of his head—was out of the water. His right hand was clenched around a cane, a walking stick. He had a death grip on it."

Herman figured he had pulled off a perfect crime. But things started to unravel when he tried to collect on John Hancock and Metropolitan policies that provided double indemnity for accidental death. The circumstances were a little too suspicious. Investigators from both companies began asking questions. How come, for example, Ralph Caruso had signed his full name on some of the applications, when he had only been able to make his mark before? How come "Herman Caruso, brother," could only provide identification as Herman *Petrillo?* The insurers forced Herman to accept part payment on the policies, merely reimbursing him for Caruso's funeral expenses. Herman had the last laugh, as he collected a generous amount from each company, double-billing them with a padded invoice. But for a year's work and all the risk, he cleared only seven hundred dollars on the Caruso job, not much of a reward, though a few hundred dollars went a long way during the Depression.

R.I.P.
RALPH CARUSO

A few months later, Herman arranged some adventure travel for the husband of a woman named Marie Woloshyn. Herman, who was something of a ladies' man, had a little thing going with

Marie and had managed to get her to invest in several insurance policies on her husband's life. On a chilly January evening, Herman took John Woloshyn out in his latest vehicle for a promised jaunt to an after-hours roadhouse. A buddy of Herman's named "Jumbo" Valenti went along to make sure it turned into a trip to California for the unsuspecting victim.

As they drove along, Jumbo whacked John Woloshyn over the head with an iron pipe. Then he picked up the unconscious man and dumped him in front of the car. A few forwards and reverses by Herman finished the job. When they found the mangled body, police concluded it had been a hit-and-run. No one was ever charged.

R.I.P.
JOHN WOLOSHYN

3
LOUIE THE RABBI

Paul Petrillo did not seem to have cousin Herman's skill for engineering death. Despite his deeply held belief in *la fattura,* despite his bevy of rabbits' feet, despite his snappy business cards, Paul knew he was a fraud. He was an abject failure as a *fattucchiere.* Not one of the objects of his affliction had died. He yearned to master the arcane arts and prove to cousin Herman that there were more refined techniques than simple thuggery to accomplish his goals. When Dr. Torricio, a local masseur and naturopath, invited Paul to attend sessions where various healers discussed their practices, he was overjoyed. It was there that Paul Petrillo met Morris Bolber.

Bolber was no *paesano,* but a Russian Jewish immigrant. Ill-kempt, rotund, and fortyish, he was a local mystic commonly known as "Louie the Rabbi." Bolber was not really a man of the cloth. But he was Jewish, taught Hebrew, and presented himself as a man of learning, a man who had arcane wisdom about life.

That was enough to qualify him for the rabbinate in the South Philadelphia Italian community where he practiced his mysticism.

What a story this Jew told! Born in Tordobis, Russia, in 1890, he was raised by his grandfather, a cantor. He entered the university at Grodno at age nine. Graduating at twelve, the youthful scholar went off on his own to the great seaport of Odessa to learn more about the world. He found work for a few years as a tutor of young children and continued his own studies.

All this time, Bolber told his South Philadelphia friends, "There was one thought that was constantly on my mind. It was of the *Kabbalah,* the ancient book on superstition and witchcraft which had been forbidden to students at Grodno. 'You are too young and not holy enough,' the instructor told us. Now that I was a teacher myself, I read it from beginning to end. It led me into far fields and explorations of the supernatural.

"On one occasion, I learned about a man who was suffering from a form of cancer. The doctors gave him only three days to live. I consulted the *Kabbalah,* and went to the bedside of the man. I felt the hardness of his stomach and saw the agony of his face. 'Do you want to live longer?' I asked him. Certainly he did. 'Very well, then,' I advised him, 'take a large glass of milk, and to that add twenty drops of pure turpentine. Drink a third of a glass of this mixture three times a day and you will live a long time.'

"It worked," Bolber bragged. "The man lived for nine months."

This masterful achievement was apparently enough to launch a reputation. Young Morris began to cure all sorts of ailments with potions of turpentine, vinegar, alcohol, and horseradish. Fortunately for his clients, these pungent mixtures were usually applied as salves rather than ingested. By the time he was sixteen, Bolber the medicine boy was ready to expand his horizons. He decided to go to China, to seek out a fabled witch doctor named Rino. He tracked down this toothless seventy-seven-year-old woman in the city of Chongogo and lived with her as an apprentice for five years, from 1905 to 1910. Or so the story went.

"From Rino, I learned everything. She taught me how to cure every kind of disease. Most important, she taught me the secret of the *knife*. With the powers of the knife—an ordinary kitchen knife that had been infused with healing spirits—I was able to perform many wonders. Once, for example, I stood in the park with friends and we were annoyed by four noisy couples on nearby benches. I waved my knife and they moved away."

In 1911, at the age of twenty-one, Bolber made the voyage to America, arriving in New York with his trusty knife in pocket. By this time, he claimed to speak ten languages, enabling him to chant incantations in Arabic and strange Asian tongues as well as Russian and Chinese. He planned to make his fortune as a faith healer. Reality caught up with him, however, in the form of Esther Checter, whom he met on the Lower East Side and married. She did not approve of witch doctoring, so Morris went into the grocery business. He ran a little store in New Brunswick at first and then in Perth Amboy. Later they moved to Brooklyn, where he also worked as a Hebrew teacher.

By 1931, he had four children, and the grocery business had failed. Morris packed up his family and moved to South Philadelphia to return to his true calling. He continued his teaching, preparing Jewish boys for their bar mitzvahs. But knowing of the large and superstitious Italian immigrant community in the area, he also sent out handbills announcing his new practice as a faith healer, expert in the *Kabbalah* and the secrets of the knife learned at the feet of Rino, the sorceress of China. It did not hurt, in this world of *il mal'occhio,* that he had a drooping lid on one eye and peculiar brown flecks in his irises, fostering rumors of mysterious powers. Clients began visiting his office on Moyamensing at Ninth.

Salvatore Sortino, the huckster who aided Herman in the Caruso job, was a typical Bolber client. At first he went to the rabbi to get some luck with his wagon, but he quickly fell under the spell of this "great man with superpowers." Whatever this Jewish witch doctor told Sortino to do, he did. "Put an egg under your arm and keep it there for nine days," Bolber commanded, "and a little devil will come out to give you luck." Sortino dutifully complied, despite the obvious inconvenience. The charms must have worked, because the huckster was soon begging the great man to teach him "the game of faith healer." Bolber asked for five hundred dollars, but when it was obvious Sortino didn't have that kind of money, the always-flexible healer chopped his fee to only fifty bucks.

Even that was high for what Bolber taught. All Sortino learned to do was hold up a knife and mutter, "In the Name of the Father and of the Son and of the Holy Spirit, Amen," while making the sign of the cross. But it was enough to make him a devoted disciple. "The knife didn't work, not always," Sortino conceded, but he didn't blame his teacher. "It's because I didn't finish paying Morris Bolber the last twenty-five dollars," he told everyone.

After giving Caruso his cold bath in the Schuykill, Sortino hotfooted it to Bolber's house. He figured he'd better protect his luck. "Before I said anything to Bolber, I offered him twenty dollars," Sortino later recalled. "I figured I better pay him. I still owed him twenty-five, but twenty was all I had."

No one could have been a better audience for Rabbi Morris Bolber, with his evil eye and fantastic stories of Chinese mystics and the knife, than Paul Petrillo, the would-be *fattucchiere.* "Professor P. Patril" listened to Louie the Rabbi's stories. Bolber told him many things, but mostly he related extravagant tales of sexual potions and charms. He could make a woman love a man and vice versa. He could turn the worst husband, one who drank and beat his wife, into a loving homebody. This had become a large part of Bolber's trade in his new Philadelphia practice. Girls whose boyfriends had spurned them would go to see Bolber. The rabbi would get a picture of the boyfriend and maybe a lock of his hair, then whisper incantations in tongues that would bring him back. Wives would come complaining of their husbands, and the rabbi would rekindle the ardor of youth.

At least this is what Bolber contended, and Paul believed. Gradually the Russian Jew and the Neapolitan tailor became close friends. The men talked of the struggles of life. The Depression was growing, money was tight. Morris had four children and Paul had seven, the youngest only four and the oldest just entering dental school. They talked of ways to earn more.

"We can make money together," Morris told Paul. "I can teach you what to tell people. You look good; you look like a professor. I look like a tramp."

The two men formed a partnership that combined Morris's *saichel* and Paul's savior faire.

4
GONE FISHIN'

Anna Arena, dressed only in a corset and brassiere, sat bolt upright in a straight-backed chair. She was in the center of the large room illuminated by candles in juice glasses with Hebrew print on the sides. Her ample flesh bulged from the borders of the undergarments and her pasta-enriched thighs spilled over the edges of the narrow chair. Beads of sweat dripped from her unshaven armpits. She stared, mesmerized, at the Russian Jewish mystic who circled around her, brandishing a table knife that flashed in the flickering light. He mumbled strange phrases, which she could not understand, interspersed with suggestions that she strip down further, which were only too clear.

Anna was typical of a string of women whom Paul Petrillo had been referring to Morris Bolber. Paul's tailor shop at number 1822 was located in a fashionable part of Passyunk, an area that drew women out on shopping trips. On one side were Max Cohen's shoe store, Victoria Stein's millinery, and Millie Giacobbe's fashions. Across the street was a row of clothing stores, ranging from Esther Miller's ladies' wear to L. Fine's fur emporium, including four small department stores. With Mileti's butcher shop and Frank DeFay's children's wear also nearby, there were good excuses for women to frequent the block on daily shopping trips, especially women who had a little money to spend.

The smooth-talking Paul, at the center of the Passyunk street action, had no trouble finding clients who could make use of Morris's *Kabbalah*-derived talents. Sometimes referrals would go the other way, when Morris had a client whom he sensed might respond better to Paul, particularly one who spoke no English, Russian, Chinese, Arabic, or any of the other dozen languages, Italian excepted, in which Bolber claimed fluency. Several clients a day were soon being referred back and forth. Nonetheless, it was difficult to turn a large profit when the consultation fees were only fifty cents or a dollar per session. The partners remained alert to better opportunities. They were open to most anything. When young women asked for magical help with unwanted pregnancies, for example, they found a way to oblige. If incantations didn't work, they lined up a regular medical practitioner willing to provide *un aborto* for an appropriate fee, and a kickback to the middlemen.

Anna Arena worked part-time as a seamstress in the Petrillo tailor shop, trying to supplement her family's income. She constantly complained to Paul that her husband, Joseph, a shoemaker, was a drunk. He did not take care of her and their six children, she moaned. Worse yet, he no longer showed any interest in her as a woman. "He used to love me," she told Paul, no doubt referring to the time when the children had been conceived, "but he love me no more." She was pathetic—unattractive, simpleminded, and incurably superstitious—a perfect subject for Rabbi Bolber's primitive form of sex therapy.

Anna found her way to Rabbi Bolber's office one evening in December 1931. When he sat her in the chair and asked her to disrobe, saying it would bring out the erotic in her, she drew the line at her underwear. No matter. Bolber had no trouble convincing the partially clothed Anna that she had latent sexual wiles. He paired her up with a male client in need of sex therapy, a man named Dominick Rodio. In a perverted stroke of genius, Bolber arranged for Anna to put her menstrual blood in a tasty dish, maybe some *vongole con salsa rossa,* which he said he would feed to Rodio and "make him crazy for her." Whatever the cause, Anna and Dominick soon became so involved that her shoemaker husband seemed a nuisance.

Paul Petrillo was alert to the opportunity for a *la fattura*-enhanced life-insurance speculation. The healthy Joseph Arena was not a good prospect for an ordinary insurance gamble. But now Paul believed he had an ability to coax the Angel of Death to the scene. Morris Bolber could make things happen. So Paul dispatched his buddy Gaetano Cicinato to Anna Arena. She signed up for a double-indemnity policy on her husband that would pay $3,200 in case of accidental death. Though the policy was in her name, Paul Petrillo paid the premiums, and Anna understood that he would be entitled to the proceeds. She didn't seem to care so long as Paul and Morris could keep the magic going.

It was a perfect setup, Paul thought, until months went by with no change in the targeted Joseph Arena. Bolber waved his knife and pronounced incantations in more languages than Paul could count. He assured Paul he would provide the needed sorcery. But Mr. Arena kept strolling down Passyunk Avenue. It was enough to shake a man's faith. Paul was annoyed. The premiums on an insurance policy of this size were not trivial. Paul kept hoping his rabbi would come though, but eventually he gave in and called cousin Herman.

"Send the man to California" was the message.

Early on the morning of June 30, 1932, Herman Petrillo drove to the Arena home to pick up Joseph for a fishing trip to the Jersey shore. Anna's paramour, Dominick Rodio, a reputed member of the Mafia-like Black Hand, came along. Herman had also enlisted an experienced assistant, a goon named Steve Crispino, whose last exploit was alleged to have been bombing the home of a prominent lawyer, killing the man's wife and several of his children. As this crew drove through New Jersey's Pine Barrens, they were free with the booze, trying to make sure that Arena's powers of resistance would be ineffectual. Herman did not drink himself, refusing when Joe Arena offered him a swig. "I never drink while driving," Herman told the shoemaker. "You're liable to hurt somebody."

The men rented a smack at Sea Isle City and set off into Ludlam's Channel for some crabbing, a form of fishing that requires one to lean over the side frequently to see what is on the line. It was a midweek morning, early enough in the season so that there were no other boats around. They didn't waste any time. As soon as Arena extended himself to check his line, Rodio gave him a shove. When he popped back up, gasping for air, Rodio and the goon assistant whacked him over the head with an oar, again and again until his body lay limp.

On a Saturday morning a few weeks later, a group convened at Paul's tailor shop—Anna, with the $3,200 double-indemnity insurance check from the policy Paul had procured; her lover, Rodio; the insurance agent, Cicinato; Rabbi Morris Bolber; and the

Petrillo cousins. They all turned to Paul, who had banking connections nearby. While Bolber stayed at the shop calmly imbibing a little schnapps, the others, who were less trusting, chased off with Paul and Anna to the local bank. Down Passyunk Avenue they went, Paul in the lead, clutching the check, with Anna next to him, and Herman, Rodio, and Cicinato tagging behind on the narrow sidewalk.

"She's an honest woman. Do me a favor and cash that check," Paul told the teller as the greedy confederates all crowded around the cage, peering over Paul's shoulder lest he do some quick switch on them. The teller, seeing that it was an insurance-company check drawn on the same bank, had no difficulty obliging.

Returning to the shop, Paul put a stack of hundred-dollar bills on the table. He and Bolber began dividing it, nine bills for Herman Petrillo (from which he paid off his assistant), nine for Bolber, nine for Paul, and one for Cicinato. When the insurance agent protested, Bolber threw another bill to him. Better not to have anyone unhappy. That left only three hundred dollars for Rodio, the actual killer. He apparently did it more for love than money.

They could hardly believe how easy it had been. With the cooperation of the wife and Cicinato, getting the insurance had been a snap. The murder had been a little complicated to arrange, but there were dozens of ways to kill a man. As for Joe Arena himself, well, wasn't he a nuisance, standing in the way of love? Their consciences clear, the men shook conspiratorial hands with gusto. They were on their way.

R.I.P.
JOSEPH ARENA

5

STRONG MEDICINE

Morris Bolber sat alone in his darkened
office, his *Zohar*—the *Book of Splendor*—opened before him. It was
time for him to begin delivering on his promise to Paul Petrillo.
The Petrillo cousins might be masters at manipulating life insurance, but only he, the savant Morris Bolber, was the master at
manipulating life itself. Bolber raised his hands high overhead in
a ceremonial prayer gesture of reaching for the highest that is
knowable, dividing the fingers of each hand into the shape used
by the high priests of the Temple. He breathed in deeply, deeply,
"exhorting the winds to fill his body from all four directions" as
the great Kabbalist teacher Eleazar had instructed. Then he
dropped his head between his knees and breathed out. Up and
down, in and out, as he chanted an alphabetic series of praises:
"Melech avir, melech adir, melech adon, melech baruch..."—King
of the air, king of blessedness, king of greatness, king of power ...
Up and down, in and out, in a ritual of frenzied mysticism, until

his consciousness was lost in a hyperventilated trance, a trance
that yielded inspiration.

The first beneficiary of these prayers would be Sophie La-
Vecchio, owner of a confectionery store at the corner of Bancroft
and Moore Streets. The shop, which was always busy with kids
from the school across the street, provided her with a nice income.
She could take care of herself in the world of business, but she
could not help her sickly husband, Luigi. The unfortunate man
had fallen from a scaffold nine years before, in 1923, and had been
hospitalized for a month with severe internal injuries. He never
really recovered. He had recurring respiratory problems, including
double pneumonia on two separate occasions.

Sophie's friends told her of the wonders that the Jew down
on Moyamensing was working in reviving fading husbands. When
they called him "Papa" Bolber, a translation of the word *rabbi* that
suggested a priestly quality, she wasted no time getting herself over
to his office. Sophie knocked on the door—there was no bell—and
Bolber admitted her to his sanctuary. It was a large room, big
enough for the bar mitzvah classes that he gave in the afternoons.
A large chart of Hebrew letters dominated one wall, and books
with the same peculiar script were lying about. To Sophie, it gave
the place an air of the occult.

The American doctors could do nothing for her husband,
Sophie told Papa Bolber. She had taken him to Dr. Spono at Broad
and Federal, but the medical man had not given Luigi long to live.
"The doctor says he's going to die soon because all his insides,
they're green like, and someday they'll bust," Sophie wept. "He's
sick a couple of weeks and then when he gets up, he's all right
again. It's been nine years all the time like that. Lay down and get
up. Lay down and get up."

Though Luigi could not return to work after his accident, he helped Sophie out in the confectionery. He also brewed homemade wine, which brought them healthy supplemental income during Prohibition. Sophie had managed to become a woman of property. In addition to her store, she owned a rental house on Bancroft Avenue and one down on the shore, in Wildwood, New Jersey. This was a well-fixed woman by the standards of that time and place, and Bolber quickly sensed her financial potential. He passed this prospect, whom he called "Sophia," with an Italian lilt, on to his suave colleague, Professor P. Patril, Spiritual Adviser and Healer.

Paul got right to work setting up the job, calling on Sophie and Luigi at their home upstairs from the candy store. It was only a few blocks from the Petrillo tailor shop–office. "I am the specialist," he assured them. "I have people who come to me from all over; they come from New York, come from Jersey, come from Delaware, from uptown. You know why? Because I am the specialist, the people come from all over to me for a cure." He visited three times over the next few days. Taking Sophie aside, he told her that her husband would be all right but that it would take some time. In the meantime, he asked, "You got any life insurance on him?"

"No, he don't believe in insurance," Sophie lied, though she did have nine hundred dollars in three small policies taken out with Prudential a year before. "Beside, he's too sick now, the insurance men won't take him."

Paul's insurance buddies had already tipped him off to the existing policies, but he didn't argue. "Don't worry," Paul advised Sophie, "I have a man who can give you insurance with no doctor. If he dies and you ain't got no money, how you going to pay us?"

A few days later, the insurance agent Gaetano Cicinato came around to Sophie's. The two were *paesani,* from the same town in

Italy, so they got on well. He took down some information and
prepared two John Hancock applications on her behalf, each for a
four-hundred-dollar policy. He forged Luigi's mark on the applications, and then put one through in his own name and another
in the name of a fellow agent. He dated them a month apart, knowing that there was very little investigation and no medical examination required on policies under five hundred dollars. By
midsummer, all was in readiness. But Paul was stumped about
how to book Luigi's final "trip to California." There was always
Cousin Herman, but Luigi showed no interest in going for an outing. He hardly ever left the house.

It was time for Bolber's genius to provide a solution, and he
was prepared. Louie the Rabbi had devised a technique for killing
that would eventually earn a preferred place for him and his partners in the hall of infamy. On a Saturday afternoon, July 30, 1932,
Bolber called Paul. "After you close the store tonight, come over,
I want to talk to you. About that Sophia." Paul was pleased with
himself as he sauntered across Mifflin to Bolber's house at Fifth
and Emily that evening, whistling and greeting friends and customers sitting on their stoops. His bank account was flush with
the Arena booty, and was soon to be supplemented with some
LaVecchio loot.

Bolber was waiting outside when he got there. "Come with
me," the rabbi told his collaborator. "I am going to get you something. You can tell Sophia that the professor from New York came
in and he gave it to you." The two men walked a few blocks north,
back up to Eshman's drugstore at the southwest corner of Fifth
and Mifflin. While Paul waited outside, watching through the
plate-glass window, Morris talked to the druggist and took a package wrapped in white paper from him.

Bolber gave Paul the parcel. It was a small package, maybe

three inches long and not more than an eighth of an inch thick. Paul kneaded it with his fingers, feeling that it contained a powder. "You tell her the professor from New York told you to give him this three times a day. Mix it in his food," Morris told Paul.

"What's in here?" Paul asked.

Bolber brushed him away. He was not about to disclose his secrets.

Paul went right to the LaVecchio confectionery. Sophie was busy with customers, kids from the neighborhood still out playing on the warm summer evening.

"Where's your husband?" Paul inquired.

"He's up in the bed, sick," she shouted above the jabbering of the kids. Paul went up. As soon as she finished with her customers, Sophie followed.

"I brought you something," Paul advised her, "from the professor in New York. It's *la fattura*. It'll take care of your husband, don't worry. What're you having tonight? You having spaghetti, you mix it in his spaghetti, you mix it in his coffee, in his *zuppa*." He handed her the package. "All the meals, you mix it in. If he needs a doctor, call Dr. Boccella. I'll write the address and leave it on the bureau."

This was what Sophie had been wanting all along, a potent potion of witchcraft and magic. She wasted no time following Paul's instructions.

That evening, Luigi began to get sick. Instead of his usual coughing and spitting, he began to vomit and he had diarrhea. Sophie gave him some chicken soup with more powder. But he kept throwing up and had more diarrhea. He couldn't make it to the outhouse in the yard. She had to keep changing the bed. So she fetched Dr. Boccella.

Boccella had an unusually busy practice. He saw thousands

of patients a month, "fifty, sixty, a hundred a day," he claimed. He did a quick examination of Luigi and found him to have gastroenteritis—probably due to the excessive garlic consumption suggested by the odor on the man's breath, he speculated—and bronchitis. The doctor prescribed bismuth for the digestive problem and tincture of camphoritis for the respiratory one. Every morning that week, Boccella came and renewed the prescriptions. After a few days, he added chamomile and morphine. He told Sophie to take the prescriptions to the drugstore over on Morris Avenue.

"Why Morris?" she wanted to know. "I got a drugstore on Seventeenth and Moore, I got one on Sixteenth and Moore, I got Fifteenth and Moore, and then I got Broad and Moore. Why send me so far away?"

"I get a commission there," Boccella unashamedly disclosed. Everyone had his little *trucco.*

Sophie dutifully dispatched her sister-in-law or a neighbor each day to procure the medicine Boccella had prescribed, but Luigi did not improve. Boccella went off to his weekend residence at Wildwood, leaving Sophie with a stack of prescriptions and instructions to call the pharmacy if there was any new problem.

As Luigi's condition deteriorated, Sophie fretted. After a week, she got Paul on the phone. "What kind of powder the professor from New York give you? My husband, he just throws up every day, and diarrhea, too. He makes dirty all my sheets." Paul told her he would call the professor and ask him.

"It's all right," Bolber assured Paul, "that's the way it has to work."

Paul had confidence in his rabbi. It was Saturday. It was August. So the tailor went off to Wildwood, where he, too, had a summer house. When he returned on Tuesday, after a relaxing long weekend, Paul checked in with Bolber. LaVecchio was still hanging on. So they visited the druggist again. This time Bolber gave Paul some capsules full of powder.

"Why capsules?" Paul asked.

"They're stronger," Morris said.

"Why no capsules before?" Paul wanted to know.

Bolber smiled. "You have to make him really sick before he'll take capsules."

Paul returned to the LaVecchio confectionery. "*Buon giorno.* How is your husband?" he asked Sophie.

"Last night I give him only milk," Sophie cried. "He eat nothing. All night he's throwing up. All night he no sleep. He no sleep and I no sleep. I no take my clothes off."

They went up to Luigi's room together. He was finally dozing, propped up on two pillows because of his cough. Paul took some of the white capsules out of his pocket. "He needs more medicine. Here, give him these," he said, thrusting them at Sophie. She refused. Paul took two and stuck them in Luigi's mouth, which was hanging open, spittle drooling from the corner. "Water," he shouted at Sophie, who grabbed a half-full glass from the dresser. Paul took the man's head in his hands and held it back while Sophie forced water down his throat to make him swallow the pills. "If anything happens, call me," Paul told Sophie. "Call me and I'll get a doctor, or I'll get my undertaker."

All that day, the wretched Luigi threw up and fouled his bed. All day, Sophie changed the linens, running down to the store and back up. Mercifully, he died at ten that evening, August 9. Dr. Boccella signed the death certificate, attributing the cause to gastroenteritis.

Paul did not attend the funeral, but a few weeks later he came by to ask if Sophie had received her insurance money yet.

When he saw she was crying, Paul tried to console her. The be-spectacled tailor fancied himself a ladies' man. This "scheming Casanova," as the *Philadelphia Inquirer* would later call him, was not one to pass up an opportunity for a well-dressed, sympathetic gentleman to assuage the feelings of a bereaved widow. "Why're you crying? You know he was no good, always sick. He was no good for you, no good. Let me show you what a good man can do for you."

But this romancing was an aside to the main game, and Paul did not forget that. Sophie showed him a check for nine hundred dollars from Prudential, payment on the policies she had taken out herself. She had no bank account and could not read or write, so she was not certain what to do with it. "I can help you out," Paul assured her. He accompanied her to the bank and held her hand while she scratched out her endorsement on the back of the check. Then he took the money and told her it was payment for the doctor and for his services.

When she protested, Paul changed his tone. "Shut your mouth," he told her. "We've got men who take care of things. You talk and we'll kill you."

Sophie worked alone in her business, all day and into the night. With no husband to protect her, she was terrified. Then Paul added an even more ominous threat. "Stay away from the *polizia,* if you got any sense. You helped do that job on your hus-band."

After that, Sophie didn't give him any trouble. The two four-hundred-dollar life-insurance payments from John Hancock were sent in due course to Cicinato. He gave the checks directly to Paul, who did a nice imitation of Sophie's signature and cashed them without even telling her. It had all worked just as the mastermind Bolber had planned. There was no need for a crude killing that might raise suspicions of foul play. There was no need to split profits with Herman Petrillo and other vulgar confederates. Professor Paul had been able to do it himself, using Bolber's magic.

Having established their basic modus operandi, the criminal couple were ready for its gruesome repetition with a proliferation of garlic-breathed, vomiting, diarrhea-stricken victims. Professor Paul's role was to arrange the insurance, with the assistance of Gaetano Cicinato and other cronies. Rabbi Morris's role was to concoct and supply the doses of *la fattura*. The only variable role was that of the prospective widow. Was she to be an active participant or a passive bystander, a *fattucchiera* herself, or a foil? Paul and Morris could work with either, so long as she enabled them to gain access to the food supply of the victim.

Which had Sophie LaVecchio been? Though Morris and Paul didn't care, the law would. But that was in the future. For now, Luigi LaVecchio lay quietly in his grave. There he would rest in peace, until his body would be resurrected to provide evidence of what had befallen it.

R.I.P.
LUIGI LAVECCHIO

6

COLONEL BOLBER

‎"‏י, הנה היום בא בער כתנורסם‎," Morris Bol-
ber chanted, his deep voice rising and falling as his finger tracked
the words on the pages of the *tikun*. The twelve-year-old bar mitzvah student sat next to him, his eyes glazed, unable to focus on
the foreign words. The boy could think only of the baseball he
might be out playing if only he didn't have to spend his afternoons
with this strange man who spoke in tongues.

"It's music, dummkopf," Bolber scolded. He grabbed the
boy's shoulder and shook him out of his reverie. "You want your
father should be ashamed of you on *Shabbes?* You got to learn your
parsha so you can be a *mentsh*. Listen to me."

Morris Bolber wore several hats. With the adolescent boy, he
was the rabbi listed in the telephone book, a Hebrew scholar who
trained bar mitzvah *bochers* in the language and traditions that
would take them to manhood in their religion. Other times he was
Papa Bolber, the Kabbalist shaman who could cure ills and trans-

form personalities. These careers brought in a steady income that enabled him to provide for his family.

But there was also the Morris Bolber who wore a fashionable bowler, a blue chinchilla coat, and a white silk scarf. This Bolber, thanks to the sartorial tutelage of Paul Petrillo, was no longer a *shlump.* These fashionable accoutrements did not come cheap. They were spoils of Bolber's third career, as a merchant of *la fattura.*

To anyone who saw through Bolber's facade of mumbo jumbo, he was a charlatan or even a buffoon. But for those who lacked such perspicacity, like the huckster Sortino, he was a genius, the source of profound wisdom and magical powers. Many skeptics were converted when they learned of the results that had been achieved with Bolber's *fattura* formulae. First it was only Paul Petrillo, but soon an ever-expanding array of faith healers and witch doctors bragged to their friends and associates about the "perfect" crimes they had managed to pull off. With these endorsements, there was no shortage of other customers who sought access to Morris Bolber's patented fountain of death.

To help with this growing business, Bolber found an assistant in a young man named David Brandt. A former veterinary student at the University of Pennsylvania, Brandt was a down-on-his-luck typewriter salesman who turned up at Bolber's office looking for spiritual guidance. Instead he found a new career marketing *la fattura.* Like so many others, Brandt was mesmerized by Bolber and would do anything the great man asked. With Brandt's help, Bolber introduced *la fattura* to a non-Italian clientele, bringing in customers like the Slavic Agnes Mandiuk, wife of Romaine; the Jewish Joseph Swartz, son-in-law of Lena Winkleman; and the first poison *widower,* Thomas Pino, husband of Jennifer.

R.I.P.
ROMAINE MANDIUK

R.I.P.
LENA WINKLEMAN

R.I.P.
JENNIFER PINO

But using David Brandt was the exception for Morris Bolber. For the most part, he remained detached from applications of *la fattura,* preferring to work through distributors. Bolber was, it seems, a man ahead of his time, anticipating the franchising techniques of Colonel Sanders by several decades, only with a somewhat different collection of herbs and spices. "Colonel" Bolber did not have to wrangle with insurance agents, or clean up vomit. Others might make the big scores and take the big risks. Bolber was doing very well, thank you, collecting a nice little fee on a high volume, and keeping a low profile.

For example, Providenza Miccichi, another of the Passyunk faith-healing coterie, carried the marketing of *la fattura* to a new level. Rather than wait for customers to come to her, she developed an outreach program. Like an Avon lady, she went door-to-door telling fortunes and, when the proper case presented itself, dispensing death. Under her influence, Dominick Cassetti sprinkled some of Morris Bolber's magic powder on the spaghetti of his beautiful young wife, Jennie.

R.I.P.
JENNIE CASSETTI

In each and every case, the death raised no suspicion. No one had any reason to doubt Bolber's claim that his potent potion was the perfect murder weapon—foolproof and undetectable. The claim had never really been put to the test. So far, only the low-level medical practitioners and undertakers had been fooled. Sooner or later, one of these corpses would die in a sophisticated hospital or otherwise find its way onto a serious autopsy table, where it would undergo a different kind of scrutiny. But this risk did not seem to concern Morris Bolber, who just kept supplying *la fattura* to an expanding list of purveyors. The Passyunk–South Philadelphia territory was being well covered by the *la fattura* pioneers, Paul Petrillo and his followers. But North Philadelphia, the natural habitat of Paul's criminal cousin, Herman Petrillo, was soon taken over by that ever-enterprising entrepreneur of crime.

x x x

"You know what it means your *haftorah?*" Rabbi Bolber demanded, thumping the pages of the *tikun* with his stubby forefinger. The frightened boy looked up in ignorance. " 'For behold, the day is coming which will burn like a furnace,' " Bolber read from his translation, " 'and all the arrogant and all the evildoers will be stubble.' " The boy didn't seem to understand. "The bad boys are going to be all burned up, turned to ashes. That's you," the rabbi warned, "unless you learn your *parsha.*"

7
THE WRONG VICTIM

It was the perfect crime. At least it seemed to be for years, as more victims fell in 1933, 1934, 1935, and 1936. Paul had achieved his dream. He was now a master of *la fattura,* and he had acquired a feminine companion, a woman named Rose Carina, who shared his interests. Pitiable, pliable creatures like the whining Anna Arena and the grumbling Sophie LaVecchio had been little more than grist for his death mill, valuable only for the sacrificial husbands they offered. They had contributed little or nothing to Paul's mortality planning. They had shown no willingness to repeat the grim experience once its horrible effects had been graphically demonstrated. Paul's new woman was a different breed. She was not a superstitious immigrant but a hardheaded, hard-hearted native-born citizen who paid more attention to the almighty American buck than to any old-world fetishes. In earning the nickname the press would eventually hang on her—the "Kiss of Death"—she would prove to have the mercenary values and strength of character that would make her a worthy partner to Professor P. Patril and "Louie the Rabbi" Bolber. Paul had arranged for Rose to live in a house at 1262 Moore Street, right around the corner from his tailor shop, convenient for whatever plotting or playing he desired.

It was the spring of 1936. Paul and Rose had just dispatched her third consecutive husband to "California." They were living comfortably on the proceeds of this latest victim's insurance and a cache of beer, beans, and tuna fish that they had looted from his grocery store. Heady with their successes, they were ready to move on to bigger game. With the aid of Bolber's amazing concoctions, nothing seemed beyond their grasp. As usual, Paul had a plan. With the help of his nephew from Brooklyn, Johnny Cacopardo, they were going to expand their activities to New York and switch from two-bit murders to the economic big leagues.

Twenty-six-year-old Johnny Cacopardo kept busy in Brooklyn playing the saxophone with his dance band, Johnny King and the Wandering Serenaders, and fooling around with the girls, following wherever his male pointer led. It had already gotten him into trouble several years earlier, when he was accused of statutory rape with a fifteen-year-old girl. But the judge, following the wisdom and morality of the time, agreed to give Johnny a suspended sentence if he would marry the girl. Johnny accepted the deal and the same judge married the youngsters in his chambers that afternoon. By 1936, the swinging saxophonist was a married man with two kids, and his style was somewhat cramped.

Johnny now had a new sweetheart, a lovely twenty-nine-year-old woman named Molly Starace, with whom he wanted to develop a more profound relationship. She was a songwriter, and Johnny had the idea that they could make beautiful music together. However, arrangements were awkward in Brooklyn, where

Johnny had to contend with his wife and two children (now five and three) and with Molly's family.

For months, Uncle Paul and his lady friend, Rose, had been encouraging Johnny and Molly to escape to the City of Brotherly Love. The reason for their interest was clear. The girl lived with her mother and a stepfather, who had raised her from girlhood and whose name she had taken. They had learned that Mr. Starace was a successful and reasonably prosperous contractor who carried $25,000 in insurance on his life. What a victim! He was worth dozens of Luigi LaVecchios or Joseph Arenas.

When the young lovers visited, Paul became avuncular, sweet-talking "niece" Molly, wheedling complaints from her about her stepfather. Mr. Starace was too strict with her, she griped. He made it so difficult for her to see Johnny that she was always sneaking around. And he was too occupied with his business and his friends to pay proper attention to his wife. Paul and Rose listened carefully. They began dropping hints about the wonderful results they and Rabbi Bolber were having in rejuvenating families, especially in making laggard husbands back into the men of their wives' courtship fantasies. The hints soon escalated to avid recruitment of Molly as a client of the *la fattura* death scheme.

But with Molly and Johnny still living in Brooklyn, it was difficult to clinch the deal. When Johnny was hospitalized with a stomach ailment at the end of August, Paul seized on the moment to send Molly a provocative note. "Dear niece," he wrote,

> *In reference to your stepfather, I see that he has had*
> *bad intentions toward you, because you did not pay*
> *any attention to him, and he turned bad now. The only*
> *way to quiet him is to send him to "California."*
> *Johnny understands what I mean and I could do it in*

24 hours or a week—any way you want it, but it will
cost your mother $500.
    Let me know if he has any insurance on his life.
If not, take all you can get and when the time comes I
will take care of it.

It might have seemed imprudent to put all this in writing, but Paul
thought he had covered his tracks by using his "California" eu-
phemism. Besides, the letter was not in his own handwriting. He
had dictated it to his insurance buddy Gaetano Cicinato, who had
written it and spruced up the English.

Molly answered a few days later, her writing tightly cramped
on both sides of a postcard that she stuck in an envelope. "Dear
Uncle Paul," she wrote, "as for my stepfather, I won't be able to
have done what you suggest. We will have to let it go for the
present." This was not what Paul wanted to hear, but Molly
continued in a friendly and conspiratorial vein: "How is your
wife and all the children? Give them my love. When you write
to me, don't put your name or address on the envelope. I don't
want anyone to know where the letters come from. Write soon."
It was signed, "Affectionately, Molly and Johnny." Hardly a dis-
couraging response. The girl may not have been as cold-blooded
and cavalier about life as Paul, but she had not slammed the
door on his plan. He was confident he could win her over with
a sustained effort. His chance came only a few weeks later when
Johnny, now recovered, and Molly agreed to come live in Philadelphia. Rose Carina was more than happy to provide room and
board.

With Johnny and Molly now on the scene, Paul and Rose
could almost smell the loot from the Starace job. The first step was
to get Johnny committed to working as Paul's protégé. One after-

noon Paul was sitting with Johnny and their cousin Herman, the hit man, in the back room of the tailor shop, which looked out on Thirteenth Street. "See that guy?" Paul said, pointing to an elderly man pushing a broom down Thirteenth. "That's Tony Zambino. I have him insured for five hundred dollars. We want you to do a job on him. He goes to that beer garden across the street." Paul gestured toward a bar called the Little Grill that was visible out of the back window. "I'll give you a powder to put in his beer. You'll get two hundred and fifty dollars, half. You don't have to worry about anything. Nobody will ever find out. Even if they have autopsies, they never show what the powder is."

Johnny demurred. But that evening he was still hanging around the tailor shop when Paul saw the potential victim going into the Little Grill. He opened the upper drawer of his desk and took out a small white paper packet. Johnny recognized it as an item he had fetched for Paul from Rabbi Morris Bolber over on Fifth Street the day before. Paul waved the packet in front of Johnny as he explained the plan in more detail. "I know him. I'll introduce you to him in the beer garden. You go over to the man's table. Get to talking with him, and while you are talking, dump this powder in his beer. Don't worry, it takes two or three hours to work." Johnny still seemed skeptical, so Paul took him over to the bar.

The two men took a table near Zambino. "Go ahead," Paul said, pushing the packet at Johnny. "You do it," Johnny said, pushing it back. Paul refused, offering a lame excuse: "I can't—too many people know me." The two men sat there, shoving the packet back and forth, until Zambino wandered out.

The next morning Johnny was again at the shop, when Herman came in. Paul could hardly wait to excoriate his nephew. "Last night the son of a bitch, he had a chance to put powder in the old man's beer and wouldn't do it." Paul pulled the packet out of his desk drawer and waved it under Johnny's nose again.

Herman chimed in, "What're you afraid of? We've been doing it right along. Nobody ever knows anything. What'sa matter Johnny, you yellow? They can't trace you. It don't leave no trace." Herman shared Paul's feeling that it was only a matter of time before Johnny would see the light.

Back at the house where Johnny and Molly were staying, Rose was after the young man, too. She seemed to think that he was already a part of the murder ring, speaking openly to him about how she and Paul had taken care of her prior husbands, and how she was thinking of marrying Paul as soon as they had "done a job" on his sickly wife. "Should I marry him?" Rose queried Johnny. "He's got seven kids." Everyone from the old man Zambino to Paul's own wife was fair game for Paul and Rose's crowd. Their nefarious activities were the primary topic of conversation.

One night the four of them—Paul, Rose, Johnny, and Molly—went to the Alahambra to catch a movie. As they went in, Paul greeted a woman named Millie Giacobbe, who was coming out of the early show. "You see that woman?" Paul said after Millie left. "I did the job on her husband. Nobody knows anything. Why are you afraid?"

Johnny still didn't want to get involved himself, but he saw no need to stop his uncle from earning a living. So he just listened, until the talk turned to Dominic Starace, the stepfather of his girlfriend. It was not so easy to ignore the plotting against Starace because Johnny was the one who had first told them about the man and because Paul was drawing the innocent Molly into the plan. Johnny felt a responsibility to protect Molly. He told this to his uncle and asked Paul to lay off. But Paul was not about to pass up this spectacular jackpot.

Molly eventually gave up on her relationship with Johnny and moved back home on Monday, December 7. The Wandering Serenader was distraught, but Uncle Paul saw an opening. "Go back to your wife," he told Johnny. The young man was a disappointment to him, less than worthless, and he wanted him out of the way so they could get on with the Starace plan. But Johnny just moped around, uncertain about what to do. It was not only the loss of Molly that concerned him. She had taken with her Uncle Paul's letter from back in August, the one that implicated Johnny in the plan to send Dominic Starace "to California." Johnny was desperate to obtain and destroy it.

Johnny called Molly and insisted that she return to Philadelphia with the letter. Every day he called, threatening that he would kill her whole family unless she brought the letter to him by Saturday. One time he got Molly's mother on the phone by mistake and threatened her. She called the police, but they scoffed at her. "Don't call the saint before the devil appears," the desk sergeant told Mrs. Starace. "The person who threatens you will never kill you." She was not exactly reassured.

"What's this letter?" Mrs. Starace asked her daughter. Molly refused to tell her. The girl was terrified. Johnny was threatening her, and Paul was trying to get her to kill her stepfather.

Then Rose Carina called Mrs. Starace. "Tell your daughter Molly not to go to Philadelphia. Johnny wants to kill her. I am coming to New York on Sunday with Paul. We will tell you everything." That was it. The Staraces made certain Molly did not set foot out of the house.

When Johnny awoke that Sunday and heard that Paul and Rose had gone off early, leaving word that they were going "to Bristol," he suspected their true destination and purpose. He ran around the corner to Paul's tailor shop and jerked open the desk drawer. The notorious packet was not there, but a gun that Paul kept handy was. Shoving the pistol in his inside jacket pocket, Johnny rushed to the Trailways Station for the bus to New York.

Johnny had guessed right. Paul and Rose had taken the train up to the city that morning, taking Rose's young daughter Rita along with them to enhance their family image. By midday they were seated in the living room of the Starace home at 28B Thirty-fourth Street in the Gowanus section of Brooklyn. The Staraces, proper Italian hosts on a Sunday afternoon, fed them a big dinner. When Mr. Starace then had to go out to estimate on a contracting job, Paul gave the two Starace boys, who were teenagers, money to take little Rita to the movies. He and Rose wanted to be alone with Molly and her mother.

Mrs. Starace turned to the gentleman tailor from Philadelphia. "Is it true, what your nephew told us, that you are a great magician?"

"Yes, they call me John Do, the magician," Paul replied. "I am a great spiritualist. I am a crystal-gazer. I perform all kinds of magic."

"How do you do it?" she asked.

Paul took out a little package wrapped in brown paper and unfolded it, revealing a smaller packet in white paper. The packet contained a powder that, Mrs. Starace recalled, "was glittering like diamonds."

"That is magic powder," Paul told her. "It is ground up from bones of dead people. When we want something to happen to someone, we light up a glass of alcohol and we use a little bit of that powder. If we want to get somebody out of the way, they're gone like that." He snapped his fingers.

"If someone dies like that in New York, so soon, so quick, they do an autopsy. Don't they do that in Pennsylvania?" Mrs. Starace asked.

Paul laughed. "Of course they do it. But I am the head of a very powerful organization. My nephew John Cacopardo is my right hand. Rose Carina is my secretary. I have my cousin with the half-Jewish, half-Italian name, Herman Petrillo. We have connections in Philadelphia, in Washington, and in Harlem, New York. We have very powerful connections in Jersey. When anybody dies like that, we have our own doctors and our own undertakers. Our doctor passes them with heart failure, and then there is nothing left for the undertaker to do but bury them."

"Aren't you afraid to tell me that? Don't you think I can go squeal on you?" Mrs. Starace asked.

"I am not afraid of squealers. I am a very powerful man. If anybody squeals, we send somebody down to see them, and we take care of them," Paul told her.

They were interrupted by a knock at the door. Mrs. Starace cracked it open, the safety chain hooked. It was Johnny Cacopardo, who had rushed to New York on the Trailways bus and, in his haste to get to Brooklyn, had taken the wrong subway line twice. After traveling for hours with a gun in his pocket and wild thoughts in his mind, he was crazed, and looked it.

"I want to talk to my uncle; I know he's there," Johnny insisted.

Mrs. Starace was not about to let him in. "Your uncle is going home now, right away. You can talk to him outside." She slammed the door and locked it. She went to the telephone table in the hall. "I better call the police," she announced as she picked up the phone.

Paul jumped from his chair and pushed her against the wall,

grabbing the phone from her hand. "Don't you call the police," he said. "Don't call them!" He opened the door and pulled Johnny in. Grabbing the lapels of his jacket, he dragged his nephew into the dining room.

"What right have you got to take him in my house against my will, when my husband's not home?" Mrs. Starace demanded. She was screaming at him. "I told you what he said to us. He wants to kill us."

Paul tried to calm her. "It is my nephew," he said. "He is not going to kill anybody. Keep quiet."

Paul motioned for Johnny to sit at the dining room table, where coffee and cake were still laid out. He pushed the cake over to him. "*Mangia,* Johnny, relax." Johnny, who had not eaten all day, grabbed a piece of cake. "Why did you come here?" Paul asked.

"I came for two things." He turned to Mrs. Starace. "I wanted to apologize to you and your husband for threatening you all the time and, second, I want to talk to Molly for a few minutes alone. Then I swear you will never see me again."

"The best apology to me will be if you leave us alone and go back to your wife and children," Mrs. Starace told him.

Johnny began sobbing. "Why don't you let me talk to Molly? I swear I won't hurt a hair on her head."

"Whatever you have to tell her, tell her in front of us," she said. The boys and Rita had returned from the movies by this time. They were all standing around staring at this disheveled intruder.

"Please, let me talk with her privately, just a minute, I promise," Johnny pleaded.

Molly looked at her mother. Then she looked at Paul. "Paul, will you come in with me?" She trusted Paul. He was now her protector. Molly walked to her room, which was on the first floor, at the back of the house. Johnny followed her, as did Paul. Mrs. Starace followed, too, and stood in the doorway.

"Molly," Johnny said, "give me that letter."

"I swear to God I don't know where it is. If I find it, I will give it to you," she told him.

"Be a good girl," Paul urged her, "give it to him." He was also interested in retrieving the potentially troublesome item.

"What do they want from you?" Mrs. Starace chimed in. "What kind of letter is it?" She assumed it must be a love letter that the girl was embarrassed to disclose. So when Paul said to her, "Mom, go out for a minute, maybe she can't talk in front of you," Mrs. Starace backed out of the room.

Molly stood there frozen, her arms tightly crossed, shivering from fear. Johnny reached out, placing his hand on her shoulder as if to reassure her. As he did so, his jacket fell open.

A moment later Mrs. Starace heard Molly shouting, "Paul, he has a gun. He has a gun!" And then she heard three shots. Paul had tried to wrest the gun away from Johnny, and in the struggle, it had gone off. Molly staggered out of the bedroom holding her stomach. Blood was gushing out of her.

"Molly's shot, Molly's shot," Mrs. Starace shrieked. "He shot Molly. Look at the blood, look at the blood." Rose Carina took Molly and pulled her into the kitchen.

One of Mrs. Starace's sons grabbed a bread knife out of a drawer and rushed back to the bedroom. Johnny was gone, having escaped out the window. The gun lay on the floor. Paul Petrillo stood there with his hands in his pockets, staring out the open window, its curtains blowing in the winter wind. But when the Starace boy picked up the gun and headed for the window to jump out after Johnny, Paul grabbed him by the neck. "Where do you think you're going, kid? Drop that." He shoved the boy back to the kitchen, where Molly was lying on the floor, and helped him and his brother carry her out to the family car so the boys could drive her to the hospital.

Paul sized up the situation. It was *molte grave*. If the cops got Johnny talking, the entire ring would be in jeopardy. Even the letter began to seem more ominous, despite his cleverness in having Cicinato write it for him. He and Rose started to search for it, but they had hardly begun when the police arrived, summoned by Mrs. Starace. Paul was his smooth best, quickly shifting all the blame to Johnny, but as soon as the police learned he was from out of town, they arrested him as a material witness.

With Paul in jail, Rose stayed in Brooklyn at the home of her new friends, the Staraces, using every opportunity to scour the house surreptitiously for the letter. It was nowhere to be found. Rose raised the matter of the letter with Molly's mother, trying to be casual. But Mrs. Starace, figuring the letter was at the root of all the trouble, wanted nothing to do with it.

"I used my quick thinking," she later told investigators. "I lied to her and said I'd burned all of Molly's papers." She had in fact found the letter, mixed in with some of Molly's song lyrics, and turned it over to the police.

Meanwhile, Molly's condition worsened. She had been struck by two bullets. One went through her arm, pierced her body, and lodged in the bed behind her. The other remained in her stomach. Within the week, she died. The situation was even more grave than Paul imagined. He was in jail, Molly was in the cemetery, his self-incriminating letter was in the hands of the police, and his loose-cannon nephew, Johnny, could be arrested at any moment. The authorities were on the verge of breaking open a diabolical murder ring, with Paul at its center.

Paul brooded about his exposure. The shrewd Bolber, he now

saw, had stayed in the background the entire time, leaving him
and Rose to do the dirty work. They found the prey. They arranged the life insurance or property manipulations that would
generate profitability. They administered the potent powders and
held the hands of the grieving widows. Now they were the ones
who would face the music.

For the time being, the situation was under control. The
Brooklyn police were concerned only with the crime in their jurisdiction, the killing of Molly Starace. The perpetrator and his
method were clear, as far as they were concerned. The only problem was tracking the man down. So they devoted their efforts to
finding Johnny Cacopardo. When they questioned Paul about the
incriminating letter, he expressed surprise at its contents. "That
Johnny is a foxy boy," Paul told the police. "He probably wrote
that thing up himself." Paul volunteered for a handwriting test to
prove that he had not written the note himself. The police were
convinced. The letter was stuffed in a folder somewhere, of no
value to the investigating officers because it provided no information on Johnny's current whereabouts. Paul Petrillo was released.

A few months later, Paul had reason to be more confident
than ever of his invincibility. When New York authorities tracked
down Johnny and arrested him, Paul got a message to his nephew:
Keep your mouth shut. We've got it fixed so you'll get a light sentence.
Johnny cooperated, taking all the blame on himself for the accident, even claiming the gun as his own. But it was a setup. Paul
and Rose both took the stand at his trial and condemned Johnny,
saying he had been planning to kill Molly all along, and that they
had gone to New York only to warn and protect her. When Johnny
heard this, he tried to change his story and turn informer. It was
too late. Even his own lawyer wouldn't believe Johnny's blathering

about sinister activities in Philadelphia. The story was too bizarre—obviously something concocted by a cornered murderer trying to distract attention from his own crime—and no one would give it any heed.

Johnny, convicted of murder, was sent to Sing Sing for thirty years to life, where he continued to pester disbelieving guards with his wild story. Paul, now the hero who had risked his life to warn the Staraces, returned to Philadelphia and his business affairs.

R.I.P.
MOLLY STARACE

PART II

La Giustizia

INDICTMENT

County of Philadelphia, ss:

THE GRAND INQUEST OF THE COMMONWEALTH OF PENNSYLVANIA, INQUIRING FOR THE COUNTY OF PHILADELPHIA, UPON THEIR RESPECTIVE OATHS AND AFFIRMATIONS, DO PRESENT, THAT HERMAN PETRILLO, OF THE SAID COUNTY, AND WITHIN THE JURISDICTION OF THIS COURT, WITH FORCE OF ARMS, ETC., IN AND UPON THE BODY OF ONE FERDINANDO ALFONSI IN THE PEACE OF GOD AND THE SAID COMMONWEALTH THEN AND THERE BEING, FELONIOUSLY, WILFULLY, AND OF HIS MALICE AFORETHOUGHT, DID GIVE TO THE SAID FERDINANDO ALFONSI ONE MORTAL WOUND, OF WHICH SAID MORTAL WOUND THE SAID FERDINANDO ALFONSI AT THE COUNTY AFORESAID, AND WITHIN THE JURISDICTION OF THIS COURT, DID DIE. AND SO THE GRAND INQUEST AFORESAID, UPON THEIR OATHS AND AFFIRMATIONS AFORESAID, DO SAY.

8

DA MCDEVITT

The district attorney of Philadelphia in 1938, Charles Kelley, was a serviceable lawyer, but he was no reformer, nothing like the zealous Tom Dewey, who was ruffling feathers up in New York. Appointed by the Republican political machine that controlled everything in Philadelphia, he was not one to seek troublesome cases, especially ones that might offend an important part of the machine's political base.

When homicide detectives came to Kelley with the unfolding story of an apparent poisoning of one Ferdinando Alfonsi, the district attorney was wary. There were already hints, based on a preliminary investigation, that Alfonsi was not an isolated case, but part of a larger ongoing conspiracy in which the South Philadelphia Italian community was deeply implicated. This was a critical Republican voting bloc, still loyal well into Franklin D. Roosevelt's second term. The growing allegations were outlandish, difficult to credit, and maybe nightmarish to prove. But they could not be ignored. He assigned the case to one of his younger assistant district attorneys, Vincent McDevitt. McDevitt was better known as a hail-fellow-well-met than as a fearsome prosecutor. Kelley thought that McDevitt understood the political culture of Philadelphia well enough to know that one did not rock the boat, at least not when it might knock over valuable crew.

As it turned out, Vince McDevitt was not a timeserver like his boss. An Irish kid from the row houses of West Philadelphia, Vince was the second oldest of four brothers. After the death of his father when he was just fourteen, he had worked to help his mother support the family. Though she worked as a seamstress, Mrs. McDevitt had an unusual qualification for that day. She had graduated from college in the 1890s. She urged her sons to do the same. After he finished parochial school, Vince enrolled at the Wharton School of the University of Pennsylvania, but only in the night-school division. There was no money in the family for full-time college.

After only a year at Penn, the aspiring college student dropped out, convinced that a law degree (which one could then pursue directly, without having first completed college) was more to his liking than a business one. Discovering that state senatorial scholarships were available to deserving students, he set out to convince his senator to award him one. He had no political or family connections, the usual qualification for these scholarships, but he somehow sold himself and won a partial grant, enough to enable him to attend Temple Law School at night. Even with this aid, he could not spare the time for a full course load. It was not until the economically doomed year of 1929, when he was twenty-eight years old, that Vince finally completed his legal education and qualified for the bar.

Three years later, while still struggling to start a practice in the declining economy, McDevitt married and quickly became a father. He was relieved when, in January 1935, he obtained an appointment as an assistant district attorney. The salary, about $3,500 a year, was not bad, considering the fact that it was only a part-time job and he could continue to develop an outside income. It gave him enough security to invest in his first house, on Drexel Road in the respectable Overbrook section of Philadelphia. A second child was born in 1936.

The position as assistant DA carried some prestige, and it enabled Vince to acquire trial experience and make valuable contacts. There were weekly informal lunches where the young assistants could meet senior members of the small Philadelphia trial bar. Through these contacts, he found his private practice growing. A big man with a handsome, clean-cut look, McDevitt was immensely personable and gregarious. He liked people and he was easy to like, good with a story and just as good listening to those of others. He began friendships with men such as Harold Kohn, later to be a prestigious antitrust lawyer; John McShane, who would become a wealthy construction contractor and long-term client; and John Kelly, the powerful contractor and political leader who would eventually be best known as the father of Grace, Princess of Monaco.

With a wife and two small children, McDevitt knew he had to devote himself to his budding private practice if he was going to move ahead financially. A poison murder case was no help in this regard. But he had a great sense of duty and responsibility; he was fascinated by the story that was emerging.

Urine specimens taken from Ferdinando Alfonsi, who lay on his deathbed at the National Stomach Hospital, confirmed the doctors' worst suspicions. He was a victim of arsenical poisoning. McDevitt moved quickly to arrest the apparent killers—Alfonsi's wife, Stella, and that jack-of-all-crimes, Herman Petrillo—on a charge of attempted murder. When Alfonsi died in the hospital a few weeks later, the charge was upped to murder one.

R.I.P.
FERDINANDO ALFONSI

9

THE SECRET SERVICE MURDER PLOT

Herman's longtime nemesis, Agent Landvoight of the United States Secret Service, laid out the Alfonsi story for McDevitt. Landvoight knew more than he wanted of the gory details because his undercover agents had become embroiled in the murder plot while trying to catch Herman Petrillo in a counterfeiting sting operation.

One of Herman's rackets was the Italian-American Political and Moral Bocce Club of Paradise, better known as the Paradise Club. With cousin Paul, Herman had founded this social club, a simply furnished room where you could have a cheap glass of wine, play cards, and lament—in the Italian dialect of Napoli— the sorry state of your wife and the world's affairs. Herman enjoyed hanging out there. It was a fertile source of contacts. But he also liked such profitable sidelines as arranging group insurance for club members. Every member was eligible for a four-hundred-dollar death benefit—"funeral insurance," they called it. It was

free. It came with the dues, if you could pass the physical examination. Herman arranged for Dr. Henry D'Alonzo, a fellow former
barber, to perform the medical examinations. Dr. D'Alonzo
screened from fifty to one hundred men a night at fifty cents a
head. Herman, who got a per-head cut from the insurance company, hoped no one would fail. He was not disappointed.

When he needed someone to help in one of his criminal
schemes, Herman would often repair to the Paradise Club. It
seemed only fraternal to cut his buddies in on the opportunities
that his fertile mind kept generating. A fellow named Ferdinando
Alfonsi had always seemed particularly interested in joining him.
Alfonsi was a family man whom Herman had first met when Ferdinando lived with his wife, Stella, on Cross Street, off Passyunk.
He had known modest prosperity as a cement contractor in the
late 1920s, when he was a young man. But now he was getting
close to forty and his business had collapsed with the Depression.
The only job he could get was as a day laborer with the WPA.
You could hardly support a wife and two sons on that.

So Ferdinando helped Herman move some counterfeit cur-
rency, and he helped him fence some hot merchandise. Herman
began dropping by the house at 2515 East Ann Street in Northeast
Philly, where the Alfonsis had moved, picking up his colleague in
whatever Plymouth or Dodge was then serving as his office. Stella
was an added inducement for these visits.

Stella Liberti Alfonsi was beautiful, with an earthy southern
Italian appeal. She had been raised by a traditional family in the
factory town of Bristol, Pennsylvania, outside Philadelphia. Her
father had been a strict disciplinarian with a violent temper. Lame
and unable to work, Mr. Liberti was home all the time, limping
around the house with his cane and raising it in anger against
anything that displeased him. While her mother was out at factory

jobs, Stella was brought up by the nuns at St. Ann's of Bristol, where she attended school. They taught her to sing and to act. She had a beautiful voice and loved to perform in church plays and the Italian operettas that local theaters staged.

Stella's father arranged her marriage to Ferdinando Alfonsi in 1926, when she was only seventeen and he was a successful twenty-seven-year-old cement and masonry contractor. It was no love marriage. "My father sold me to Alfonsi for two thousand dollars" was the story she told her family in later years. The couple moved to Philadelphia, into the house at 914 Cross Street. Stella quickly bore two sons, Ralph and Leo, but she and her husband did not have much of a relationship. Ferdinando was out with his buddies almost every night, and she was often out with girlfriends like her neighbor across the street at number 919, Rose Carina (later to become known as the "Kiss of Death," but now just another struggling housewife).

The Alfonsi marriage was rocky, with frequent breakups. Stella paid little attention to her children, leaving them home alone or sending them off to the movies by themselves. Sometimes they would return home to a locked house and sit on the doorstep for hours waiting for their mother. The responsibilities of motherhood seemed more than she could tolerate. Stella was a gregarious child-woman who lived for the moment.

Herman was not one to resist the allure of a woman like this. At first, he just befriended the lovely Stella. When he learned that Stella was unhappy with her husband, it seemed almost too good to be true. He figured he could woo her with his charm, and charm her with his chivalry in ridding her of an unwanted husband. The only problem was that Herman was tight with Alfonsi. They were lodge brothers and business partners. They hung out together. It wasn't easy to kill a man who was your pal. So, after arranging for a couple of thousand dollars of life insurance on Alfonsi, Herman began looking for someone else to finish the job.

George Myer (aka Newmyer) seemed the right kind of guy. The times were not good, and he was just looking for a few dollars to keep body and soul together. Myer was flexible. He had been a forger, worked with bootleggers, and been a police informer. This time he looked up a friend of his, Dominick Policino. The two men had done time together back in 1927, when Policino was in for beating up his son-in-law and Myer for forgery. Policino was now running a little spaghetti diner at 1802 East Thayer Street in South Philadelphia. Policino couldn't offer his ex-prison *compagno* anything directly, except maybe a plate of spaghetti carbonara. But he took Myer outside and introduced him to Herman Petrillo, who was sitting there in his "office," the greenish gray Dodge purchased with the proceeds of his latest arson caper. Policino passed on the kind of recommendation that counted in their world: "This man is all right. He took good care of my whiskey during Prohibition. He saved me from getting arrested a lot of times."

Petrillo invited Myer into the car to discuss affairs. Myer promptly offered a hot Hoover vacuum cleaner for twenty-five dollars. But Herman countered with a grander proposal. "Why stop at twenty-five bucks?" he said. "I got a chance for you to make five hundred."

"What d'you got in mind?" asked Myer.

"Nothing much, you just bump a guy off. It's all set up."

"Who d'you want bumped off?"

"A fellow named Ferdinando Alfonsi."

Herman took Myer around to the back of the car and removed a piece of pipe from the trunk. It was about eighteen inches long, with a flange at the end. The plan was straightforward.

"You do it in his house. Hit him with the pipe." Herman

swatted the pipe into his palm a couple of times for effect. "Then carry him up the steps and throw him down. It'll look like an accident." Herman apparently had decided to go for double indemnity if he was going to have to split with Myer.

"Why don't you do the job yourself if it's so simple?" asked the skeptical Myer.

Herman was offended by the idea. "I know the guy. He's a friend of mine. I just knocked a guy off five days ago, but I didn't know him so good."

It didn't much matter to Myer. A job was a job. Besides, he did not really plan to go through with this murder. He was just trying to work Herman for an advance. When they discussed the plan, Myer volunteered a perceptive insight. "We can't use the pipe. It'd leave an impression on his head. They'd notice it right away." Herman knew that wasn't true, because he and Jumbo Valenti had used the very same pipe on John Woloshyn a few years earlier. But he wasn't one to quibble. If Myer didn't like denting pipes, he'd give him something softer.

Surmising that a sack packed with sand might fill the bill, Herman had his tailor cousin, Paul, sew one up. Herman assured Myer, "The bag won't kill the man, but it'll knock him out, and it won't leave no mark. The doctor will say he had a cerebral hemorrhage. Then you can take him in back of the house and push him down the cellar steps and break his neck." Herman definitely liked the idea of the steps.

Myer continued to press Herman for an advance. But Herman was too cheap or too cagey. They kept planning the job, and Myer kept coming up with excuses why he had been unable to go through with it. One time he said he could not find the house. Herman said that Alfonsi's wife, Stella, was in on the plan, and he would have her tie a white towel to the back fence. Myer found

the towel, but he said neighbors were outside and he couldn't
sneak in. All the while, they talked about payment, as Myer fished
for his advance. Finally, Herman upped the ante. He said he would
pay Myer an extra $2,500 in counterfeit dough if he would just
get the job done.

Counterfeit dough! Myer loved the idea, because he was an
old informer for the T-men. He knew they would appreciate a lead
to some big game. When Agent Landvoight learned that the long-
sought prey Herman Petrillo was finally in his sights, he quickly
set up a plan. By the beginning of August, Stanley Phillips, a street-
smart agent of the United States Secret Service, was working undercover with Myer. Two other agents were detailed to follow and
cover them.

Myer arranged a meeting at Policino's spaghetti joint on
Thayer Street. It was August 1, 1938, ten o'clock in the morning.
Myer and Phillips, who arrived first, were sitting at a table having
coffee. Herman joined them, but quickly suggested that they ad-
journ to the privacy of his Dodge, which was parked outside. Myer
introduced Phillips as "Johnny" Phillips, a friend of his just out
of Trenton State Prison from a murder rap. He convinced Herman
that the two of them could deliver when Myer alone had been
unable. Since the price was still to be the same, Herman did not
care.

The conversation turned immediately to the subject at hand,
how to bump off Alfonsi. Herman led with his stair proposals. He
also suggested that, because he was friendly with the man, he could
"entice him to go to some beach on the Jersey coast" where they
"could take him out in the surf and drown him. His clothes would
be discovered in the locker of the bathhouse and it would appear
as an accident." Phillips, trying to establish his bona fides, proposed that an auto accident would be a better gimmick, a proposal

that Myer embraced because he figured he could get Herman to supply them with a car. The idea was that they would take Alfonsi out for a ride and ask him to look at the headlights. When he walked to the front of the car, they would step on the gas and keep going. Herman liked the scheme, having used it himself in the past, but he didn't want to invest in a car. He told Myer to steal one.

The three men kept conspiring all through August, meeting three or four times a week, with Herman pushing and Phillips and Myer stalling until they could get some evidence for their counterfeiting case. To keep Myer on board, Phillips slipped him a dollar or two from time to time, a total of ten dollars over two months. It didn't exactly take big money to satisfy a punk like Myer. They kept pressing Herman for an advance to buy a car, which they now said they'd need for a getaway even if they didn't use it in the act. The T-man didn't want to mess up Herman's murder plan before he could get *his* job done. Everyone had his own priorities.

On August 22, they convened again in a booth at Policino's on Thayer Street. As usual, Herman was late, timing his appearance to make an entrance. This time, he had something dramatic to show them. Reaching into his trousers, he pulled out a counterfeit Lincoln-head five. Myer was so impressed with its quality, he called over Policino for a look-see. A sophistication in judging counterfeits, with a connoisseur's appreciation for fine work, was part of their ethos. Herman let the men examine it as he extolled the quality of the workmanship, but he wouldn't let them keep it. Agent Phillips could barely control his excitement. "You get us a stack of those, we could use them to buy the car," the agent suggested, finally seeing the end of this interminable mating dance with his prey.

Herman was amenable, but he was no patsy. "It's thirty

bucks for a hundred," he told them. It was a good deal. Thirty per hundred was an average price, and these notes were far better than that. Phillips agreed to take two hundred dollars' worth.

Herman apparently had a bit more difficulty than usual in connecting with his source in Harlem, and two weeks went by. In the meantime, the Secret Service learned that Alfonsi's health had taken a sudden turn for the worse. Myer had discovered it himself. He had been looking all over for Herman, and when the murder maestro could not be found at any of his usual haunts, Myer decided to see whether anything had happened with their waiting victim. He went by the Alfonsi house on Ann Street and knocked, posing as someone interested in a construction project. "Is the contractor here?" he asked when Stella answered the door.

"He is very sick; he's been sick since Friday" Stella told him. "You can't see him."

"Oh," said Myer, feigning surprise, "I just saw him yesterday. This is the house of Periniti, the contractor, isn't it?" Myer asked, dissembling as he backed away.

Myer rushed the information to the Secret Service. The covering agents immediately went to the Alfonsi home, posing as WPA officials worried about his absence from work. They found the man writhing in pain.

"Alfonsi lay there on his bed," the agents reported. "There was a distinct yellow cast to his face. His eyelids were purple, his eyes bloodshot, and his pupils bulging. His tongue had a coating over it, and he talked with great difficulty. When he spoke, he would attempt to gesticulate, but he didn't have the strength to continue. His hands would collapse back on his chest. It was almost impossible to understand him because of the thickness of his speech."

All the while, Alfonsi's beauteous wife, Stella, stood beside him, stroking his forehead. She brushed the hair back out of his face and patted the pillow. Mrs. Alfonsi seemed very anxious to make her husband as comfortable as possible and keep him out of the hospital. She said she could give him as good care as anyone and saw no need for him to go elsewhere. That was enough for the T-men. They turned the matter over to the Philadelphia police.

Meanwhile, Herman finally arranged for a delivery of counterfeit money to be made in Trenton, halfway between New York and Philadelphia. Myer and Phillips met him there at the bus station, just behind the Stacy-Trent Hotel, on September 18. Herman, who was parked and waiting, motioned them into his Dodge. He handed them a small white envelope. It contained forty counterfeit five-dollar bills. Phillips was very pleased. His case was about to be closed. But trying to maintain his cover as he quietly counted the money, he raised the Alfonsi matter as if he had no knowledge of the victim's declining condition.

"Now what about that job?" Phillips asked.

"Oh, forget about that part," Herman said. "The man's in the Stomach Hospital, and he's not coming out."

After months of fooling around with Myer and Phillips, Herman had finally taken matters into his own hands.

10
CHEMOTHERAPY

When DA McDevitt confronted Stella with this story, she clammed up and denied everything. But Herman Petrillo opened wide, trying to talk himself out of trouble and willing to talk anyone else into it. He was innocent himself, Herman claimed, but he knew who was guilty. Herman reeled off a list of victims that astounded even jaded homicide detectives, and he fingered his tailor cousin, Paul Petrillo, and the Jewish mystic Morris Bolber as the evil masterminds responsible for dozens of deaths. Brought in for questioning, Paul Petrillo amenably added to the list. He was innocent himself, Paul assured the prosecutor, but he, too, could name names, such as those of Morris Bolber and his cousin Herman and their myriad victims. Paul's nephew Johnny Cacopardo, stewing in his Sing Sing cell, read about the Philadelphia arrests and contacted McDevitt. At last, Johnny had found someone who would listen to his story.

McDevitt's pad began to fill up with dozens of leads. No one had ever even imagined something like this. It was not only Ferdinando Alfonsi who had been—to use a term that came into vogue—"Petrillo-ized." Mostly, the deceased were husbands. One batch consisted of Dominic Carina, Prospero Lisi, and Peter Stea, all late husbands of the true femme fatale Rose "Kiss of Death" Carina, who had lost three spouses in quick succession and was now working on a fourth. But Rose's prey were only a few entries on a long antimatrimonial roster. There was Joseph Arena, late husband of Anna Arena; Luigi LaVecchio, late husband of Sophie LaVecchio; and Charles Ingrao, late common-law husband of Maria Favato. There was Antonio Giacobbe, late husband of Millie Giacobbe; Guiseppi DiMartino, late husband of Susie DiMartino; Antonio Romualdo, late husband of Josephine Romualdo; John Woloshyn, late husband of Marie Woloshyn; Romaine Mandiuk, late husband of Agnes Mandiuk; Pietro Pirolli, late husband of Grace Pirolli; and Salvatore Carilli, late husband of Rose Carilli, a widow from Wilmington. There were a few wives, Jennifer Pino, late wife of Thomas Pino; and Jennie Cassetti, late wife of Dominick Cassetti. And, for good measure, one boarder, Ralph Caruso, late tenant of Christine Cerrone; one child, Philip Ingrao, late stepson of Maria Favato; and one mother-in-law, Lena Winkleman, late annoyance of Joseph Swartz. All, except Arena and Caruso (both of whom had drowned) and Woloshyn (who had been run over), had died of sudden illnesses like the one that had stricken Ferdinando Alfonsi.

The deaths strung out over the thirties: Carina in 1931, Arena and LaVecchio in 1932, Lisi and Giacobbe in 1933; Caruso in 1934; Woloshyn, Mandiuk, Pirolli, and Charles Ingrao in 1935; Winkleman, Stea, Pino, and Romualdo in 1936; DiMartino in 1937. There was a lull from February 1937 to June 1938. Then Cassetti, Philip Ingrao, Carilli, and Alfonsi dropped in quick suc-

cession over the summer, until the case broke in September 1938.
McDevitt literally didn't know where all the bodies were buried.
It was a daunting task. For a prosecutor who had never before
handled a major case, it was an opportunity to make, or break, a
legal career.

There was clearly more going on in this case than McDevitt
understood. Someone was sending death threats to the informer
George Myer and his wife, craftily composed of individual letters
cut out of newspaper headlines (not prepared on a traceable typewriter as the notorious 1932 Lindbergh kidnapping notes had
been). "ADVISE HUSBAND TO STAY Out OF COURT OR Death, 4 TWO.
WE DARE YOU TO SEE Detective," read one such missive.

Then, in January, the threats became more than just artful
clippings. Myer's battered body, his arms and legs bound and his
mouth taped shut, was found on Erie Avenue near I Street. The
victim told police he had been brutally beaten for five hours and
then tossed unconscious in a deep snowbank. He had been revived
by the cold snow, Myer said, and managed to roll out into the
street. Had he not been discovered by a passing motorist, who
rushed him to the hospital, the state's case against Herman Petrillo
and Stella Alfonsi would have been missing a key witness. Myer
could not (or did not want to) identify his attackers, but obvious
suspicions were raised. The police put him in protective custody.

Meanwhile, neither the police nor Vincent McDevitt had
managed to get the Petrillo cousins to admit anything; all the rats'
talking had simply been to point the finger at others. But McDevitt
could add one and one, and, as he saw it, the evidence he had
added up to enough to convict Herman Petrillo. McDevitt was
ambitious, too. He knew that these cases would have to be parceled
out among several prosecutors and that the first case to come to
trial was the one that the public would remember. The only solo

transatlantic pilot anyone cared about was the first, and Vince McDevitt wanted to be the prosecutorial Lindbergh of this murder conspiracy.

February of 1939 was a remarkable month, full of history-making events that displaced poison murders in the minds of Philadelphia citizens. Neville Chamberlain was appeasing Hitler, who thundered threats in the Reichstag. President Roosevelt was attempting to aid Britain and France, while the ever-perspicacious Herbert Hoover, not content to rest on the laurels of his 1928–1932 presidency, lobbied on behalf of isolationism. Jewish leaders, dismayed by the events in Germany and the world's lack of concern, sought a place of refuge for mass resettlement, even proposing Alaska and British Guiana as alternatives to Palestine. Harvard terminated the fellowship of Granville Hicks because he proclaimed himself a Communist. Eleanor Roosevelt resigned from the Daughters of the American Revolution because they refused to allow the Negro soprano Marian Anderson to sing in Constitution Hall.

But Assistant District Attorney Vincent P. McDevitt of Philadelphia was concerned with none of this. He thought of only one thing—preparing his case against Herman Petrillo. Autopsies had been completed on Ferdinando Alfonsi, whose unhappy fate had launched the entire process, and on the exhumed bodies of Charles and Philip Ingrao, the late husband and stepson of Maria Favato. They were all found full of arsenic. On February 17, 1939, the grand jury returned murder indictments against four coconspirators, the Petrillo cousins—Herman and Paul—and the widows of the autopsied men, Stella Alfonsi and Maria Favato.

These indictments were in large part a public-relations effort by the district attorney, an attempt to show the voters that legal authority was in control. In reality, the cases were still very much under investigation and new charges were emerging almost daily. But by March, McDevitt was ready to begin, with Herman Petrillo selected as his number-one target. The indictment was narrowed to charge him with only the murder of Ferdinando Alfonsi.

x x x

McDevitt began to educate himself about arsenic. The notorious substance, he learned, was a common element, a gray metal in its pure natural state. Throughout history, it had been widely used in industrial and household preparations. It was available in solid form as arsenic trioxide, or "white arsenic," the component of various rat poisons, ant pastes, and veterinary preparations. As sodium arsenite, it was mixed in liquid solutions for weed control and other agricultural purposes. Copper acetoarsenite, or "Paris green," was a popular wallpaper dye as well as an antirat weapon. In low doses, arsenic was used for medicinal purposes. Salvarsan, an arsenic-based medicine, was then the chief medical weapon against syphilis. They called it "chemotherapy." Women even used it secretly to capitalize on the way it attacked blood vessels. It brought a rosy glow to their cheeks.

Arsenic had acquired a diabolic reputation as the weapon of choice for those who chose to kill by stealth, probably because it was both odorless and tasteless yet toxic in small doses, making it easy to slip into food or drink or even mix with sugar so that the victim could help himself. A mere 120 milligrams—4/1,000 of an ounce, comparable to a third of an ordinary aspirin tablet—was considered a lethal dose, so a teaspoon of laced food or a cup of coffee with this satanic sugar substitute could easily be fatal. Yet it was not so overwhelmingly toxic as to prevent the killer from tasting a bit of a laced dish himself—just a taste, mind you—

thereby reassuring his prey. Better yet from the murderer's perspective, the symptoms of an arsenic death mimicked those of ordinary causes such as food poisoning, bleeding ulcers, and heart failure.

McDevitt read the bleak abstract in standard medical manuals:

> Gastrointestinal effects include inflammation of the mouth, pharynx, and esophagus, burning abdominal pain, thirst, violent gastroenteritis with vomiting, copious rice-watery or bloody diarrhea containing shreds of mucus, and dehydration with intense thirst and muscular cramps. Central nervous system effects include headache, dizziness, muscle weakness and spasms, hypothermia, lethargy, coma, convulsions, delirium and even mania. Cardiovascular manifestations include shock, cyanosis, and cardiac arrhythmias. These effects result from the action of an arsenical metabolite on blood vessels generally, causing dilation and increased capillary permeability.

In other words, arsenic burned its way through the digestive system and then insidiously destroyed the blood vessels. An acute dose killed fairly quickly, usually within one to three days, but lower doses could cause symptoms to drag on for months or even years. Liver damage, skin diseases, and severe weight loss from anorexia often resulted. Every adverse human condition from dandruff to cancer had been attributed to this appalling agent of the Grim Reaper.

Unless there was reason to suspect foul play, as there had been in Ferdinando Alfonsi's case, most doctors simply attributed the death to routine causes. Luigi LaVecchio's death certificate read "gastroenteritis." In other cases involving Bolber and the Petrillos, the cause had been listed variously by innocent physicians as "cardiac decompensation," "myocardial degeneration," "lumbar pneumonia, myocarditis," "influenza," and "diabetes." The only really telltale symptom of arsenic noted in the manuals was "a garlic odor to the breath," hardly a noteworthy matter in the Italian immigrant community.

McDevitt also learned that another poison had been used in some of the cases, antimony. This was a gray metallic element like arsenic that also had medicinal uses. Antimony compounds were used to treat parasitic infections and as vomit-inducing emetics. Antimony killed in the same secret ways as arsenic, with similar symptoms, but it had ten to twenty times the toxicity of its better-known cousin. One reporter, fascinated by this alternative toxin, called it "an exotic and elusive poison—a poison so secret that it is rarely named—that scarcely leaves a trace in the bodies of its victims."

The reporter was alluding to the one property of both arsenic and antimony that prevented them from becoming the basis of the perfect crime. As inorganic elements, they did not decompose. They collected in bodily tissue and were easy to find on autopsy, even years after death. Because antimony was toxic in smaller doses than arsenic, it could be more difficult to detect. Yet both arsenic or antimony murderers had to maintain a low profile and avoid any basis for suspicion. They were best advised to avoid sophisticated medical care for their victims. They did well, if at all possible, to have the body cremated immediately and the ashes scattered.

However, even if these cautions were ignored and the poison was identified, an arsenic or antimony killer had one final factor working in his favor. The presence of the poison might establish the cause of death, but it could not prove how the evil element had gotten there. The prosecutor faced a formidable double challenge. He had to prove both a negative and a positive—that it *did not* come from some accidental source (such as workplace exposure) and that it *did* come from a particular person, the defendant, with evil intent. This last task was seriously impeded by the fact that administration of poison was always a covert act, with none of the drama and evidentiary richness of a stabbing, gunshot, or other violent assault. All this and "reasonable doubt" favoring the defendant, too.

As DA McDevitt continued to research his case, he was dismayed to learn how often poisoning prosecutions stumbled over these proof problems. The accused were, more often than not, acquitted. He saw that extraordinary preparation would be required.

"We had a complete working unit," McDevitt later reported. "It consisted of twenty detectives, six insurance company investigators, two chemists, two physicians, one pathologist, a toxicologist and an undertaker, as well as a score of helpers. In order to meet coming attacks in Court, we read the testimony of every poison case that had been tried and lost in Philadelphia since the famous *Williams* case of 1905, in which a couple accused of poisoning their children had won acquittal. We found the answer as to why they were lost. The State would build a good strong case of circumstantial evidence plus the direct evidence available against the defendant and then the State's case would slowly but surely melt and evaporate under the expert testimony of the medical men and chemists for the defense."

In past cases, he learned, the evidence had become compromised because of inadequate controls in the testing process. The exhumed body had not been watched carefully the entire time, the receptacle into which bodily organs were placed had not been properly cleaned, the organs had been left unattended on the au-

topsy table while doctors left the room, or the embalming fluid had
contained arsenic. In the *Williams* case, the defense claimed that
there was arsenic in the dye in the children's clothing, in the air,
and in the soil, as well as in the embalming fluid.

"Most criminal cases are won in the office," McDevitt observed, "but ours was also won in the laboratory. As each body
was exhumed, in the presence of two homicide detectives and the
superintendent of the cemetery, a police photographer took a pho-
tograph. Samples of the soil or water lying in the bottom of the
grave were taken and delivered to the chemist. The casket was
removed to the morgue in the presence of the detectives and received by the coroner's physician and two chemists. In the presence of two identification witnesses who knew the decedent in his
lifetime as well as the undertaker who furnished the casket, the
box was opened. The coroner's physician then received samples
of clothing worn by the decedent and of the lining of the casket.
Bits of metal were removed. These were given to the chemist to
be tested for arsenic along with samples of the soil and bits of
wallpaper taken from the room where the decedent had died.

"Then the physician donned rubber operating gloves known
to be chemically clean by him, and using sterilized instruments,
removed an organ one at a time, weighing it in the presence of
the chemist and then placing it in a chemically clean hermetically
sealed glass jar. This jar was held by the chemist who was to make
the test. By this procedure we were prepared for medical and
chemical experts for the defense for we knew and could prove, if
necessary, that everything the victim's body touched from the time
of death to its exhumation was tested and found negative for arsenic."

At least that was the goal. McDevitt met with Dr. Martin
Crane, who performed the autopsies, and with the police-lab chem-

ists and others involved in the process to impress upon them the importance of conducting precise and meticulous examinations. They confronted a tedious, and unappetizing, task. The internal organs—stomach, liver, kidneys—had to be removed from rotting bodies, some of which, such as that of Luigi LaVecchio, had been in the ground for more than six years. Portions of each organ then had to be sliced off (several slices randomly distributed from around the organ) and ground into a fine mush with a sterilized meat grinder. Some of this mush was then subjected to qualitative tests in order to determine if it contained any poison at all. If this proved positive, more of the same mush was subjected to more elaborate quantitative tests to determine the precise amount of the toxin.

The tested specimens all had to be painstakingly weighed, because the quantities found in the tested portion would have to be multiplied, based on relative weight, so that a conclusion could be stated about the amount in the entire organ. With results expressed in a thousandth of a gram, or even a millionth of a gram in some cases, the slightest error would fatally corrupt the results. Each of these tests took days, and they had to be separately conducted for each possible poison and for each of the organs.

Despite these demands, McDevitt and his team worked quickly. They had to. With daily stories in the newspapers about a murder ring, the pressure on the district attorney to do something to bring the case to a head increased. It was difficult to do so when key participants had yet to be located. Herman and Paul Petrillo told such incredible and often conflicting stories that McDevitt and his colleagues did not know who or what to believe. Among the accusations that Paul made against Bolber, for example, was that the oddly named "Louie the Rabbi" wanted to have intercourse with all the women who came to him.

"He told me he used to go see Sophie LaVecchio all the time,"
Paul told the DA. "What do you call it, he had relations with her.
Bolber told me he went to Sophie's house and gave her some of
his nature in a drink of milk. Do you understand what I mean?
His own nature, in a drink, in a glass of milk, to make her go
crazy for him. He had another woman, Rose Smigel, and he had
that poor woman crazy about him, and had plenty of intercourse.
He used her himself in my store, in the dressing room. Irene Block
was a young woman, came to Bolber to help patch up a lover's
quarrel, and he kept her for two years, used her sexually. I know
because he used me as a lookout. He used to go with the girl inside
and I watched for his wife to come in so I could tell him to quiet
down. Another time a seventy-year-old woman came to Bolber,
and when she couldn't pay, Bolber said, 'Give me your body.' "

McDevitt had no idea what to make of these bizarre sexual
allegations. But the dead men and women were dead, for sure.
Who had been murdered and who had died otherwise? What role
did the spouses of the deceased play in the deaths? Were they
dupes or demons? Who was the mastermind? For someone like
McDevitt, who prided himself on his objectivity and his ability to
get to the bottom of things, it was all a muddy, murky pool of
charges and cross-charges, of fact and fantasy.

It was easier for the press, which jumped on this tale of an
"Arsenic Murder Ring" as a surefire circulation booster. Day after
day, the papers, from the tabloid *Record* and *Daily News,* to the
broadsheet *Evening Bulletin* and *Ledger,* to the relatively staid *Inquirer,* barraged readers with updates on the unfolding horrors.
Hardly a day went by without at least a report like WEIRD STORY
TOLD AT POISON HEARINGS, or FIFTH BODY EXHUMED IN POISON INQUIRY. When there were wild claims to offer, the headlines grew
larger, screaming, POISON RING SOUGHT DEADLY GERMS, or RING

KILLED AT LEAST 100, even though such were just thirdhand rumors of what someone might have said. If the DA's office and police investigators produced no news at all, reporters assigned to fan the flames kept the blaze alive with background stories. BLACK MAGIC USED BY ARSENIC KILLERS, reported David G. Wittels of the *Bulletin* in a four-column feature spread, advising his readers that Paul Petrillo's "abracadabra was a strange mixture of Palatinate German black magic, African voodoo, and the lore of the superstitious of old Italy." An enterprising investigative reporter, Betty Hurd Renshaw, showed how easy it was to buy arsenic, easily acquiring, as the headline read, ENOUGH ARSENIC TO MURDER 250 PEOPLE IN AN HOUR—FOR JUST 97 CENTS. Even the blithest residents of Passyunk began looking askance at their spouses and eating their food more gingerly.

The much-talked-about trial of Herman Petrillo began on March 13, 1939. The whereabouts of Morris Bolber and other prime suspects, including the triple poison widow, Rose "Kiss of Death" Carina, were still unknown. Stella Alfonsi and the other indicted coconspirators remained deep in their jail cells. But the now-chubby, dapper Herman Petrillo was there for all to see in Room 453 of Philadelphia's City Hall, the Court of Quarter Sessions.

11
HERMAN ON TRIAL

POISON RING TRIAL TOMORROW TO BARE WEB OF WITCHCRAFT, blared the *Philadelphia Record*. Curious citizens thronged for admission to the spacious fifty-foot-square courtroom with its impressive twenty-five-foot-high ceiling and enormous arched windows. They clogged the broad corridors of City Hall, vying for one of the 150 or so places available in the spectator section. But Herman Petrillo, the one man with a constitutionally guaranteed seat, was almost casual about the whole thing. When he had beaten the rap in his arson trial two years before, he had seen how difficult it was to prove a case "beyond a reasonable doubt," and he had always been careful to avoid damning himself. When the police arrested him, he had been smart enough to mark the genuine money they took from him. That way they could not frame him by substituting counterfeit ones. He was always thinking ahead. He knew he was a lot smarter than the cops. And he had a smart Jewish lawyer, Milton Leidner. As he saw it, a Jew lawyer could run circles around a dumb mick prosecutor like McDevitt. So why should he worry?

There were a few reasons. For one thing, there were rumors that the judge, named Harry McDevitt, was the prosecutor's uncle. In addition to sharing a last name, Judge McDevitt had sworn in the assistant DA when Vince had joined the prosecutor's office. In any case, Judge McDevitt was notoriously severe and pro-prosecution. Like-minded observers declared, "He does not believe in some of the modern ideas of penology, which he regards as coddling and pampering the criminal too much." Around the courthouse they were not so kind, describing him as "tough and vicious," even "evil," and dubbing him "Hanging Harry." He was obnoxious to defense lawyers, embarrassing them with rude comments while he bent over backward to favor the prosecution. He was intensely political and not above using whatever power he had to further his goals. One lawyer remembers him as cut from the same cloth as J. Edgar Hoover, possessing information on everyone and an unscrupulous willingness to use it. Rumor has it that, after his death in 1950, a fortune in ill-gotten greenbacks was found stashed behind pictures in his Atlantic City retirement villa.

x x x

For any defendant or defense lawyer in 1939 lacking the wherewithal to buy justice, Judge Harry McDevitt was the most feared judge on the bench. Leidner knew this, but he did not file a motion to disqualify. He felt he was on good terms with the judge, even thought he was a personal friend. You could get mileage out of that sort of a relationship. That's the way it was in

Philadelphia in 1939. Another judge and lawyer were commonly
known as the "Great Divide" because of the way they were said
to share bribes. It was a town where you went along to get along.

Leidner hoped Judge McDevitt would have the good sense at
least to avoid showing bias against the defendant. But he was
wrong. Though the rumors of a familial relationship turned out to
be unfounded—the judge and prosecutor were not related—the
judge's major concern seemed to be ensuring that the prosecutor
did not blow his big case. Whatever the prosecution wanted, the
prosecution got.

Not that the DA needed this unfair advantage. He had a
formidable array of witnesses to present. Thomas J. Shearn, agent
for John Hancock Mutual Life, told how Herman had taken him
to the Alfonsi house on February 9, 1937, to write a policy. When
Ferdinando said he wasn't interested, Herman told the reluctant
prospect, "Just fill in the application, that's all. The man's in a
contest. Let's help him," and Alfonsi complied. He took the maximum that could be written without medical examination.

Luigi Cissone, an agent for Monumental Life Insurance, told
the jury how he had met Herman at their hangout, the Paradise
Club. Herman said, "I have this guy, he's a little bit against insurance, but I'm going to take you there, and you talk to him." Herman took Cissone to the Alfonsi home on February 24, 1937, along
with a bottle of vermouth ("which is some Italian liquor," Cissone
thoughtfully explained to the jury). The two men and the vermouth convinced Alfonsi to apply for two thousand dollars more
in life insurance. Constantine Avellino and Achilles Tedesco,
agents for Home Life, told how Herman had sent them to the
Alfonsi home in May 1937, to write another policy on Ferdinando,
and how Herman had said they "would have to resort to some
means" to get the man's signature because he was opposed to in-

surance. They succeeded in getting an application for another seven hundred dollars' worth of insurance. Anthony Fiascatore, the president of the Paradise Club, told how Herman had arranged for Ferdinando Alfonsi to join up in June 1937 and qualify for the four-hundred-dollar death benefit granted to all members.

All this could have been innocent, just a friend helping friends. But the Secret Service informer George Myer and the undercover agent Stanley Phillips testified about Herman's attempts to lure them into killing Alfonsi during the summer of 1938. DA McDevitt had Myer and Phillips relate the story of the conspiracy in detail. He had Myer hold up the sandbag that Herman had commissioned for the deed. It was all black, and Myer swung it ominously. And then Myer told of seeing Herman Petrillo a few days after the Secret Service visit to the sick man blew the matter open. The brains of the operation was sitting in his office—his Dodge—at the corner of Ontario and Kensington Avenue, unaware that the Homicide Bureau was now looking into his affairs.

"What's the chance of going ahead with that job for the five hundred dollars?" Myer had asked.

"Oh, you don't have to bother with that now, because the man's in the hospital," Herman bragged. "The fools think he's got influenza or pneumonia. But I gave him enough arsenic to kill six men."

On the subject of poisons, Benjamin Winokur, a pharmacist, told the jury about the time in 1936 when Herman had just returned from his investigatory trip to Italy. The journey had apparently given him ideas.

"What's conium?" the curious Herman inquired of the druggist.

"It's the poison hemlock that Socrates drank," Winokur told him.

"Have you got any?" Herman asked.

He seemed disappointed to learn that it was not in the usual stock of pharmaceuticals. A while later, Herman returned to Winokur and asked, "What do you know about typhoid germs? Do you know where I can get some?" Winokur advised him that the drugstore did not have any call for this item and that he thought it would be inadvisable to carry it because "a broken vial could destroy an entire community." But the druggist seems not to have thought there was anything odd in the inquiry. A few weeks later, Herman was back.

"Hey, Ben, I got a formula for a hair restorer and it uses hydrocyanic acid." He said he needed a solution stronger than the 2 percent the druggist had in stock, something like a 50 percent solution.

"That would be enough to kill anybody," Winokur told him.

"So, can you get it for me? I really need it for that hair treatment," Herman persisted. But Winokur couldn't.

Judge McDevitt seemed concerned that the jury might not have gotten the point. "That hydrocyanic acid, is that the stuff that sends off lethal fumes that produce death?" he interjected.

"That's right, Your Honor, it produces death," the witness confirmed. The judge gave the jury a knowing look.

There was more corroborating testimony from Dr. Henry E. D'Alonzo. He was the former barber turned medical doctor who had performed the medical examinations required for the Paradise Club's death-benefit program. D'Alonzo was well known by Herman and his cronies. Dr. D'Alonzo told the jury that Herman had come to him, ostensibly for a medical examination, but then had asked, "Hey, Doc, can you get me some typhoid germs?"

"What the hell do you want with typhoid germs?" D'Alonzo demanded.

Stella Alfonsi.
"Lies, lies, I can't stand
this pack of lies."

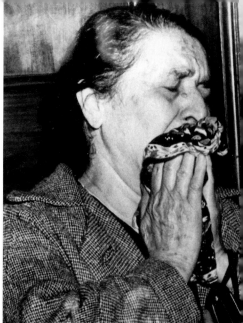

Christine Cerrone.
"Oh, mother of mine,
all this money!"

Josephine Romualdo.
"It was a love drink."

Sophie LaVecchio.
"Cure, not kill, please."

Millie Giacobbe.
"He's making sounds in the
cellar now."

Agnes Mandiuk.
"Rabbi Bolber told me to hang a fish in
moonlight for four days."

Grace Pirolli.
"You could hear him scream from
Ninth Street to Tenth Street."

Maria Favato.
"Love potion? It gives death."

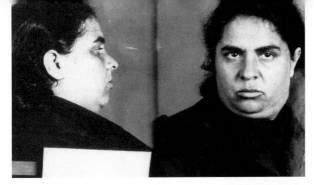

Josephine Sedita.
"Aska Wanna
Jinksa Hoo."

Joseph
Swartz.
"Oh, God,
help me...."

Susie DiMartino.
"Hey, Guisep."

Certificate of death.
"Pneumonia, myocarditis"
...and garlic breath?

Above: Herman Petrillo. "How would you like to go fishing?"

Below: 1822 East Passyunk Avenue. The Little Shop of Horrors.

Above: Paul Petrillo. "Professor P. Patril— Divine Healing, Private Readings."

Morris Bolber.
"Louie the Rabbi."

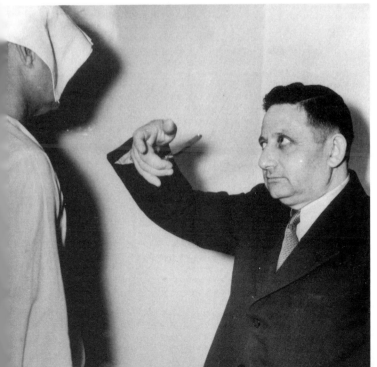

Top left: "Put
an egg under
your arm and
keep it there
for nine
days."

Left: "From
Rino I learned
the secret of
the knife."

Right: Dominick Rodio.
A taste for *vongole con salsa rossa.*

Below: Anna Arena.
"He don't love me no more."

Right:
Rose
"Kiss of
Death"
Carina.
"I want
to be an
angel
now."

*Far
right:*
Jennie
Cassett.
Avon
lady
calling!

Above: Exhumation of Romaine Mandiuk. Digging up witnesses.

Below: A Passyunk guide.

Above: DA Vincent McDevitt. "Any woman would have done the same thing."

Below: Bringing in Josephine Romualdo. "My, what a long hallway you have, Mr. McDevitt."

Right: The spirits counterattack.

Below: George Myer, the informer.
"You want to buy a vacuum cleaner?"

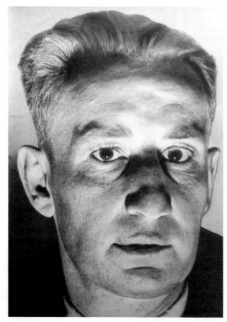

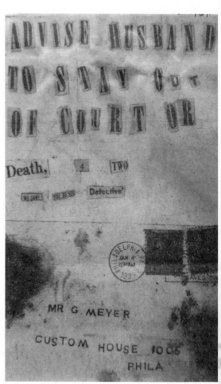

ADVISE HUSBAND TO STAY OUT OF COURT OR

Death,   TWO

Detective

MR G. MEYER

CUSTOM HOUSE 1005
PHILA

Above: Displaying the evidence. Nice sewing
on that little black sack in the foreground.

Right: Widowed Stella Alfonsi.
"I can take as good care of him as anyone."

"Don't get excited," Herman said. "If you can get them, there is two or three hundred dollars in it for you."

"Listen, Petrillo, if you came here on a professional visit, that's one thing. But if you came here for any discussion like that, you get the hell out of here."

The prosecutor wanted to emphasize this point. "Did he want live germs or dead ones?"

"Live germs," the doctor answered.

Dr. D'Alonzo also told about when he was summoned by Stella to the Alfonsi house late on the night of Sunday, August 29, 1938, to treat the ailing Ferdinando. When a week of treatment failed to rally the patient, Dr. D'Alonzo took him to the National Stomach Hospital, up at Fifteenth and Jefferson, a proprietary institution run by Dr. Isaac Strawbridge and his son, Rendall. Dr. D'Alonzo drove Alfonsi up in his own car. The pathetic man was so debilitated from a week of fever, vomiting, and diarrhea that he could hardly walk.

He was admitted by the senior Strawbridge, who turned him over to Nurse Alice Shearer. Nurse Shearer described how she pumped out his stomach and gave him an enema to obtain a stool sample. She marched Alfonsi to a urinal and stood there while he passed a specimen for her. Then she stuck some needles in his arm to take blood. She forced a tube down his throat to gather some vomitus, but Alfonsi obliged by barfing around the tube. She scooped it up.

That was enough for juror number two, a housewife named Maie Letzerick. She fainted dead away and, when revived, told them she would do it again if they kept discussing such things. She was replaced by an alternate.

Dr. Strawbridge said he suspected some form of toxemia. The urinanalysis confirmed it, revealing large quantities of arsenic. They tried activated charcoal to absorb the metal and more alkaloids. But it was too late. After a week, the patient's spleen became enlarged and tender, and his joints swelled up so much, he lost use of them and experienced unrelenting pain. "He was a most cooperative patient," Dr. Strawbridge said. "The poor fellow tried so hard to get well, but as the condition of his bones and limbs became more severe, he had to have morphine in rather increasing doses until he died." Alfonsi suffered for eight weeks, until he finally slipped away on October 27. "The final outcome, in my opinion," the doctor said, using medical terminology, "was caused by paralysis of the muscles of respiration induced by profound toxemia." Put simply, he had suffocated, after two months of absolute misery. When they did the autopsy, they found arsenic in his stomach, liver, and kidneys—the obvious cause of his horrible death.

Detective Michael T. Schwartz of the Philadelphia Homicide Bureau added a devastating bit of circumstantial evidence. He had accompanied Secret Service agents in a search of Herman Petrillo's house on September 28, 1936. They found two chemical catalogs— the *Mallinckrodt Price List, March 1938, of Chemicals for Medicinal, Photographic, Analytical and Industrial Uses* and the *Merck Chemicals—Medicinal, Analytical, Technical, Photographic Price List of April 1938.* Glancing through the Merck catalog, Schwartz noticed penciled tick marks next to several items—including acid arsenic and acid arsenic trioxide (white arsenic). He confronted Herman with the book and opened it to the marked items.

"What's these marks mean, Petrillo?" he asked.

"Well . . ." Herman stalled. "There's lots of things checked off in there."

Schwartz pursued the subject. "There's lot of things not checked off, too. Why'd you check off particularly poisons?"

Herman asked to see the book. He said he was interested in

some prescriptions for making rejuvenating pills. He held the book in his left hand and turned the pages with his right, looking for these prescriptions. But with a dampened left thumb, he surreptitiously rubbed away at the arsenic tick marks. Schwartz let him go on for a while, then he abruptly pinned Herman's left hand to the table, the thumb caught in its act. "You are a wise guy. What do you mean rubbing that off?" Schwartz demanded, flipping the book open. Herman just sat and stared at the marks, now covered by a smudge that made them even more obvious.

On top of all this, Judge McDevitt accepted an innovative legal theory put forth by the prosecutor. The assistant DA was permitted to introduce evidence of Herman's involvement in other killings under a theory of "system." All the deaths, the prosecutor argued, were part of one large system of killing. Based on this theory, the jury heard the grim details of the poisonings of several victims—Charles Ingrao and his son Philip, and Guiseppi Di-Martino—in which Herman was involved only indirectly. They even heard about deaths that did not involve arsenic, such as the drowning death of Joseph Arena, when Herman chauffeured him on that unlucky fishing trip to the Jersey shore. These other killings had been years before Alfonsi's death. There was no evidence, only McDevitt's general allegations, of any common plan engineering them all. But of course Judge McDevitt barely paused before ruling in favor of the prosecution. There was hardly anything that the judge would not admit.

Most important, the judge ruled that autopsy details regarding the deaths of the Ingrao duo and DiMartino were fully admissible. This was critical to the prosecution because the autopsy of Ferdinando Alfonsi had been conducted before DA McDevitt had learned of the proof problems that so often foiled poison-murder prosecutions. As a consequence, it was incomplete, yielding no specifics as to the amount of arsenic found or other details. It might have been highly vulnerable to attack by the defense. But the Ingrao and DiMartino autopsies had been carried out with utmost care.

Dr. Edward Burke, the Philadelphia city chemist, recited the details regarding the Ingraos and DiMartino, to the hundredth of a milligram—Charles Ingrao, 45.74 milligrams of arsenic in the liver, 13.43 in the stomach; Philip Ingrao, 46.21 milligrams in the liver, 5.35 in the stomach; Guiseppi DiMartino, 72.98 milligrams in the liver, 4.04 in the stomach, and 19.24 in kidneys. He tested the wallpaper from the men's bedrooms, the embalming fluid used on them, and the earth from their graves; all were found negative for arsenic. Dr. Martin Crane, the coroner's physician, and Dr. John A. Kolmer, a professor of medicine and expert on arsenic, explained how the poison first goes to the stomach, then to internal organs, and is then excreted through the urine, feces, and skin. Within six to eight weeks, it is almost all gone. It was a formidable technical presentation. The implication was clear. For a residue of 50 to 100 milligrams to remain in only a few internal organs, much larger doses must have been administered, far in excess of a lethal dose.

The prosecuter was also free to present evidence that Herman helped collect the insurance on these other victims, facts that would otherwise have been completely irrelevant. This process reached its peak with the testimony of Domenick Corigliano, a Home Life agent who had refused to pay a suspect insurance policy obtained on the life of Guiseppi DiMartino. Corigliano told the jury that Herman had pulled up next to him as he stood outside a barbershop at Twenty-third and Indiana in North Philadelphia.

Herman called out to him, the insurance agent said, through

the rolled-down window of his green Dodge: "Yo, Domenick, I want to talk to you about how the company refused to pay that DiMartino claim. It seems this company is getting cheaper day by day."

"I asked him," Corigliano testified, " 'You interested in this claim, too? How come you're still free? Ain't you got the electric chair yet for what you're doing?'

"Herman said to me, 'What's wrong? All we do is, when a wife wants to get rid of her husband, she gives him a little bit of whiskey and puts him to sleep forever.'

" 'Someday they're going to pick you up,' I told him.

" 'You think wrong,' Herman said to me. 'They have Italian law in Italy—you have to discharge yourself. But in the United States the government has to prove it; otherwise, you get off even if the case has *basta* evidence.' "

Herman, who had been fuming at this testimony, finally sprang to his feet. "What a lie. Why don't you tell the truth?" he shouted at Corigliano.

"Shut up," DA McDevitt snapped back at Herman.

Leidner, who must have been sleeping through Corigliano's lengthy denunciation, finally woke up. "I object, Your Honor, this testimony is inadmissible."

But the judge was enjoying it all. "Let him rave," he said smugly as he overruled Leidner's objection.

"That's right," the witness continued proudly, as if the judge's ruling was a personal vindication. " 'Five dollars to a doctor if they have an investigation, and it's pneumonia,' that's what Herman told me."

When the time came for him to present his defense, there was not much that Herman could offer. Leidner, his lawyer, strove to discredit the key witness, the informer Myer, which was not too difficult. Even Myer's pal Dominick Policino, the restaurant owner who had introduced him to Herman, said, "Everyone knows Myer lies too much." Beyond that, Leidner wanted to intimate that Alfonsi had received Salvarsan, the arsenic-based treatment for syphilis, or that his condition was caused by a gassing during the war. But he could produce no evidence in support of these theories, and the judge brought him up short whenever he tried to plant unfounded suggestions. Judge McDevitt had the defense on a very short string.

Each night, when Leidner went home after trial, he would receive calls from an anonymous informant offering defense tips. This mysterious source tipped him off to one of Myer's grander fabrications. Just a few months earlier, in January 1939, Myer had gone to the police and filed a complaint against his wife. She had conceived a child/puppy after intercourse with a dog, Myer told police, and when the midwife saw this offspring, she took it away and destroyed it. He wanted them charged with infanticide. Detective Joseph Hartzell, called as a witness, confirmed that Myer had in fact made such a statement.

"This story is absolutely untrue," Leidner told the judge.

"How do you know?" the judge teased.

"Mrs. Myer will prove that," Leidner said.

"Naturally, who else?" the judge acknowledged.

But he did not let Leidner bring in Mrs. Myer to pursue this wild tale.

x x x

Leidner subpoenaed Herman's putative coconspirator, Stella Alfonsi, to come and help in the defense. Leidner asked her if she had conspired with Herman. But Stella, who was in prison awaiting trial herself, took the Fifth Amendment on advice of counsel. She would tell her story another day.

Herman took the stand and denied everything, of course. He stood up in the witness box, his hands outstretched and resting on the rail, and for three hours and fifteen minutes he answered repeatedly, "No," "No, sir," and "No, never" as Leidner asked him if he had been involved in various aspects of the crimes. He worked for the Maroni Macaroni Company, selling their products. It was true, he admitted, that he had helped his friends get life insurance, but was that a crime? Asked about the scheming to get insurance on Alfonsi, Herman just chuckled and reminded the jury, "Them insurance agents do all kind of tricks as long as they get the business."

It was not a bad story, as stories go, but when DA McDevitt cross-examined Herman about all the witnesses who had tied him into murders, including Secret Service Agent Phillips, Dr. D'Alonzo, and the insurance agents, he could only say that they were lying. They were all lying, especially George Myer.

"Myer is a liar?" asked the prosecutor in mock surprise. Herman guffawed. The whole courtroom laughed at that one.

The Italians in the courtroom snickered again when DA McDevitt tried to catch Herman in a lie about Guiseppi DiMartino. "If you don't know any DiMartino, who's this here in your address book?" he asked, pointing at a name that looked like DiMartino. But the entry said "Piazza dei Martiri." That was the Plaza of Martyrs in Naples that Herman had visited on his trip a few years earlier.

No one laughed when the prosecutor asked Herman to read from an insurance-claim letter and the defendant had to admit he could not. "Could someone else read it?" Herman asked the judge plaintively. "I don't read so good." This rueful admission was probably the only moment of the trial that evoked sympathy for the defendant.

The outcome was never in much doubt. "Guilty," announced Mrs. Margaret Skeen, a forty-two-year-old housewife, the fore-woman of the jury, "with a recommendation of death."

"You lousy bitch," Herman snarled. Guards grabbed the raging defendant as he leapt toward Mrs. Skeen.

When the courtroom settled down, Judge McDevitt congratulated the jurors. "You can see how mean and vicious this man is," the judge told the jurors. "You now realize that was the only verdict you could have returned." He sentenced Herman Petrillo to die in Pennsylvania's electric chair.

"I'm sorry," Herman's lawyer told the judge, "I wouldn't have defended this man if I had known he was such scum."

12

FOR THE DEFENSE,
RAYMOND PACE ALEXANDER

Vince McDevitt was exultant. His masterful prosecution of Herman Petrillo was a front-page triumph, as important in Philadelphia as the dictator Franco's contemporaneous victory in the Spanish Civil War, or Clark Gable's conquest of Carole Lombard a few days later. McDevitt's careful preparation seemed to have paid off, and he had no doubt of the importance of his work. "The wholesale murders of this fiendish arsenic ring will prove the most atrocious series of crimes ever committed," he advised the *Philadelphia Evening Ledger*.

But the victory was somehow tainted by the presence of Judge Harry McDevitt on the bench, ruling in the prosecution's favor at every turn, allowing them to throw the kitchen sink at the defendant. The real test would not come until there was a trial before a more neutral judge. There was grave doubt, in fact, that the prosecutors could sustain Herman's conviction on appeal. Review by the Pennsylvania Supreme Court was mandatory in a capital case, and the court had a reputation for thoroughly protecting defendants' rights, even those charged with loathsome offenses. With the right defense lawyer, one who knew how to raise such issues, Herman Petrillo's appeal would have a strong chance of succeeding.

For example, a few years earlier, in 1933, a sixteen-year-old black boy named Willie Brown had been charged with raping a seven-year-old white girl, a horrendous crime that had revulsed the public. In a trial before the same judge, Harry McDevitt, Willie Brown was convicted and sentenced to death. The conviction had been based on formidable evidence, including a confession. But Brown got a new lawyer for his appeal, who challenged the manner in which the trial judge had overwhelmingly favored the prosecution. The Pennsylvania Supreme Court agreed, overturning the verdict, chastising the trial judge, and awarding Willie Brown a new trial.

X X X

The lawyer who had handled Willie Brown's appeal was a brilliant advocate, possibly the most skilled criminal lawyer in the city. His name was Raymond Pace Alexander.

Alexander's mother had died when he was a boy and he was sent to live with an impoverished aunt, who resented the burden. He supported himself doing menial jobs from age twelve, working as an errand boy for pushcart vendors. He later told friends that he was paid with unsold vegetables, which often would be his only dinner. But he managed to get a good education, first at Philadelphia's elite public Central High School and then on a scholarship to the University of Pennsylvania. He finished the challenging four-year curriculum of the Wharton School in three years, while working five nights a week backstage at the opera, and graduated with highest honors. The Department of Economics wanted him to remain for graduate work, but he had higher aspirations. He secured admission to Harvard Law School and got a job as researcher and lecture assistant in the Harvard Economics Department that would enable him to work his way through. On graduation from law school, he returned to his native Philadelphia and began a practice that would be studded with impressive and groundbreaking legal victories for forlorn clients such as Willie Brown.

Another of Alexander's clients was Louise Thomas, a nineteen-year-old "Negress" who had been convicted of murdering a married Negro police patrolman, with whom she was living as a mistress. She was the first woman sentenced to the electric chair since it had been adopted by Pennsylvania in 1904, and the first woman sentenced to die since one had been hung in 1889.

Taking the appeal of this seemingly unsympathetic soul only a year after he graduated from law school, Alexander obtained a reversal of the conviction on technical grounds, by challenging the manner in which the prosecutor had unduly assailed the character of defense witnesses. In the process, he established a precedent that would protect all future criminal defendants from overly zealous district attorneys. Then, on retrial, Alexander won an acquittal for his client on grounds of self-defense.

By 1939, Raymond Pace Alexander was an experienced trial lawyer who had built an impressive and successful practice winning cases no one else wanted to touch. Many of his cases, such as the representations of Willie Brown and Louise Thomas, paid nothing. But the financial rewards of major victories in negligence cases that others rejected as unpromising, and other work, had enabled him to acquire his own office building and to head a firm of busy lawyers. It was a Horatio Alger story, in the best American tradition, with one additional twist. Alexander was a black man.

There were only a handful of black lawyers in Philadelphia. Between 1920 and 1945, only twenty-one had been admitted to the bar, out of a black population of 170,000. In this small circle, the law firm of Raymond Pace Alexander stood out as a beacon. Its four partners were all graduates of Ivy League law schools (two from Harvard, one from Yale, and one from the University of Pennsylvania). The firm operated out of its own office building, located "uptown" at 1900 Chestnut Street, among white businesses, not down in the black business district around Lombard Street. Even the secretaries and receptionists at the firm, all black, were educated and well-spoken, always answering the phone with an elegant *Alexandaar* pronunciation rather than a clipped *Alexandr.*

In 1936, a feature article in *The Brown American* referred to the firm as "a Philadelphia institution," noting that "in Philadelphia, when one thinks of the law in connection with Negroes, the trend of thought usually goes directly to 1900 Chestnut Street." The NAACP magazine, *The Crisis,* in a 1939 article, called the firm "one of the most skillful, best-trained, and successful law firms in America." Alexander himself had become a distinguished, courtly man, learned and dignified in his legal manner. His prosperity showed in his elegant personal style—from his active support of the opera and upscale hobby of horseback riding to his custom-tailored English suits and shirts and his chauffeured Lincoln Zephyr. He "walked like a king," someone said, dominating any room that he entered.

Despite his personal success and refined lifestyle, Alexander remained a man of the people, never forgetting the poor clients whose legal woes undergirded his practice. His aristocratic manner was a statement on behalf of his people, not something to separate himself from them. He had the common touch. "How's that boy of yours getting along in school?" or "Is your wife feeling better?" he would never fail to ask the janitor or the clerk.

He was famous for opening his home in the evening to clients who could not get time off during the day from jobs they desperately needed. They lined up the hall stairs, catnapping, while Lawyer Alexander listened to their problems, one by one, at his dining room table. "I don't care," he once told his wife when she grumbled about dirt some clients had dragged into her living room. "The people who soiled the carpet are the ones who paid to have it laid."

Vince McDevitt knew that he would have to face an appeal of the Herman Petrillo conviction that would raise issues of fundamental fairness. He knew that his advantages at trial would become his disadvantages on appeal. But at least he did not have to worry about facing the formidable and elegant Raymond Pace Alexander. Virtually all Alexander's clients were black. Colored lawyers did not defend white people, especially not murder defendants. Not in Philadelphia, not in the 1930s. Not yet.

x x x

But any appeal was in the future. Right now, the office of the district attorney and that of the Philadelphia police had more than enough to keep them busy as they forged ahead with their investigation. They exhumed the body of a grocer named Peter Stea, latest deceased mate of "Kiss of Death" Carina. The murderess was still on the lam, but that was no reason to let the evidence against her just rot away. McDevitt himself turned his attention to his next quarry, whose trial was to begin in less than three weeks. The defendant would be Maria Favato, charged with the murder not only of her common-law husband, Charles Ingrao, but also his son Philip, as well as a few nonfamilial unfortunates. The press had names for her: the "Witch," and "Borgia."

13
THE WITCH

Born in Italy in 1896, Maria DeLuca first came to the United States as the child bride of Joseph Favato in 1910. The couple returned to Italy in 1915, where she became pregnant and had a son by another man. When Joseph left her and things did not work out with the new father, Maria DeLuca Favato picked up her child and returned to America, coming to live in Philadelphia. She was still relatively young, in her twenties, and a good cook and housekeeper, so she had no trouble finding another man. Eventually Charles Ingrao, a thirty-one-year-old baker, became her common-law husband. Maria moved in with Ingrao the day before Christmas in 1925. They treated December 24 as their wedding anniversary.

Ten years later, in 1935, it was fortunate that "Witch" Favato could attract men with her housekeeping, because she was no longer anything in the looks department. "Stout and dumpy" was the way the press described her, with good reason. She was not much more than five feet tall, but weighed more than two hundred pounds. Ingrao seemed fed up with her, treating her coarsely, even beating her in fits of temper.

Maria seemed to be a simple woman. She could not read. Her English was barely functional. She lived the narrow life of a modest immigrant housewife, having little contact with the New World and an intense devotion to the traditions of the old. She was deeply superstitious, believing in the power of *la fattura* and *il mal'occhio*. She tried, without success, to call upon these mysteries to salvage her relationship with Ingrao. There was something more, however, to Favato than this plain facade.

For one thing, she had the practical sense to buy a considerable amount of life insurance on her husband. As the longtime wife of an apparently healthy man, she had no trouble purchasing substantial policies. First came a one-thousand-dollar policy with Prudential, then a five-thousand-dollar one with the same company. There was also a one-thousand-dollar policy with Monumental Insurance. These were quarterly-premium policies. She also had four small industrial weekly-premium policies, issued by Prudential and Metropolitan. All this insurance was purchased and paid for in the name of Maria Favato, as wife of "Charles Favato." The package was worth almost nine thousand dollars.

Maria also had hidden charms that won the heart of a boarder in the house, Raphael Polselli. The fifty-one-year-old Polselli was a scrawny, almost emaciated little man, only five foot four, slightly taller and much narrower than the corpulent Favato. But he would, and did, kill for her. It began when he saw how Charles treated his common-law wife, smacking her around and generally abusing her. "Why you take that?" Polselli asked, but the battered woman shrugged. It was now the spring of 1935, and Polselli's heart was full of love. He appreciated her, he told Favato, he could take care of her, and he had a friend who could take care of Charles.

This helping hand was Jumbo Valenti, the thug who had done the job for Herman Petrillo, bashing John Woloshyn over the head with an iron pipe and tossing him in front Herman's office *del giorno*. Nothing was too much for Caesar "Jumbo" Valenti, a lumbering 250-pound, six-foot-three-inch monster with a heavy black mustache, huge gnarled hands, and a barrel chest. It was said that he had had eleven criminal convictions in Italy before he came to the United States as a young man, illegally of course. Jumbo Valenti loved America, the land of opportunity.

"This is a good country to murder people," he told his wife. "It's not like Italy, because here you can kill somebody, get on a train, and go to another part of the country where the police can never find you." But it didn't work out so well for him. Shortly after he arrived, in 1915, he was caught mauling some *michione*. He got a suspended sentence because it was his first offense (in America, where you get a fresh start). But a few months later, the police in New York got him for carrying a pistol, and he spent two years in Clinton Prison. When he got out, he moved to Media, Pennsylvania, near Philadelphia.

Less than a year later he slipped again. One day he came home to find his wife in a compromising situation with a local shoemaker. He opened fire and emptied a six-shot revolver at them, wounding her and killing the poor shoemaker. True to his theory, Jumbo fled to Connecticut, but the police tracked him there, and he wound up serving eleven years in the Eastern Pennsylvania Penitentiary for second-degree murder. After emerging in 1931, he returned to New York, where he was convicted twice more, for felonious assault with a knife and for running an after-hours club. Valenti had spent half his life in jail.

Polselli invited his friend down from New York for a visit, sending him ten dollars for the fare. Jumbo came to Philadelphia with a small suitcase that looked like a purse in his enormous hands. Maria greeted her behemoth guest with a finger to her lips, cautioning him to be quiet lest he wake her irascible husband. She let Jumbo sleep on a sofa in the living room, his feet hanging over the arm. When Ingrao went off to work in the bakery each night, the three plotters discussed his future. Just "punch him in the face, tro him down the stairs, and go back to New York" was little Raphael's idea. Apparently he had the same belief in interstate invisibility as Valenti. But Jumbo wasn't going to depend on that again.

"No," he bragged to them, "I have a friend who do anything with a bottle. He can give you something make someone love you, make someone dead."

The friend, of course, was Herman Petrillo. Valenti had been talking with his sometime partner in crime. Herman, who had learned of his cousin Paul's newfound ability to summon the angel Gabriel, had been extolling the virtues of *la fattura* over *una macchina* for travel to California. It was the perfect instrument, Herman said, never raising any of the suspicions that had caused him such troubles in the Caruso case. "I can get it for you," Herman told Valenti, "a hundred and fifty dollars for a treatment." Jumbo quickly figured in a little profit and told Polselli it would cost three hundred dollars for this magic, half down and half when it worked.

Polselli advanced the money. A few days later, Valenti brought a small bottle to the house. "This is guaranteed stuff from Washington, D.C.," Jumbo proudly proclaimed.

"It'll make Charles good to you, or it will make him die," Raphael told his inamorata, Maria.

It was morning, and Charles Ingrao was expected home from the bakery for his breakfast. The plotters went in the kitchen to prepare a feast. Maria roasted three spring chickens and broiled five pounds of steak with hot peppers. She scrambled two dozen eggs. Jumbo, who had been a cook, fixed a salad and made a huge pot of coffee. The four of them—Valenti, Polselli, Favato, and Ingrao—consumed all this, washing it down with two gallons of wine. Valenti mixed the *fattura* in Charles's coffee.

That night Charles was too sick to go to work. He suffered from intestinal agonies, pain in his throat and chest, fever, thirst, and gas and diarrhea for nine days before he died on August 14, 1935, with his loving wife ministering to him all that time. The doctor saw nothing unusual in this condition and attributed it all to pleural pneumonia.

Just as Herman had promised, no suspicions were raised. Polselli was satisfied. He thanked Valenti and gave him the other $150.

R.I.P.
CHARLES INGRAO

With some of her insurance money, Maria went to a "sorceress" named Bridget Caprana at Fifth and Venango. Caprana had *il mal'occhio*. She could change herself into a black cat and visit the devil. She promised to put Favato in contact with the deceased Ingrao. That night, Maria saw Bridget marching around her bed "accompanied by seven men with horns." She locked the door, but "black cats with gleaming eyes" still prowled through her bedroom.

But the sorcery didn't work. Favato paid Caprana thirteen hundred dollars over a period of several months, and all she got were nightmares and some pieces of cloth in which the powdered bones of the dead man had supposedly been wrapped.

Other women had written such expenses off to bad luck. They were *sfortunato*. But Maria Favato hired a lawyer to sue Caprana, the sorceress without sorcery. Maria had seen that Polselli and Valenti could produce results with their witchcraft, and she expected other practitioners to do the same.

Whatever guilt Maria may have felt over the manner of Charles Ingrao's passing, she was not sorry to have him gone. Polselli, her new lover, was a man who treated her right. Out of gratitude, she used fifteen hundred dollars of her insurance loot to set Polselli up in business. He became an undertaker. Raphael was, however, better at plotting deaths than burying the victims. His business soon collapsed, and the lovers needed more money. They knew how to get it.

Maria no longer had a husband, of course, but she had love-lorn friends and neighbors. After making sure he was well covered by life insurance, Maria drank coffee with the husband of her friend Josephine Romualdo, and soon the husband was under a doctor's care. His unexpected demise, after a weeklong illness, was attributed by the unsuspecting doctor to "pneumonia and myocarditis."

R.I.P.
ANTONIO ROMUALDO

Three months later, Susie DiMartino, another of Maria's acquaintances, watched as her husband suddenly fell ill with a horrible cough and cold. Maria Favato and Raphael Polselli, good neighbors to the end, came to the bedside to care for the sick man.

When he began having convulsions, Susie summoned Dr. Frank Massaniso. All the doctor could do was sign the death certificate, ascribing the death to "influenza and pneumonia."

R.I.P.
GUISEPPI DIMARTINO

Raphael Polselli had sent insurance agents to the DiMartino house, where they had convinced the illiterate Guiseppi to put his mark on applications for several small policies. To minimize the risk of questions from the home office, the agents wrote some of the applications in the name of Joseph DiMartino, with the beneficiary as his wife, "Asundi"—neatly cross-switching English and Italian usages. This sort of trick, like the artificial spacing out of application dates, was the kind of thing at which all the agents were adept.

After a while, Polselli and Favato got bolder, inviting the agents to Maria's house, where an accomplice impersonated DiMartino and signed his name. "Hey, Guisep," they would shout upstairs when the insurance agent asked to see DiMartino, and the impersonator would trot down, ready to sign any and all papers. By the time they were done, in August 1936, they had accumulated nine polices, amounting to $5,317 coverage. Polselli and Favato paid all the premiums directly, telling the agents that DiMartino had left the money with them.

Maria and her boyfriend, Raphael, collected most of the insurance on these men without a hitch, but Home Life somehow learned of forged signatures on some of DiMartino's policies and refused to pay. Maria stormed down to the insurance office with simple Susie DiMartino in hand. Herman Petrillo arranged for his

helpmate, Stella Alfonsi, to go along as interpreter. But the superintendent, Benjamin Koran, turned them over to his Italian-
speaking assistant, Domenick Corigliano.

Maria did not mince words once she could let them fly in
her native tongue. "You son of a bitch," she told Corigliano.
"You're the same crook who ten years ago refused to insure my
brother. I know more about insurance than you. I insure lots of
people. I pay the premiums. I never have any trouble. Now you
give me trouble. If you want to make a living, do it the right way;
otherwise, I'll send a boy down here to knock you off." When
Mrs. Alfonsi tried to intervene and smooth things over, Favato
told her, "You talk to the Jews. This one's Italian. We understand
each other." But there was nothing Maria could do. Under the
circumstances, she was lucky that Home Life just returned the
premiums and did not take any other action.

Even with these little annoyances, it was a good business,
this *la fattura* racket. The biggest problem was in coming up with
a supply of victims. But Maria and Raphael already had the recipient of their next treatment waiting at home. He was Philip Ingrao,
the son of Maria's first "cure," her common-law husband, Charles
Ingrao. When Charles had deserted his first wife, Philip had been
taken in by the Catholic Charities, which placed him with foster
parents. These foster parents, who received a small monthly fee
for taking care of him, remembered Philip as a nice, healthy kid.
As soon as she had rid herself of her husband, the bereaved stepmother, Maria Favato, had gone to the Catholic Charities and offered to take Philip off its rolls.

Thus, in August 1936, a year after Charles Ingrao dined on
his last breakfast, sixteen-year-old Philip Ingrao came to live with
his stepmother and her new boyfriend, Raphael Polselli, undertaker. Maria put him right to work, finding a job for him as a

porter in a movie theater and then as an apprentice baker. He had to pay his way in the household.

She also began immediately to take out life insurance on him. The first policy, five hundred dollars of industrial insurance with Home Life, was applied for on September 16, less than a month after Philip's arrival. Over the course of the next year and a half, Favato applied for more than twelve thousand dollars of life insurance on her stepson. Some of the applications were rejected, but by taking out many small policies with different companies, and making some applications in the name of Felice Ingrao, rather than Philip, she managed to accumulate $6,382 in valid coverage. The policies were cheap on a young man, only twenty-two cents each week per five hundred dollars' coverage. By the spring of 1938, the limits had been reached. The premiums were getting close to three dollars a week, and the kid only earned five dollars. It was time to act.

Philip took ill on June 7, 1938. He was sick, vomiting for almost a month, until he died on the morning of June 25, 1938. Dr. Massaniso, the same man who had treated Guiseppi Di-Martino, saw Philip from time to time during this period, prescribing sedatives and tonics. But Favato did not bother to call the doctor during the final days; she just waited until she was certain her stepson was dead, then called the Errichetti Funeral Home.

When the undertaker, a woman named Josephine Errichetti, arrived, she complained, "You are only calling now? You see the boy is going bad. He is going green."

"Well, I didn't see as it made any difference when I called you. The boy's dead, ain't he?" Maria huffed.

There wasn't much doubt of that, but the undertaker told her she'd need a doctor to confirm it. Maria called Massaniso, but he was out. His young assistant, Dr. Schwartz, came over instead.

He found Philip to be very dead, cold to the touch and strange in appearance. "His skin was rather yellow and mottled, very blotchy in appearance." Schwartz didn't like the look of it. It looked like the result of some kind of jaundice or liver condition. He pronounced the young man dead but refused to issue a certificate, telling them to wait for Dr. Massaniso. "He was just here last night," Favato lied. "Well then, there won't be any problem," Schwartz told her.

But then a hitch developed. Dr. Massaniso came the next morning, but since he hadn't seen Philip for over a week, he refused to issue a death certificate. Josephine Errichetti and her men were there, too, waiting to haul the boy off. "Why don't you just make it pneumonia?" Favato asked the doctor, recalling how easily matters had gone with DiMartino. But Massaniso only gave her a look. He had never seen a case like this before. He asked her why, if the boy had been so sick, she hadn't called him back earlier. "I had a *fattucchiere,*" she told him, "and I was ashamed to let you know." Massaniso knew Italian; that was a "hex doctor" to him. That made him even more wary.

"This ain't getting me anywhere," Errichetti complained. She had already spent too much time hanging around on this case, which she knew wasn't going to produce much of a fee. "I got to take the boy down to the morgue if Dr. Massaniso ain't going to give me a certificate."

"What'll they do down there?" Maria wanted to know.

"They will open your son up and I will get my cause of death so I can bury him," Josephine said.

Favato didn't like that, so she resumed arguing with the doctor. Back and forth it went, until Josephine finally told her men to pick up the body. Over Favato's protests, they carried it out to the hearse and drove it to the morgue for the coroner to inspect. Stepmother Favato went along.

An autopsy could be disastrous for those so near but not so dear to Philip. The moment of truth loomed. But Maria Favato remained cool as a marble slab. My name is Mary Ingrao, she told the deputy coroner, thinking it was better to sound like an American mother than conjure up an image of a wicked Italian stepmother. "My son's been going for some time, always suffering from the boils and weakness." She sobbed. The official diligently took the information down. He performed a perfunctory autopsy, with no examination of internal organs or chemical tests that might have revealed the presence of poison. Why bother? Who would suspect a poor mother of killing her son? The death certificate read "rheumatic fever," and Philip was buried the next day.

R.I.P.
PHILIP INGRAO

Again, however, there was trouble with the insurance. Herman, a reputable businessman who stood behind his product, had to intervene. When there was a delay in getting the death certificates that were needed for the insurance claims, Herman drove Maria over to the funeral home. It was early in the morning, only half past eight, and Herman came barging into the place, with Favato in tow. "What's going on?" Herman demanded of Domenick Petaccio, the assistant undertaker. "Where's those certificates?" When Petaccio stalled, Herman slipped him five dollars to get the job done.

Later, when Home Life delayed paying the insurance on Philip, Herman went to see Nick Del Buono, an insurance agent buddy who had helped him out in the Caruso matter. "How the hell is it the company don't pay this claim here?" he demanded. Del Buono demurred and said he would have to see the superintendent. Herman took the Home Life agent aside. "I want she should get this check, because she owes me money. What can we do, you and me? How the hell can we fuck the life-insurance company?" Del Buono, getting nervous, sent Petrillo away. But the company eventually paid the claims.

The pleased Maria Favato, with her new loot in hand and her nickname—the "Witch"—well earned, treated herself to a fur coat. And she contemplated Charles Ingrao's younger son, Michael, whom she had also taken in from the Catholic Charities. The insurance pot on Michael was up to $1,750. She also had a thousand dollars riding on her own son, twenty-seven-year-old Joseph Pontarelli.

14

THE CAGED BIRD SINGS

Quite a story. Yet the guards at the Philadelphia city jail, Moyamensing Prison, where Maria Favato was awaiting trial, thought her a peasant simpleton. They taught her to cut out paper dolls, and she sat for hours enjoying her newfound skill. Favato told her lawyer she wanted to go into the paper doll–making business when she got out. That was one side of her. Could she have been merely a dupe in the hands of Polselli and Herman Petrillo? But there was also the Maria Favato who brazenly confronted the insurance agent Domenick Corigliano when he refused to pay on a policy she had fraudulently obtained. There was the Maria Favato who the assistant undertaker Petaccio called "dumb like a fox" because she had helped trick them out of a large fee for burying Philip Ingrao. There was the Maria Favato who self-righteously sued Bridget Caprana when that sorceress failed to "turn herself into a black cat and visit the devil" as promised. "Queen of the Black Widows," "Witch," and "Borgia," the newspapers called Maria as they filled their columns each day with lurid details of her toxic tendencies.

Which was the true Favato? She moved quickly as she was led into the courtroom, with a spry step that belied her two-hundred-plus-pound heft, as if she was anxious to do battle. But from the moment she settled into her seat, she showed nothing discernible in attitude or emotion. Even when testimony was in her native Italian, she sat stony-faced, looking straight ahead or up at the ceiling, not commenting upon nor apparently even caring what the lawyers were doing. Her apparel was as unrevealing as her demeanor. Every day she wore the same dark brown print dress and black coat with a cheap fur collar, which she either threw back over her shoulders or folded in her lap.

"An occasional flutter of the eyelids was the only movement noted in her immobile face," complained the *Inquirer*. Vincent McDevitt had brought Herman and Paul Petrillo to the courtroom, hoping the presence of their notorious visages, which had been emblazoned across the front pages as the men who "Petrillo-ized" victims, would help taint Favato. Herman constantly glowered and clenched his fists, as if enraged by lies being told on the witness stand. Paul smiled and chuckled to himself, as if amazed by the inventive prevarications propounded in testimony. But Favato just sat. When McDevitt said he would prove she was a kingpin of the ring, head of its North Philadelphia branch, she "remained disinterested," said the *Inquirer*. When he said he would ask for the death penalty, "Mrs. Favato just kept staring into space, motionless."

She just sat, until 4:25 P.M. on the fourth day of the proceedings. Then, in midtrial, Maria Favato stunned the courtroom. "I am guilty," she confessed, guilty of the three murders with which she was charged—Charles and Philip Ingrao, and Guiseppi DiMartino.

"She was cold as ice," said her lawyer, former City Councilman Edward Kelly, "but she insisted she was innocent and I believed her. She told me she had gotten nothing from the insurance on DiMartino." When he learned Favato had in fact fleeced the victim's wife, Susie, of all her insurance benefits, Kelly told reporters, he advised his client to plead guilty. Maybe that way, he said, she could avoid the chair.

"I'm sorry," lawyer Kelly apologized to the court. "Had I known what I know now, I would not have been so zealous in defending her." It was certainly no case for a city councilman. This was still Philadelphia in 1939.

Now there was no stopping the district attorney's office. They were two for two on murder convictions and had just secured the prosecutor's dream, a bird who knew everything and was literally singing for her life. The Witch Favato, who had felt no misgivings about doing in her husband and stepson, was hardly the sort to show restraint in attacking her former colleagues in crime. To encourage her, McDevitt had Favato appointed a "deputy investigator" and gave her a makeshift little badge and card. The prosecutors listened as she fingered thirteen women who supposedly had joined with her in killing their husbands.

In some instances, like that of Dora Sherman, wife of a kosher chicken merchant, the investigation quickly revealed a false accusation. The autopsy on Dora's husband established that his gastric distress was merely the natural outcome of her cooking, not fortified by any nefarious substances. She was summarily released. But in most instances, Favato's allegations seemed reliable enough for McDevitt to press forward with an interrogation of the accused woman.

McDevitt was a man who knew how to get along with everyone, and get what he wanted from them. His friends tell a story of the time that McDevitt was being audited by the IRS about a disputed deduction for a tree damaged by lightning. He wanted to claim the lost property value, not just the cost of a new tree. "You are a handsome boy," he told the auditor. "Your teeth are beautiful; I bet all the girls love your smile. Now how would you feel if your center tooth was knocked out? You'd have lost more than just the cost of some false replacement, wouldn't you?" That was classic Vince McDevitt. He brought the same skills to bear in mastering the psychology of interrogation.

Naturally he used time-honored tricks, such as "good cop/bad cop." The prosecutor would alternate a rough Irish cop like Lt. James Kelly with someone like Tony Franchetti, an Italian-speaking detective from the Passyunk neighborhood. Beyond this, McDevitt was blatant in his use of flattery and small material rewards to charm potential informants like Maria Favato. Life for ordinary prisoners in Moyamensing Prison was bleak. Locked in their two-person cells all day, with only one fifteen-minute exercise period and no entertainment, not even a radio, there was nothing for an inmate to do except sit around on the stone floor and play cards with her cellmate. Required to fold their straw mattresses in half during the day, they had not even the modest comfort of a soft seat. McDevitt could easily mitigate that existence with little treats—a ride in the park, maybe even a meal in a restaurant as a reprieve from the slop the prisoners knew as food.

McDevitt would brag for years about how he had tricked one suspect, Dr. Horace Perlman, into confessing. Perlman, a respected gynecologist, had found himself snared in the activities of the ring, a classic casualty of the slippery slope of illegality. It began when the notorious Petrillos and Morris Bolber enlisted Perlman's help with a sympathetic abortion. But then they started blackmailing the doctor to do other favors, from performing more abortions to facilitating poison-murder plots.

Dr. Perlman had been arrested on the basis of detailed accusations from Thomas Pino, a "poison widower" who had confessed to murdering his own wife, Jennifer. But then Pino suddenly took ill and died. With Perlman's lawyer cruising City Hall trying to locate him so he could get out a writ of habeas corpus, McDevitt had to improvise. He quickly coached the Italian-accented Detective Riccardi to impersonate the prematurely deceased Pino. As soon as this actor was ready, they brought Perlman in for a lineup.

McDevitt proudly described the scene that followed: "Strong klieg lights illuminated the lineup so that a person standing in it could hear everything said, but was prevented from looking out into the audience. Chief Connelly, whom Dr. Perlman had met, stood out in front and said, 'Bring in Pino.' As soon as 'Pino' (the Italian detective) entered, he began shouting, 'There's the man that murdered my wife; I paid him and Paul Petrillo. He gave me the pills. Oh! Why did I ever kill Jennie?' Perlman all but collapsed. He confessed and signed a full statement."

When it came to questioning the accused "poison widows," McDevitt developed a carefully tailored strategy to gain what he called "maximum psychological advantage." Each female suspect was arrested late at night, "usually around midnight," said McDevitt, and then taken to the old City Hall, a massive, menacing stone structure full of shadowed archways and long, echoing corridors. She was taken to a darkened room deep in the bowels of the building, far removed from sight or sound of the outside world. There, in a setting perhaps better adapted to communicating with the spirits than the truth, these superstition-obsessed suspects were confronted by the twin powers of the police and a powerful witch, Maria Favato. They accused each widow, in gruesome detail, of complicity in the death of her husband. As the strength of these charges sank in, the kindly McDevitt would come on the scene and "make light of them, as if it were the thing to do, that any other woman under the same circumstances would probably have done the same thing."

A few of the alleged poison widows held out, but most succumbed to McDevitt's combination of intimidation and blarney, offering a full confession or at least damaging admissions. Thus, bragged McDevitt, did each "pneumonia death become a murder." Of course, it didn't hurt that many of the women had no lawyers, could hardly speak English, and couldn't read the confessions they were asked to sign. It didn't hurt that these simple women were assured that their cooperation could help avoid a drastic sentence. The circumstances had dealt the prosecution a powerful hand, and Vince McDevitt was playing it for all it was worth. There were, as a factual matter, gross distinctions among the widows in terms of culpability. But all that disappeared in the heat of the moment. Every remaining defendant, from the ringleader, Paul Petrillo, to the most ingenuous widow, McDevitt decided, would be charged with first-degree murder, and in every case, the Commonwealth would aggressively seek the death penalty.

Confronted with this ultimate charge, Maria Favato's lover/ henchman, Raphael Polselli, collapsed and figured he had better make a deal while he could. Polselli confessed to his involvement in the killings of Charles Ingrao and Guiseppi DiMartino. He also implicated a onetime boarder in DiMartino's house named Emedio Muscelli. Muscelli was the accomplice who had answered the "Hey, Guisep" calls and impersonated DiMartino in applying for insurance.

When Muscelli refused to talk, McDevitt confronted him with Maria Favato. "He's the one," she said. "It's Emedio what gave the poison to Guisep. He loved Susie. After her husband was dead, Emedio was in the house alone with her. 'I'm the boss of the house now,' he told me."

Muscelli lunged toward Maria, crying, "Liar!" but the detectives restrained him. He glowered at her, and shot her the *mal'occhio*. At that, the two-hundred-pound woman leapt at Muscelli like a cat, her claws extended. She raked her hand across his face, then clenched her fist and smashed him with all her might while the startled police still held him down. The embarrassed detectives had to explain in court the next day why the glowing shiner on Muscelli's left eye was not the result of police brutality.

15

RUN, RABBI, RUN

When the Alfonsi case had first broken, with the arrest of Herman and Stella back in September 1938, Morris Bolber had folded his tent and slipped back to Brooklyn, where he had friends who could give him a place to hide. He knew the Philadelphia police were looking for him, but as yet they did not have a specific warrant out for his arrest. He supposed he might eventually have to speak with them, but he preferred to do so when he was ready, not when they happened to find him.

The story of the "poison murder ring" was attracting growing attention outside of Philadelphia. The *New York Daily News* had given extensive coverage to Herman Petrillo's trial in March and Maria Favato's in April. So long as none of the key conspirators gave evidence, Bolber held out hope that the prosecutors would never be able to convict anyone except Herman. But the landscape altered drastically when Maria Favato threw in the towel and Polselli followed. On April 26, the *Inquirer* reported that the police were now focusing on a "search for the ring leader, a man of middle years, and a practicing witch-doctor, known as 'The Rabbi.' " The next day, the same paper reported that Herman Petrillo had begun "squealing his head off." This rumor was not true, not insofar as it implied Herman was willing to confess. His only squealing was to complain about the "injustice" of his trial. Nonetheless, the story raised Bolber's level of anxiety. He realized his options were narrowing. He could try to slip out of the country. But where could he go?

In some circles life might be going on as usual. Tyrone Power married the French film star Annabella, and Douglas Fairbanks, Jr., took a socialite as his new wife. Philadelphia comic-page fans could chuckle as Dagwood Bumstead discovered the idea of slicing a loaf of bread horizontally and filling it with sandwich fixings from end to end. "You eat it like a harmonica," he told Blondie.

But the noose was tightening on Jews. Hitler had just rolled over Czechoslovakia and was openly mocking Roosevelt, who could not muster enough political support to oppose him. Britain, rather than resist, showed signs of returning to appeasement. The only line they drew in the sand was *against* Jewish emigration to Palestine; a six-month moratorium was imposed. As desperate Jewish leaders sought some haven, America, the immigrants' promised land, was perhaps their most sought-for objective. But this country showed no interest in opening its doors.

For a Jew already here, it was no time to leave. Morris Bolber decided to take his chances with the Philadelphia police. By surrendering voluntarily, he hoped he might be able to make a deal. On April 30, 1939, a throng of 600,000 people attended the opening of the world's fair in New York. They heard Roosevelt's turn-the-other-cheek response to Hitler's taunts, blandly ignoring them and calling for peace. Bolber was not among the onlookers. He had taken the train to Philadelphia.

On May 1, Morris "Louie the Rabbi" Bolber strode unannounced into the office of the Philadelphia district attorney, removed an elegant chesterfield coat, carefully folded it, and doffed a pearl-gray bowler. "I would like to see Mr. Vincent McDevitt," Bolber said. "I am a psychiatrist. I have some information that may be of interest to him."

16
THE GREAT BOLBER

DA Vincent McDevitt had shown he was a master at getting people to talk, not by the third degree, but by beguiling and cajoling them. McDevitt rose to the challenge of drawing out Morris Bolber, recalling, "His character was one of the most amazing I ever saw, shrewd, talented, and fascinating, but unpredictable and utterly fantastic. He spoke fourteen languages and had a remarkable memory." McDevitt knew how to reach a man like the great Bolber. He would treat him as a dignitary.

"His position in the organization required certain amenities," as McDevitt put it. "He wasn't questioned in a cell or dingy room in City Hall. A suite of rooms was taken at the Bellevue-Stratford Hotel. Dinner for Chief Connelly of the County Detectives, Bolber, and myself was served in the room. Being a vain man, we played to his vanity. Chief Connelly appointed him a deputy investigator. Proudly he accepted the assignment, promised to help us clean up the ring, and agreed that he would tell all. He did."

If Bolber ever flagged, McDevitt knew how to get him going again. The assistant DA was a great raconteur himself, with a stock of stories and a big booming laugh. He knew that sometimes you had to entertain a little to be entertained. He could keep things moving along with an anecdote, and he knew when to feed Bolber such lines as "You were more important than that, weren't you?" or "A man like you would know a lot more than that, wouldn't you?"

"For two straight days Bolber talked," McDevitt told reporters when he emerged from the marathon session. "Pacing the floor of the living room of the hotel suite, he dictated to two stenographers, who alternated, murder after murder. He gave all the details, circumstances and little by-plays and incidents of each case. Altogether he made six statements, each one twenty to fifty pages in length."

That was not all. Louie the Rabbi also pleaded guilty to first-degree murder. He had a lawyer, but he made the deal himself, figuring he was smarter than any *goniff* shyster. He figured he had cut a good deal when McDevitt accepted his plea to a single murder, that of Romaine Mandiuk, and agreed to drop all other charges. Bolber would have to testify against his coconspirators of course, but that would be a pleasure, an opportunity for the world to view the genius of Morris Bolber. In the meantime, McDevitt would keep him happy. He would have a private cell "to keep his mind clear," and conjugal visits with his wife. And there would be no trial for Bolber himself.

A psychologist, Professor Thaddeus L. Bolton of Temple University, evaluated this bizarre character who had swung from leader of the gang to leader of its downfall.

Bolber is a man short of stature, plainly overactive, and his color is not good. A closer physical examination would probably reveal the fact that he is a case of hyperthyroidism and that his kidneys have not remained unaffected. He is the type of man who seeks to draw notice to himself and seems to glow with satisfaction and to increase his demonstrations just in proportion to the amount of notice he can draw to himself. He is only a higher type of the morbid egoist familiar to all courtrooms in large cities, the "court show-off." Some technical writers might call him a case of megalomania.

He displays the phenomenon of exact memory and he insists stoutly upon having his words correctly recorded and repeated. In fact, he shows the phenomenon very common among defective persons, that is know as "exact answer." When his language is in any way changed, he breaks out in violent protest. On such occasions he begins a kind of oration and this takes the form of what we will call megalo-lallism—that is, he is a violent and demonstrative talker, with the intonations of oratorical speech.

The courtroom will be a haven to him. It is not possible to tweak his nose, twist his arm or crack him over the head with a night stick. In a short time he will have the courtroom in a kind of confusion and disorder. His diabolical cunning is such as to topple over the dignity of the court and disconcert the bar.

Professor Bolton closed with a warning to Vincent McDevitt. "There is, for Bolber, no self-control. With no external control, in fact he could go to an extreme. He might even be judged an irresponsible person and escape the punishment that awaits him."

x x x

McDevitt had no time, however, to worry about Bolber's craziness. He and the homicide detectives now faced an information avalanche. Maria Favato and Raphael Polselli were giving them names. Morris Bolber was giving them essays. They were combing death records of the past seven or eight years for South Philadelphia decedents who had died of pneumonia, flu, or heart conditions under suspicious circumstances. The coroner's office went to work overtime autopsying exhumed bodies. The FBI crime lab was called to help test kidneys, livers, and stomachs for poison traces.

The FBI had also tracked down the fabled Rose Carina, the last major suspect.

17
ROSIE BANANAS

$\mathbf{F}$rom the moment of Herman Petrillo's arrest in September 1938, Rose Carina had been wary. At first, she thought it would blow over, that the vaunted undiscoverability of *la fattura* would protect her and her covillains from the sanctions of the law. For a time, she continued as normal, taking on another husband, the widower Isadore Tropea, in October 1938. The fifty-year-old Tropea was a mild-mannered man, a part-time violin teacher and vulnerable single father in need of someone to help make a home for him and his eight-year-old son, Gaetano. Rose had known Tropea around Passyunk for many years, but they had lost touch until they met again in the summer of 1938, while both families were on vacation in Atlantic City. Tropea worked at the John B. Stetson Company, a generous employer, which, as Rose well knew, provided a one-thousand-dollar death benefit for every worker.

"Rose sent word to me through her little daughter Rita that

she would like to see me," Isadore Tropea told reporters. "She had lovely manners, talked well, and we got on well together. I felt so sorry for her because she told me she had hard luck, with three husbands dying, and she was all alone. She told me, 'I want to be an angel now. I am proud to have you as my husband. There is nobody like you. You are wonderful.' I fell for it."

Only a few weeks after their marriage, however, Rose learned of the results of the Alfonsi autopsy. Arsenic had been found, and both Herman and Stella were being held for murder. "When Rose began reading about the poison arrests in the papers, she started crying and wouldn't tell me what was the matter," Tropea continued. She preferred not to stick around for the rest of the story. On December 9, 1938, only two months after she and Tropea were married, he returned from work and found a note from his wife. She had been happy with him, she wrote, but she wanted to see the world again. Some of his furniture and his first wife's diamond ring were also gone.

When Tropea went to the police, he told them he had seen a physician because of pains in his stomach only a few weeks earlier. He also said Rose had asked him to make her the beneficiary of his one-thousand-dollar life-insurance policy—in place of his son—and to take out another, even larger policy with her as beneficiary. Tropea had had the foresight to refuse. "I am a lucky, lucky man," he sighed.

Rose had taken off for Washington, D.C., traveling with her ten-year-old daughter, Rita. The heat was on, and the Kiss of Death had reason to want to see other parts of the world. Rose was not easy to track down. Her parents claimed not to have seen her in years and could offer the police no leads. Husband number one, a piggery worker named Antonino Carbonato, offered the tip that she had an easily identifiable scar on her lower right leg from a burn received in a powder factory where she worked as a girl. But he, too, knew nothing of her present whereabouts.

Rose's neighbors were shocked when police came to question them. They recalled her not as the "Rose of Death" but as "Rosie Bananas" because of her proclivity for bringing fruit to friends. She was, they told reporters, "a devoted wife and mother, an unsurpassed cook and housekeeper, and a sympathetic friend." She was always "the first one on the scene to help" when anyone got sick, they said. Maybe they were thinking of how she had helped minister to some arsenic sufferers in their final hours.

The search for Rose intensified after the convictions of Herman Petrillo and Maria Favato in March and April of 1939, because testimony at those trials deeply implicated Rose in the killings. Convinced that she had left the state, the Philadelphia police called in J. Edgar Hoover's fabled FBI to help track her down. The Bureau, reported the *New York Daily News,* "notified authorities in Mexico, Cuba, and throughout Latin America to be on the lookout for the elusive 'kiss of death' woman." On May 17, the FBI had a tip that she was back in her old New Jersey neighborhood, and they raided a diner in Lakewood, where she was reportedly working as a waitress. But they were one day late. Rose, still accompanied by Rita, now eleven, had fled just in time.

But the trail was hot. Acting on a new tip, the FBI burst into a Greenwich Village "love nest" early the next morning, where they found the Kiss of Death in bed with a dapper new male companion, Antonio Mastro of the Bronx. Rita was asleep on the couch. The G-men whisked the threesome to Philadelphia in two cars, while a throng of spectators waited up all night outside City Hall to get a glimpse.

What a disappointment! Rose "Kiss of Death" Carina was double-chinned, bespectacled, and frumpy. If she was the woman

of a man's fantasy, it was the fantasy that leads him to tattoo
Mother in a heart on his bicep. "My goodness, I must be an awfully
important woman," Rose gasped. The cops turned Rita over to the
children's bureau, then began grilling Rose. Meanwhile her father
celebrated. "I'll not work tomorrow," he said. "I'll kill a couple of
chickens and have a celebration. If Rose comes down here, I'll
shoot her. She's been nothing but trouble."

Police concluded that Mastro knew nothing of Rose's activities. He thought her name was Mary Jonas. But Judge Harry
McDevitt ordered him held for a week anyhow. "Anyone careless
enough to associate with such a woman should be locked up for a
while, for his own good," the judge said. Rose, of course, was
charged with murder and held without bail until trial.

x x x

It was now May 1939. The DA's office decided to postpone further
trials for a few months, until the fall, by which time they hoped
to get all the overlapping and conflicting stories sorted out. The
investigators were accustomed to an absence of information, to
ferreting out facts and witnesses. This situation was the opposite.
There were more stories and twists and bodies than they could
comprehend. McDevitt still suspected that there was some higher-
up who was coordinating the ring. He could not believe that the
gang of fools he was questioning had been able to do it on their
own. He imagined instead that he had found his way into a criminal conspiracy that would break open the notorious Black Hand.

At one point, McDevitt had Paul Petrillo released from jail
and put under twenty-four-hour surveillance. He hoped the tailor
would lead him to bigger game. For weeks, detectives tailed Paul,
watching him go around to a series of women in the community.

They would later learn that he was threatening each one to keep silent. He called on Sophie LaVecchio Davis, the now-remarried widow of his first arsenic victim, and reminded her, "Keep your mouth shut, or I'll get someone to kill you. You open your mouth and you're dead."

He also asked each woman to sell chance books for him in a lottery he was running, trying to raise two thousand dollars to pay his lawyer. Nobody ever said the Petrillos weren't enterprising.

Later that spring, Lou Gehrig voluntarily benched himself after playing in 2,130 consecutive games over fifteen years. The investigators wondered if it would take them that long to finish the arsenic murder cases. Perhaps inspired by Gehrig's baseball exploits, they posted a big investigative scoreboard on the wall, filling it with a chart listing the name of each suspect, his or her victims, and his or her connection with other suspects. It was exciting, and they were getting famous. The *Inquirer* gave Lt. James A. Kelly and Detectives Samuel Riccardi and Anthony Franchetti of the Philadelphia police Homicide Bureau special awards for heroism and brilliant investigative work.

As the months of 1939 slipped by, Philadelphia took little note of Hilter and Mussolini's "Pact of Steel" solidifying the Axis powers. The Munich treaty of September 1938 had lulled the American public into complacency. Pan American Airlines began the first transatlantic air service. SAILINGS FOR EUROPE INCREASE AS WAR RUMORS QUIET DOWN, reported the *Philadelphia Inquirer,* amid stories of the Bolber-Petrillo axis, reminding readers that depravity was not far from home.

However, by September, complacency about world events had turned to alarm, as the war in Europe begain with a German invasion of Poland. The blitzkrieg loomed. In Philadelphia, DA

McDevitt, too, planned a blitzkrieg, with nine murder trials in three weeks. The first defendant on the agenda was a kingpin, Paul Petrillo, tailor and insurance speculator *straordinario*. He was charged specifically with the murder of Luigi LaVecchio, the first man to fall victim to the arsenic scheme, seven years earlier.

18
HANGING JURIES

Herman Petrillo and Maria Favato, the two previous defendants, had been represented by experienced criminal lawyers, but not ones who were accustomed to high-profile cases. However, as the arsenic murder ring grew in notoriety, the cases became increasingly attractive to the luminaries of the Philadelphia criminal bar, whose reputations and fortunes were made on the most visible, most celebrated cases. Even Herman's conviction in the spring of 1939 and the flurry of guilty pleas that followed (accompanied by the defense lawyer's nightmare of coconspirators turning state's evidence) did not seem to change the situation. When the state led off its new round of prosecutions in September, the star defendant, Paul Petrillo, was represented by a star lawyer. It was not Raymond Pace Alexander, whose race still made him unsuitable, but the mighty Lemuel B. Schofield, who agreed to take it on pro bono.

Major Schofield, as he was always addressed because of his

experiences during the World War I, had spearheaded an exposé of police corruption in the twenties and been appointed police commissioner. Serving in that capacity from 1928 to 1932, he acquired a formidable reputation for rectitude, becoming the darling of the Women's Christian Temperance Union for his zealous enforcement of Prohibition laws. Reporters relished such attention-grabbing acts as his raid on the "swanky" Manufacturers' Club, of which he was a member. Schofield loved the press, even (or especially) when they reported on such matters as the reputed wealth of his heiress wife. The front-page status of Paul's trial was a magnet for him.

The major was a pudgy, thick-necked man, with close-cropped hair, wire-rimmed glasses, and a Prussian bearing. He would do anything to gain an edge for his client. On one notorious occasion, while defending a judge against charges of corruption, he brought in several of the defendant's fellow judges to testify as character witnesses. When the court denied him the right to call the witnesses, he turned to each, addressed the man by name and title, and thanked him personally for coming in. Although he was held in contempt of court for this charade, Schofield prevailed for his client.

Schofield was also well known as a bulldog on cross-examination, going after every detail of a witness's testimony and character, and willing to try almost anything to shake a witness's confidence. Once, while defending a doctor charged with raping a patient, he demanded that the unfortunate female victim climb up on a table and demonstrate her position while the act took place. They still tell the story around the courthouse of the hulking Schofield standing over that woman sprawled out on the table with her legs spread apart.

In representing Paul Petrillo, Schofield was favored with a

fair-minded trial judge, Albert S. C. Millar, who was willing to give the defense some leeway in presenting its case. The defense lawyer took full advantage from the outset, arguing with vigor to obtain a jury that was not disposed to hanging his client. The attitude of the jurors as to the death penalty was critical because they would control its imposition.

Schofield explained the situation to the panel of prospective jurors. "Ladies and gentlemen, the law in Pennsylvania has been changed. It used to be that a person convicted of first-degree murder automatically received a sentence of death, but now the legislature has allowed the jury to select the punishment." The profound choice was up to the twelve selected men and women— the electric chair or life behind bars for a convicted murderer.

Although ostensibly well intentioned and merciful in its intention, this procedure had become the nemesis of defense lawyers. By placing the critical death-penalty decision in the hands of the jury, it gave prosecutors a reason to bar any juror who had scruples against imposing that ultimate penalty. They had a morbid name for this process; the jury had to be "death-qualified." The issue came up immediately as Vincent McDevitt opened the questioning of the first venireman.

"Your name is Charles Shapiro?"

"Yes."

"Mr. Shapiro, are you opposed to the death penalty?"

"Yes, sir."

That was it. "Challenged by the Commonwealth for cause," proclaimed McDevitt.

Without hesitancy, Judge Millar agreed. "The challenge is sustained."

Each side, prosecution and defense, was limited to forty peremptory challenges—discretionary challenges for which no reason needed to be given. But there was no limit to the challenges for cause. McDevitt could sit there and knock off anti–death penalty veniremen until the crack in the Liberty Bell disappeared. All the scrupled Quakers of Philadelphia could not sit as jurors in a murder trial, leaving only more harshly minded citizens available to decide the defendant's fate.

In subsequent years, lawyers would attack the death penalty on various constitutional grounds and achieve some success, including ameliorative modification of the Pennsylvania law, which might have aided in the defense of Paul Petrillo and his fellow *fatturiste*. But it was not until 1985, following one of the great sagas in American jurisprudence, that the Supreme Court finally ruled on the legality of the "death qualification" process itself. Although ample evidence supported the conclusion that the process did, in fact, produce juries that were more prone to convict, the Court nonetheless upheld it on grounds of efficiency. The alternative, warned the Court, would be complete retrial of the case before a second jury to determine punishment. So death qualification was found lawful, and it is still practiced today.

Lemuel Schofield could not, of course, predict these results. Neither he nor any other defense lawyer of the time even raised the notion of a constitutional challenge to the death penalty or to death qualification. It was simply not within the contemporary frame of reference. Schofield's battle would be fought not in the hallowed halls of the Supreme Court but in the trenches of the voir dire, the jury-selection process. There he struggled to obtain jurors who at least indicated flexibility on exercising their right of clemency. Even that was not an easy job, given the public acclaim that had been bestowed on Vince McDevitt and his prosecutorial team over the preceding several months.

Schofield had to contend with women like Mary Hill, who
said she would impose nothing but the death penalty.

"Could you consider whether the punishment should be life
imprisonment or death?" Judge Millar asked her in disbelief.

"Death" was her adamant monosyllabic response.

The judge struck Mrs. Hill for cause. Some open-mindedness
was necessary. But that is about all that Schofield got. There was
no chance of getting a venireman like Simon Monblatt, who confessed he was against the death penalty but said, "Maybe I would
give in," if the crime was bad enough. His anti–death penalty leaning was enough for him to be excluded by McDevitt's challenges.
With all the squabbling over the fine points of each juror's moral
convictions, or lack thereof, it took four days and 178 veniremen
to pick the jury, portending a long trial.

When the proceedings commenced in earnest, Schofield confirmed that he was a master of all the defense lawyer's tricks. He
knew the art of obfuscation, of confusing and distracting the trial
proceedings with so many objections and technicalities that the
prosecution's evidence could not be presented cleanly and simply.
He was a vicious cross-examiner, homing in on any small malfea-
sance of a witness to demonstrate his or her unreliability and
catching every testimonial inconsistency. He was dogged and relentless in attacking each aspect of the prosecution's case. There
is an old saying among lawyers: If the facts are with you, argue
the facts; if the law is with you, argue the law; otherwise, bang on
the table. Schofield was a maestro of table banging.

The trial went on for weeks. The kindly judge tried to ease
the burden on the sequestered jury. He attempted to arrange for
them to be shown a movie, but the lawyers could not agree on a
selection, so Judge Millar had them taken for a bus ride in the

park instead. He gave them an afternoon off to vote in a primary election on Tuesday, September 19. It was not much solace for this miserable group holed up in dormitorylike rooms atop City Hall. Each day, they would come down and observe more of the seemingly endless parade of witnesses being put on by the prosecution.

Gaetano Cicinato and a dozen other insurance agents told of Paul sending them to write policies on men who would soon die, sometimes with Paul himself as the beneficiary. Schofield wore away at the credibility of these agents by showing how they "took shortcuts," such as vouching for a man's good health without ever having laid eyes on him, or posing as a health inspector to get a reluctant but illiterate client to put his "X" on an application. Schofield tried to smear the agents with loaded questions that would plant suggestions of impropriety in the jury's mind: "How long did you stay around drinking with her?" he asked Cicinato about his visit to one woman, as if that had anything to do with the case.

Given the chance, he would try to make a witness appear foolish, like Dr. Boccella, who had attended Luigi LaVecchio in his final illness. This was the medical man who claimed to see "fifty, sixty, a hundred" patients a day.

> QUESTION: Doctor, do you have any record of this case?
>
> ANSWER: No, I never keep any records. It would be impossible for me.
>
> QUESTION: You are too busy, I suppose?
>
> ANSWER: Too busy.
>
> QUESTION: Too much work?

ANSWER: Terrible.

QUESTION: You send out lots of bills?

ANSWER: No, I don't, because I never recall how much it is to be.

QUESTION: Never sent a bill?

ANSWER: Never did.

QUESTION: How do you get paid?

ANSWER: If they pay me, all right; if they don't pay, I never care.

"No wonder you are busy," Judge Millar interjected.

All these agents and doctors offered only circumstantial evidence. The heart of the case came when Paul's alleged coconspirators offered eyewitness specifics. Sophie LaVecchio, who was also charged with aiding in the murder, described how Paul thrust little white capsules down her husband's throat as he lay dying. She also testified that Paul later forced her to turn over her insurance checks. "He took me to the bank and held my hand and made me sign the name. Then I was waiting for the money, but he put it in his pocket and he walked out." When she complained, he threatened to kill her, him "and his big gang."

Schofield made sure the jury knew that Sophie was also indicted and was trying to save her own skin. "That lady over there dressed in white, who came with you, she's not a nurse, is she? She's a warden from the jail, isn't she?" he asked rhetorically. Schofield also brought out that Sophie had been taken out to lunch at Linton's Restaurant the day before, suggesting that McDevitt was somehow improperly soliciting her testimony. It was

part of McDevitt's style of treating cooperating witnesses as dig-
nitaries.

For six hours Schofield battered Sophie with accusatory questions, calling her a "wicked woman." He read from her first statement to police, just after her arrest. Her story then was that Bolber
and Petrillo had come to her house with guns. "Paul and Morris
bring me the pills. They both stuck guns in my side and gave me
pills to give to my husband," she had said.

But now her story included no guns and no Bolber present
at the crucial moment. "All I want is the truth," Schofield told
her, "and I'll sit here until I get it." That backfired when Sophie's
response provoked laughter.

"Sit there as long as you like," she told him.

Despite Schofield's best efforts, it was Sophie's plaintive final
note that stuck with the jurors. "I went to Petrillo because he was
a specialist," she said. "I believed it. You give me a card, it says
you're a lawyer, I believe you. I believed him when I saw his card;
I believed he could cure my husband. I would try anything, anybody, any drugstore; I was trying to help."

"Did you say you wanted to kill your husband, or cure him?"
McDevitt asked.

"Cure, not kill, please," she sobbed.

Then she smiled at reporters as she was led from the courtroom.

Drs. Martin Crane and Edward Burke, who performed the
autopsy on LaVecchio, told of finding arsenic and antimony in the
vital organs of this long-buried corpse. It was not easy to get this
testimony past the tenacious lawyer that Paul Petrillo had defending him. Major Schofield challenged every aspect of Crane's and
Burke's credentials. He questioned Burke, who had gotten his

Ph.D. in chemistry while working at a regular job, about such petty facts as how many hours he spent at the job and how he had managed to juggle school and work. He tried to imply that Crane's medical education, which had included a sojourn in Germany, was somehow tainted by Nazi influences. No tactic seemed beneath Schofield's dignity.

When it came to the technical procedures used to determine the presence of arsenic and antimony, the major made sure that the jury was presented with mind-numbing detail. Not satisfied with raising questions about the Reinsch and Gutzeit tests, which Burke had used, Schofield also cluttered the court record with questions about the Marsh, Rupp and Lehman, Fuhner, silver ammonium nitrate, Fleitman, Betendorf, copper ammonium sulfate, and Seryczowski ignition tests.

He probed and questioned every aspect of the process. The pathologist, Crane, had sliced off pieces of internal organs and given them to the chemist, Burke, for evaluation. This was standard procedure. But the major launched an all-out assault on it:

MCDEVITT: Dr. Burke, did you analyze the liver?

DR. BURKE: I did.

MCDEVITT: Of Luigi LaVecchio?

BURKE: Of Luigi LaVecchio.

SCHOFIELD: I object. He does not know it was Luigi LaVecchio. He examined a specimen of a liver that was given to him by Dr. Crane.

So McDevitt was required to bring in all the witnesses who could document the trail of the organ sample from cadaver to

chemist. When McDevitt then tried to get back to the real issue,
Schofield still would not let up.

> MCDEVITT: What did you do and what did you find,
> Dr. Burke?
>
> BURKE: I made a chemical analysis of the liver.
>
> SCHOFIELD: I object. He did no such thing. He made
> a chemical analysis of a small part of the liver, not
> the liver.
>
> MCDEVITT: Is that what you mean, Doctor?
>
> BURKE: I made a chemical analysis of a sample of
> the liver.
>
> SCHOFIELD: I ask that he refer to it specifically; not
> as the liver, because it is very misleading to the jury.
>
> MCDEVITT: What do they think it is? His right foot?

A good part of the day was gone before McDevitt could get
Burke to the substance of his testimony. Yet Schofield showed no
signs of relenting. At the trial of Herman Petrillo six months earlier, Burke had simply recited his ultimate findings. Now he was
required to describe his analytical procedures in exquisite detail.

> MCDEVITT: Describe what you did.
>
> BURKE: I took twenty grams of liver, then ten grams
> of potassium permanganate, ten cc of the dilute
> sulfuric acid, placed in the water bath and heated
> until it came to a powdery consistency, then added 25
> cc of concentrated sulfuric acid in about 5 cc
> portions. I then added 30 cc of 3 percent hydrogen

peroxide solution, brought this to a boil, placed it in a
Kjeldahl flask, rinsed with 30 cc of concentrated
sulfuric acid, added 10 grams of ferro sulfate, crystals
of ferro sulfate, cooled, connected the distillation
apparatus and distilled into a solution of sodium
bicarbonate. . . .

On and on, for dozens of pages, with the major standing
there, alert to pounce on any flaw or inconsistency, and prolonging
the agony by making the witness speak at a torpid pace. "I ask
that this witness give his testimony a little slower so that I can
follow it," Schofield kept insisting.

No one got away with anything, not even the judge when
his tongue slipped.

SCHOFIELD: I object. The witness hasn't explained
that test yet.

JUDGE MILLAR: (interjecting) It takes four years to
go through law school and you don't get everything
on the first day.

SCHOFIELD: How many years?

JUDGE MILLAR: Oh, go ahead.

The defense lawyer raised an objection to virtually every
question, forcing the judge to rule against him constantly. At one
point Schofield even objected to Burke's saying that he had multiplied two sums. "He is a expert chemist, but he is not called here
to multiply."

"Overruled," said Judge Millar.

"Exception," said Schofield, preserving his right of appeal.

Again and again it happened.

There was a method to Schofield's madness. It put the jury to sleep, so that they would be less likely to be attentive to important points in the testimony. It gave the defense various openings to nitpick the procedure and cast doubt on its credibility. And it drove the prosecutor and the judge to distraction, which, Schofield hoped, might force them into some appealable error.

But even this master obstructionist could not prevent the testimony from finally coming in. And when it did, it clearly established poisoning as the cause of death. Luigi LaVecchio had a total of 5.6 milligrams of arsenic in his liver, kidneys, and stomach. That amount was one-tenth of that found in the victims of Herman Petrillo and Maria Favato, maybe not even a fatal dose. But LaVecchio was also full of antimony, with 15.54 milligrams in his liver and kidneys alone.

Dr. Crane contrasted the two poisons. Antimony was the more powerful toxin, he explained, but the problem with administering it was that it was a "powerfully nauseant drug." Victims tended to vomit it out before it could take effect.

"Antimony was quite common back at the turn of the century," said Dr. William Wadsworth, an old-timer in the coroner's office. "It was commonly seen in shoo fly given in grog shops back before the drought."

In 1939, only six years after Prohibition had ended, everyone knew what the "drought" was.

"Shoo fly," Dr. Wadsworth explained, "which is full of antimony, was slipped in beer by shakedown artists. The result depended on the man, not so much what the man had to drink, but whether he vomited it off or not. It generally knocked him out, and he collapsed."

The killers of Luigi LaVecchio, the experts theorized, had

weakened their victim with arsenic at first and then finished him off with antimony when he was too far gone to react. That neatly explained the switch from powders to capsules at the end. It also suggested that someone with a fair amount of expertise was behind the plot.

19

WITNESS FOR THE PROSECUTION

As if on cue, the great man with the expertise, Morris Bolber, took the stand. He was not there, of course, to claim well-deserved credit for developing Paul Petrillo's poison formulations, but to exhibit his brilliance in other ways. Louie the Rabbi relished his time in the limelight, taking the opportunity to show his sagacity and superiority, and his lack of complicity. "Voluble and excited, Morris Bolber, he of the 'evil eye' and magic powers" was how the *Inquirer* described him. "His voice boomed out in a dialect which is a thick mixture of Russian and English, blended with less pronounced portions of the seven other dialects he speaks. The jurors, who had been restless, showed signs of renewed interest as the irrepressible Bolber, leaning back indolently, his eyelid nearly covering one cast eye, gushed out his story."

"I am not the brains of any arsenic ring," Bolber told the jury, "but I am the brains of the arresting bureau. When you talk to me, you are not speaking to a murderer. My name is Morris Bolber, and everything you want by way of information I can give you."

Bolber was one man whom Major Schofield could not intimidate. The rabbi was contemptuous on cross-examination, treating Schofield like an old fool. "What do you mean you didn't get it?" he spat at the defense lawyer one time. "You have cotton in your ears?" Later, Bolber repeated a point, explaining, "I said that again because I was afraid you would forget, and I wanted to remind you. I am sorry for you."

When he spoke about Paul Petrillo, Bolber was indeed the source of all information for the prosecution. He pointed the finger directly, in as quotable a manner as he could muster with his broken syntax. "Paul Petrillo's shop, the front was a tailor store and the back was a butcher shop to kill people, you understand?" Bolber testified in detail how Paul had masterminded the deaths of not only LaVecchio but also Joseph Arena, Antonio Giacobbe, Ralph Caruso, and Jennie Pino.

He was only an unwilling, unwitting, and peripheral character in all this, Bolber assured his audience. He had confessed to the murder of Romaine Mandiuk, but only because "my conscience was bothering me." This was not because he had anything to do with this Mandiuk murder, but because he knew about it. "I took seven hundred dollars from Herman Petrillo for keeping quiet. I came forth to clean myself up, and I am glad I came." When Schofield pushed him, he stuck to his story and got in a little dig. "I didn't kill nobody. The killer is sitting next to you. You are representing him."

This line began to fray a little when Schofield got Bolber to admit that he had also been paid eight hundred dollars in connection with the LaVecchio case and some more for the Pino case.

"That adds up to eighteen hundred dollars," Schofield ventured.

"I got more than that," Bolber volunteered proudly. "I been keeping statements. Altogether I got two thousand six hundred and twenty dollars during the seven years for keeping quiet. Eighteen hundred and fifty dollars came from Paul Petrillo, and seven hundred dollars came from Herman Petrillo, and from David Brandt came fifty dollars and twenty dollars. Altogether is two thousand six hundred and twenty dollars, Mr. Schofield."

The crowd was roaring with laughter.

"And twenty dollars here," shouted Salvatore Sortino, the disciple, recollecting a sum he had slipped into Bolber's hand after the Caruso drowning. Sortino was seated in the phalanx of other defendants that McDevitt had propped up in the front row.

"You still owe me five," retorted Bolber, obviously enjoying himself.

When the merriment subsided, Schofield resumed. "Now, you got this money although you did not do anything at all?"

"Only in order to keep this mouth closed. To be sure that I will be a good boy and keep quiet. But don't forget, I received money in only five cases. I gave the district attorney seventeen murder cases."

Bolber would have talked endlessly, but they had to bring his testimony to a close by sundown so that he could begin his observance of the Jewish holiday of Yom Kippur, the Day of Atonement. Louie the Rabbi was a religious man.

While the Paul Petrillo jury was being thus entertained, other facets of the McDevitt blitz were under way in nearby courtrooms. The results did not augur well for Paul. Caesar "Jumbo" Valenti pleaded guilty to murder in midtrial and began trying to make a deal. The collapse of the rock-hard Valenti was a shock. Only two weeks earlier, while attending a hearing with Herman Petrillo and Rose Carina, Valenti had taken off in anger at a newspaper photographer. While the photographer kept snapping, Jumbo picked up a heavy wooden chair in his right hand, brandishing it like a club. Thus armed, he chased the photographer around the courtroom, dragging Herman, to whom he was handcuffed, along as if he were a rag doll. But now even Valenti had succumbed to Vince McDevitt's onslaught.

Outside the Philadelphia courthouse, the world marched on to war. The United States, which was protesting Japanese aggression in Asia, announced that it was relocating its Pacific Fleet from the West Coast to Hawaii as a show of resolve. All the while, the trial of Paul Petrillo proceeded in Room 453.

20
THE LOST LITTLE LAMBS

The worst events, as far as Paul Petrillo was concerned, were not those in Europe, but those in nearby courtrooms, where the first trials were beginning for "poison widows." These were the women who had, on the advice of one of the ring's faith healers and with the aid and connivance of one of its facilitators, sprinkled the mysterious all-powerful powder on their husbands' spaghetti or used it to sweeten their coffee.

Maria Favato had already pled guilty, but she was special, more middle manager than client of the ring. Eleven other women were scheduled for trial in the Philadelphia courts and a twelfth in Wilmington over the next three months. All these poor little lambs, even Rose Carina, asserted their innocence. Each one claimed to have wanted only the best for her husband, and to have gone to a faith healer only for help in curing illness or reviving love. They were not ringleaders like Herman and Paul Petrillo. They were not hardened criminals with long records like Caesar

ROSTER OF POISON WIDOWS

WIDOW	INFLUENCED BY	COMMENT
Stella Alfonsi	Herman Petrillo	Her case broke the ring open. Did she hang that towel on the fence?
Anna Arena	Morris Bolber Paul Petrillo	Joe Arena drowned at the Jersey shore. And wife Anna packed a nice lunch for his one-way fishing trip.
Rose Carilli	Paul Petrillo	The Wilmington widow.
Rose Carina	Paul Petrillo	The "Kiss of Death." Three out of five husbands down, and counting.
Christine Cerrone	Herman Petrillo	Landlady, not wife, of Ralph Caruso. He got "the cold bath," and she was in on the policies.
Maria Favato	Herman Petrillo Caesar Valenti	The "Witch" who hexed husband, neighbor, and stepson alike. Having pled guilty, she was now working her powers as a prosecution informer.
Susie DiMartino	Maria Favato Ralphael Polselli	Susie welcomed Maria Favato's neighborly interest in the health of her husband, Guiseppi. But so much interest?
Millie Giacobbe	Paul Petrillo	A corseter who was Paul's kind of woman, until the ghosts scared her off.
Sophie LaVecchio	Morris Bolber Paul Petrillo	Her husband, Luigi, was the first poison victim, and now Paul had become the victim of her testimony.
Agnes Mandiuk	Morris Bolber	Louie the Rabbi gave her his personal attention. How much attention did she give him?
Grace Pirolli	Josephine Sedita Rose Carina	Her husband benefited from the tender care of *sorella* Josephine Sedita and "Kiss of Death" Carina.
Josephine Romualdo	Maria Favato Ralphael Polselli	Another beneficiary of Maria Favato's neighborliness. A friend in need, or a friend in greed?
Marie Woloshyn	Herman Petrillo	Herman and Jumbo Valenti went for a bumpy ride with her husband, John.

Valenti. Except for Rose Carina, they were not accused of involvement in multiple murders, and their trials could not be conducted on the legal theory of system, with witness piled upon witness and crime piled upon crime. Other than Rose, they were just simple women whose only involvement with the law and killing was a single grim experience. Their cases were to be, by far, the greatest challenge to the prosecution.

Vincent McDevitt would have liked to have taken on the challenge of the first poison widow himself. But he could not hold off all the trials. The first one would have to begin while he was still grappling with Major Schofield and Paul Petrillo.

The leadoff widow defendant was Josephine Romualdo. None of the widows was more pathetic than Josephine, wife of the lamplighter Antonio Romualdo. The *New York Daily News,* in a feature story on "The Black Widows of Philadelphia," classified the women, labeling them "the fattest," "the youngest," "the coolest." Mrs. Romualdo qualified as "the slowest," referring to her mental acumen, not her speed afoot. From the time of her arraignment in May 1939, the "frail, sallow-faced woman, dressed entirely in black, wearing thick-lensed gold spectacles," proclaimed her innocence. WIFE SAYS POISON WAS "LOVE DRINK," headlined the *Philadelphia Evening Bulletin.*

In defense, Josephine reiterated her innocence. "I was perfectly happy with my husband and didn't want to kill him," she swore to the jury. "Mrs. Maria Favato told me she would make my husband love me as he did the day we were married."

But the eight men and four women on the jury showed no mercy. Antonio's body was laced with arsenic, and Josephine had a stack of insurance policies on him. That was all they needed to hear. After only a few hours' deliberation, their verdict was "guilty of first-degree murder, with the penalty fixed as death in the electric chair." Justice had been swift. The entire trial, including jury selection and deliberation, took only two days. In that brief time, Josephine Romualdo, the second defendant to let a jury be master of her fate, became the second person to receive a death sentence.

Word of the Romualdo conviction reached Paul Petrillo as Sophie LaVecchio was completing her castigating testimony against him. The debonair Paul, who was noted for wearing a different finely tailored ensemble to court each day, began to wear a visage that closely matched his gray suit. Then, as he sat listening to Morris Bolber's scintillating syntax, the trial of still another poison widow opened in a courtroom down the hall.

x x x

This time, the defendant was a forty-six-year-old naïf named Grace Pirolli. Grace had been lucky. Her husband, Pietro, was one of the few men with a steady job in 1935. He earned twenty dollars a week at Merck and Company. Grace also worked, at the Bayunk Cigar factory, packing cheap stogies. To keep her luck going, she took a little of her money each week to *sorella* Josephine Sedita, a Passyunk *fattucchiera*.

Sorella Josephine was known for wearing a "magic coat," a dirty, oversize blue housedress that hung limply over her broad frame, and for casting spells when she met clients. The coat, she told them, enabled her to perform miracles. When one Alphonso De Jesse went to see her about stomach ulcers that doctors could not treat, she stood there in this blue garment and proclaimed that no case was hopeless.

"She told me I had a sponge in my stomach that was someone else's jinx," De Jesse said, "and she could purge it. She said something magic; it sounded to me like 'Aska Wanna Jinksa Hoo.'"

Josephine gave him two rabbit skins and told him to keep them on his stomach to drive the jinx out. "I kept them on for three days," De Jesse admitted, "until my wife complained of the odor. Then I went back to Mrs. Sedita. She pricked my finger, smeared the blood on eggshells, and told me to string the shells over my bed. She told me to put the inside of a lamb's stomach next to my skin."

For this cure, De Jesse paid Josephine $266. But when it accomplished nothing, he sued her. Maybe that's why Josephine Sedita became so enamored of Papa Bolber's new way of "fixing" men. The Bolber-Petrillo magic worked, and the clients never sued in the end.

Over time, the enterprising fortune-teller learned a few things from Grace Pirolli—among them, that Mr. Pirolli had some small life-insurance policies and that he had heart problems. "Give me one of the little insurance policies to hold," she told Grace. "You give it to me and I will help your husband get better. I will fix him." Grace acceded, giving her a four-hundred-dollar policy.

It seemed a perfect situation for application of some of the magic *fattura* that Paul Petrillo was touting. Paul agreed to supply Josephine with the necessary potion, but only on the condition that his confederate Rose Carina go along to make sure the ghastly final days went well.

A few days later, Josephine dropped by the Pirolli house for a little coffee klatch with Pietro, whose wife, Grace, was out. When she returned home, Pietro was feeling ill. By the next evening, the familiar pattern had emerged. "He was retching," as Grace described it. "He was vomiting. He was quivering all over. He wasn't able to get off the toilet. He was crying, 'Get me a doctor, get me medicine.' " And there was that garlic odor, unremarkable as always. Grace called a doctor, who, in keeping with the apparent uniform medical practice, prescribed stomach powders.

When the prescriptions did no good, Grace summoned *sorella* Josephine. The next morning, Josephine arrived at the Pirolli house accompanied by her coach, Rose Carina. They were there, they told Grace, to care for her husband. The two women moved in and stayed for the next three days. They sat by Pietro's bedside and gave him his medicine. They even cleaned up his "greenish yellow vomit" so that Grace would not have to come upstairs and deal with it. "Grace, Grace," the miserable man would call out to his wife, "it's time for my medicine." But Rose Carina would answer the call. The doctor, Dr. Zeffrino Aversa, came back each day to check on his patient. What he had at first thought was acute indigestion now appeared to be a heart condition. By Friday night the situation had become grim.

"Your husband has only a few hours left," Dr. Aversa warned Grace, then advised her to take him to the hospital. Grace refused, saying, "If he has to die, he is going to die in his own bed."

R.I.P.
PIETRO PIROLLI

x x x

The case against Grace was even weaker than that against Josephine Romualdo. No insurance had been taken out on Pirolli in anticipation of his death. Unlike Josephine Romualdo, Grace had never admitted giving any powder to her husband, even in ignorance. From the moment of her arrest, her story had been consistent. The healer Josephine Sedita had come to her house with a promise of witchcraft that would help her husband with his heart problems. Sedita gave him the cup of coffee that brought on his horrible final illness. Sedita and Rose Carina ministered to Pietro and controlled his medicines during his final days.

"You could hear him scream from Ninth to Tenth Streets," Grace cried in dramatic testimony. As she clutched at the Bible and began to pound it on the rail of the witness box, she screamed out her defense. "He was sick. He believed in the witch doctors. He wanted them to help him. Anybody would have done the same thing. Anybody would have done the same thing!" Then she reached for a glass of water and fainted dead away. Court attendants caught her just before she hit the floor. When she was revived, Grace told how she had spent over twelve hundred dollars on Pietro's funeral, blowing most of the fifteen-hundred-dollar death benefit paid to her by Merck.

Sorella Josephine refused to return the four-hundred-dollar insurance policy that Grace had given her to hold; instead, she collected the proceeds as compensation for her services.

When Grace protested, "You said you'd cure my husband," the faith healer shrugged.

"You have to pay the doctor, don't you?" Josephine told Grace. "Didn't we take care of him?"

To make sure Grace stayed quiet, the four-foot-six-inch Josephine brought around her six-foot-three-inch, 236-pound boyfriend. This ox, named Guiseppi Pane, but also listed on police blotters for various raps as Pepe Ulongo, Joseph Sadia, Bruno, Gio Borell, and Joseph Borrelo, was not to be taken lightly. He was well known locally as a "tough guy" and an "intimidator," the sort who put a knife to your throat when he asked you questions, to encourage a more forthright answer.

The Mutt and Jeff team of Josephine and Guiseppi moved into Grace's house so that they could keep an eye on her. They stayed for weeks, when Pane, trying to help around the house by replacing a lightbulb in the ceiling, fell and broke his leg. Guys like him obviously were not meant to do good deeds.

The basics of Grace's story were confirmed by a boarder living in the house, and not really denied by anyone. Grace was a pawn in the hands of these vicious viragoes, who did their jobs thoroughly. Pietro's autopsy showed an awesome 268.1 milligrams of arsenic in his liver, stomach, and kidneys alone, triple the amount found in the next-worst victim.

The only evidence that Grace had any idea what was going on came from the testimony of homicide detective Frank M. Lynch, who guarded Grace during her initial interrogation. One afternoon, as he was escorting her back to her cell after questioning, Grace volunteered a comment to him.

"Rose Carina and Josephine Sedita put me in trouble," Grace told Detective Lynch.

"How do you mean?" the detective asked.

Grace was weeping. "Well, they got me in trouble for that policy."

"You knew they were killing your husband?"

"Yes, but they made me, because they knew I had this small policy."

That is all Detective Lynch recalled when he testified at trial months later. Nothing had been transcribed, and Lynch had not followed up with any other questions. Exactly what Grace, whose English was rudimentary, might have said or meant was far from clear. Yet it was the reed upon which the prosecution based its entire case.

It did not seem that Grace had much to fear. Michael Marchesano, Grace's scrappy young lawyer, was confident of an acquittal. He had been excited to get the appointment as her lawyer when he had taken over her case from more experienced lawyers on September 1, only four weeks before trial. The prosecutor in the case, Ephraim Lipshutz, had tried to rattle Marchesano, taunting, "I have been practicing law longer than he has been in the world," and calling him "impudent" and "irresponsible." But the novice had thrown himself into the defense with the energy of ten men, trying to compensate with enthusiasm for his lack of seasoning.

Grace was moved by his soaring summation rhetoric on her behalf. Among other things, Marchesano compared her payments to Josephine Sedita with Charles Lindbergh's recent payment of ransom in his vain attempt to protect a loved one. At this, Grace broke out in tears again, requiring her lawyer to pause. "Please stop, Mrs. Pirolli," Marchesano asked. When she could not, he was forced to finish with this fitting but nonmusical accompaniment as a backdrop. In the end, he believed he had succeeded in his efforts to paint his client as a woman guilty only of "stupidity and ignorance in allowing faith healers to go near her husband."

The jury began deliberations at 6:30 P.M. on Tuesday evening and continued through the night. Court attachés said they heard voices from the jury room until five in the morning. When court convened at ten o'clock the next morning, they were ready with their verdict. As the bailiff uttered his call, "Jury, look upon the prisoner; prisoner, look upon the jury," Marchesano nudged his client to her feet. She was wearing the same dark blue coat and flowered blue dress that she had worn since the trial had begun two days before.

The voice of Joseph Farrell, the jury foreman, was barely audible as he uttered the verdict. "Guilty."

"And what penalty say you?" the bailiff asked.

Farrell's face was ashen and his voice scarcely rose above a whisper as he stated their solemn decision. "Death."

Marchesano demanded a poll of the jury. He listened as they all concurred, some hesitantly and some with gusto. Several had wanted to limit the penalty to life imprisonment. But a strong-minded cadre, led by a seventy-three-year-old ironworker named James Magee, had convinced them to go the limit. Magee was an old hand at the process, having been foreman of the jury that convicted Josephine Romualdo a week earlier. Only a neophyte like Marchesano would have let him slip by on voir dire. With Magee's consistent help, the prosecutors were now three for three in jury verdicts, all death-penalty grand slams.

x x x

Grace's lawyer, Marchesano, was distraught. But no more so than Paul Petrillo. As Paul's case dragged on, delayed by the relentless tactics of Lemuel Schofield and the copious witness list of Vincent McDevitt, he received the devastating news of Grace Pirolli's conviction. Another astonishingly brief trial and another jury exercising its deific discretion to call for the supreme penalty. Later the same day, another jury returned with the verdict on Emedio Muscelli. Muscelli, who had impersonated the husband of Susie DiMartino for insurance purposes ("and in other ways," commented McDevitt), was a peripheral accomplice to the murder of Mr. DiMartino. Nonetheless, he was found guilty of first-degree murder. The only solace was that the Muscelli jury (without the hard-hitting James Magee in the lineup) had recommended life imprisonment.

All this news was too much for Paul. Just after lunch on the

fourteenth day of his trial, the day after these latest awesome verdicts were announced, Paul gave up. "Guilty," he said, throwing
himself on the mercy of the court. He hoped that he might have
a better chance with the judge than with the hanging jury that
had sat listening to all the evidence.

All three real kingpins—both Petrillo cousins and Morris
Bolber—had now been found guilty of first-degree murder, either
by their own word or that of a jury. All that remained for the
McDevitt team were the rest of the poison widows, nine more in
all, and a few marginal characters.

Although it had initially seemed that the widows would be
difficult to convict, the Romualdo and Pirolli cases proved otherwise. The prosecution had an apparently insurmountable advantage. The flood of publicity that surrounded the affair, and billed
it so dramatically as the work of a "poison murder ring," tarred
everyone with the blackness of guilt by association. In each case,
Vincent McDevitt and his colleagues could easily show that the
victim had received substantial doses of arsenic (and sometimes
antimony). In each case, the prosecutors had one or more of the
leading conspirators—first Maria Favato, then Morris Bolber, now
Paul Petrillo—ready to say that the defendant on trial had administered the poison. This trio of confessed killers willingly offered
any music the prosecutor wanted to hear. They knew well that
the extent of their cooperation as well as the degree to which they
could deflect responsibility would surely help gain favorable treatment when the time came to determine their sentences. Each of
the widows thus found herself having to combat a formidable
prima facia case. And they had to convince a hardhearted jury,
one that was—thanks to Pennsylvania law—innately stern and
puritanical.

The next defendant scheduled for trial in Philadelphia was

Providenza Miccichi, the *la fattura* Avon lady. Her lawyer saw what was coming, and he wisely persuaded her to plead guilty. With her plea, plus those of Salvatore Sortino (the stooge who had shoved Ralph Caruso into the Schuykill River) and the poison widower Dominick Cassetti, the McDevitt team had quarried an even dozen first-degree murderers with not a single acquittal. Three of them—Herman Petrillo, Josephine Romualdo, and Grace Pirolli—had already been assigned to the electric chair by juries. The fortunate Emedio Muscelli had gotten away with a life sentence. All the others had pled guilty and were awaiting determination of their sentences by a panel of judges. It was an astonishing streak of prosecutorial triumphs.

DA McDevitt felt very confident. His office now had a three-week break to prepare for the final round of cases. The next defendant on the schedule was Stella Alfonsi, the poison widow whose husband's death had broken the case open. The case against her, which would include testimony of Secret Service agents, was particularly strong. McDevitt had no qualms about assigning it to his colleague Charles Gordon.

21

STELLA GETS HER MAN

Lovely Stella Alfonsi had been sitting in Moyamensing Prison for more than eight months, held without bail on a charge of first-degree murder. She could not have been encouraged by what she had been reading in the newspapers. One after another, her fellow defendants had come to justice, and one after another they had heard the dread result: guilty of murder in the first degree. It was now October 13, 1939, Friday the 13th. Her lawyer, Frank Marolla, came to speak about her trial, finally due to begin in ten days.

Marolla was young, only twenty-nine, and he had relatively little trial experience. He would go on to become president of the Trial Lawyer's Association and a bar leader, but at this stage of life, he was in over his head. He also knew, from painful personal experience, how difficult it was to win one of these poison widow cases. He had been the lawyer for Josephine Romualdo ("the slowest"), had believed in her innocence, and had struggled to convince the jury of it, to no avail. He told Stella of this, and he told her that he did not foresee any better outcome in her case. That was the bad news. But he told her how even the most guilty witches of the ring had managed at least a chance to escape maximum punishment by pleading guilty. The death penalty, he advised, was final, but life imprisonment was not. There was always the possibility of parole or commutation. Stella was a young woman, only twenty-nine. With good behavior, she could see the outside world again, in ten, fifteen, or twenty years.

Stella thought about it. She was not like the other poison widows. She was by far the youngest. All the others were over forty. All the others were drab and dowdy. She was attractive and stylishly dressed, "a sultry beauty," said the *Philadelphia Daily News*. She loved parties, like the ones given by Rose Carina across the street back in the Passyunk neighborhood, full of men and fun, where she could sing and be the center of attention.

Maybe that was what dissuaded her from pleading—the thought of losing her youth and beauty to prison, with only the hope of freedom as an old woman. She could not do it, she told Marolla. Was there any other lawyer who might do better? she asked. In Stella's world, men were dominant, even domineering, but they were protective. They took care of beautiful women like her. If Marolla was not up to the job, she would find someone who was.

As a murder defendant, Stella had a right to court-appointed counsel. But she did not have the right to demand any lawyer she wanted. If her trial judge had been "Hanging Harry" McDevitt, he might have sneered at a request from her for a new lawyer. But her case had been assigned to Judge Eugene Alessandroni. He was a different type of jurist, one who tried to be evenhanded. He was not the most liberal judge, not like Judges Curtis Bok, Gerald

Flood, and Louis Levinthal of Common Pleas Number 6. But he was skilled in the law and administered his court so as to earn respect for it. Beyond that, he was a vivid presence in the South Philadelphia Italian community, working hard to improve respect for his countrymen.

Judge Alessandroni was concerned about the direction in which these poison murder cases were going. He could see that the prosecutorial momentum was acquiring freight-train force, rolling over not only the individual defendants but the entire reputation of his Italian community, which, in the public's mind, was becoming universally involved in this ever-expanding scandal. There were limits to what he could do about this disturbing trend, given the constraints of his judicial role, but one thing he surely could do was ensure that Stella Alfonsi had a lawyer who might give her a chance.

When it came to lost causes, to inspired and creative defense of unpopular criminal defendants whose cases seemed beyond help, one could not help thinking of the famed black lawyer Raymond Pace Alexander. No one knows who first proposed him for Stella Alfonsi. It could have been Stella's original lawyer, Frank Marolla, who might have welcomed a more experienced colleague to get him out of an unpleasant role. It could have been Judge Alessandroni, who had his reasons for aiding Stella. It could have been Stella herself, who had heard Alexander's name through the prison grapevine. Whatever, when Stella Alfonsi stood up before Judge Alessandroni and said that she wished to discharge her present counsel and have Raymond Pace Alexander appointed in his stead, the judge hesitated only momentarily before phoning Alexander to come immediately to his courtroom.

"Raymond, how is your trial schedule for the next few weeks?" the judge asked ominously. Alexander's offices at 1900

Chestnut Street were only a few blocks from the court, and the lawyer answered the summons within the hour. The court was declared in session, and the distinguished forty-two-year-old Negro attorney, dressed in his customary three-piece suit, saw a beautiful dark-haired young woman rise and look across the table at him.

"Your Honor," Stella repeated in open court, where there was no doubt that she could see what she what asking for, "I wish to be represented by Raymond Pace Alexander. I wish him to defend me."

Alexander had never before met Stella. But he knew, as did every other informed Philadelphian, of the poison murder ring and of Stella's alleged participation in it. "I knew of the twelve previous convictions," Alexander later recalled, "and the hostility and adverse public feeling against the defendants, and the fact that it would take from a week to ten days to try the case, and I did not want to take it, especially in view of the fact that the fee would not be more than two hundred dollars under the statute in our state."

It was one thing to sacrifice oneself for a just, if unpaying, cause. Alexander had fought the state attorney general for two years over the segregation of schools in the nearby suburb of Berwyn. But Stella's cause was not his cause, and as far as he knew, it was not even a just one. Judge Alessandroni would not let him off easily, however. "The state is asking for her life," the judge said, "and it would ease her mind to be represented by someone in whom she has confidence. Then, whatever the result, she would have at least been a participant in her own fate." This was hardly an overwhelming plea. "It gave me an indication of what the judge thought about the probable outcome of the case," Alexander told friends.

There were, however, other forces at work. Alexander had

a reverence for the law and, even more, for judges who administered it impartially. *Non sub homine sed sub deo et leges,* it said over
the entry to Harvard Law School—Not under man but under God
and the law. Raymond Pace Alexander believed it. He believed
that the law could set his people free, and, at least so far, experience had proved him right.

Fresh out of law school in 1924, he was denied admission to
a movie theater—denied, ironically, the right to see *The Ten Commandments.* The refusal violated the law in liberal Pennsylvania,
but no one had ever done anything to enforce it. Not until Raymond Pace Alexander came along. He arranged a test case, choos-
ing his plaintiffs with political savvy. Within the year, all the
major downtown theaters were admitting blacks. The legitimate
theaters, beginning with the Schubert, succumbed to the same tactic under the young lawyer's prodding. As a founder and leading
lawyer for the local NAACP, Alexander continued these efforts
for years, integrating restaurants and hotels throughout the city.

Alexander was not always successful. In 1929, he took on
the case of two colored amateur golfers who had come to Philadelphia to play in the Amateur Public Links Championship. After
the two players had won their early-round matches, tournament
officials disqualified them on a trumped-up technicality. Rushing
into court with a motion, the young black lawyer obtained an immediate hearing and a ruling that the disqualification was improper and illegal. Alas, the decision was not rendered until 3:00
P.M. on the final day of the tournament, just after the last round
had been completed. Alexander's clients were reinstated to a tournament that was over.

But the upbeat lawyer was not discouraged. "They won't do
it again," he told friends.

Raymond Pace Alexander was an integrationist. His friends

were integrationists. They believed, deeply, that the generation of educated Negroes had finally come, the generation that, with university training and professional credentials, would finally lay to rest black stereotypes and gain not merely citizenship but true parity for their race in all walks of life. He had been born only thirty-four years after emancipation, the son of ex-slaves. The nineteenth century had been the time to win freedom. The twentieth century was the time to win equality, in practice, not merely on paper. And Alexander was the paragon of the new twentieth-century Negro. Victory, he knew, would not come overnight. But he planned to do his part to make it happen with all deliberate speed.

There were some sweet moments along the way. In 1933 his law firm was looking for new, larger office space. They had relocated to an "uptown" location a few years earlier. But when their lease came up for renewal, the landlord, under pressure from other tenants, who did not appreciate the heavy flow of black clients into the building, told them to look elsewhere. Other landlords were no better, including the owners of the noneponymous Lincoln Liberty Building, who told them, "We have no racial prejudice—but . . ." Right across the street at 1900 Chestnut Street, however, Warner Brothers' plans to erect a new movie theater had collapsed, the victim of Depression economics. Alexander was able to buy the dilapidated old structure on the site for a fraction of what Warner had paid. He built his own office building there, giving his firm a secure and prominent location, and making him the landlord for white-owned businesses housed on the lower floors. From his office window, he could look down on the grand Aldine movie palace, where he had triumphed in his struggle to see *The Ten Commandments* a decade earlier.

Bit by bit, the twentieth-century vision was being realized.

Not least of Alexander's dreams were those of black judges sitting on Pennsylvania courts, where there were then none. "There is no authority in the English speaking world mightier than or more powerful than that of a Judge in American courts of record," Alexander wrote in 1931. "There is no position of greater dignity. The Negro lawyers of the country have noticed with great interest the elevation to the bench of the Municipal Court of New York City of two of its members. Today in that city one can hear young Negro boys in the lower grades in school saying that they are going to study law so that they may some day be a Judge, an entirely new experience in youthful selection of future occupations."

In 1936 he had spearheaded an effort to have a slate of three black candidates, himself included, chosen by the Republican Party for election to the Court of Common Pleas—the highest trial-level court in Philadelphia. He had long worked for the Republican Party (which then was, for Negroes, still the "party of Lincoln"). His early mentor and idol was William H. Lewis, a pioneering black lawyer who had been a Harvard football captain and assistant attorney general in the Theodore Roosevelt administration. Through this contact, Alexander had been national chairman of Young Republicans in 1928 and had labored hard for the election of Herbert Hoover. As an established Republican loyalist, he thought he could convince party leaders of the political wisdom of catering to the growing black vote as well as the moral soundness of this action. It had not worked. Despite all his efforts, the party leaders had told Alexander, "Philadelphia is not ready." Seventy years after the Civil War, the northern city of Philadelphia, home of the Liberty Bell and seat of the First Continental Congress, was not ready to see a distinguished, Harvard-educated member of the bar, who happened to be black, run for judge.

An even harder blow had come two years later, in 1938,

when Raymond Pace Alexander and his wife had tried to enroll
their first child in nursery school. Alexander had married Sadie
Tanner Mossell. Her ancestors had not been slaves, but successful
professional achievers, a family of firsts. Her maternal grandfather
was Henry Tanner, the renowned painter, who would become the
first black artist to have his work hung in the White House. Her
father, Dr. Nathan Mossell, was, in 1888, the first man of African
descent to graduate from the University of Pennsylvania. Sadie
was a proud daughter of this distinguished line. She earned a Ph.D.
from the University of Pennsylvania, the first ever granted to a
black woman in the United States, and went on to earn a law
degree at Penn, becoming the first black woman admitted to the
Pennsylvania Bar.

Sadie expected no less of her daughters, and she shared her
husband's belief in education as the key to progress for black
Americans. But when the moment came for four-year-old Mary
Elizabeth to begin that education, they found a white establishment less than fully committed to their view. The Quaker-led Germantown Friends School rejected the application outright as soon
as they learned of Mary Elizabeth's race. When Raymond Alexander wrote a temperate and well-reasoned protest, the only response was from the Quaker Committee on Race Relations,
apologizing for the society's attitude. "There is one ray of encour-
agement, however," the committee reassured him. "Certainly in
the case of Germantown Friends School, ten years ago, the committee would likely have dismissed the application with far less
soul-searching than today."

The progressive Oak Lane School in suburban Philadelphia
was no better. When the Alexanders approached that school
through an influential intermediary, they were told that the direc-
tor "feels it is not wise" for him to accept Mary Elizabeth. "He

has been working desperately hard to get recognition for Oak Lane
and to raise its social level, and he feels it is in too precarious a
state to take any chance on losing the ground he has gained. . . .
In another four or five years he will be in a position to take outstanding colored children. . . . Mr. Ivins is a very understanding
person and knows well the problem of the Negro, as he worked
with them for five years in the Virgin Islands. He has many good
friends among prominent colored people." The Alexanders were
instead referred to Miss Illman, head of the kindergarten run by
the School of Education at the University of Pennsylvania, their
joint alma mater.

Turning to Penn, it seemed that they had found solace. Mary
Elizabeth was accepted to the Illman School, and Raymond or Sadie scribbled "very nice" in the margin of the letter. Their relief
was short-lived. The progressive Miss Illman, it seems, had not
known all the facts of Mary Elizabeth's case. When she learned,
she tried to back out.

"I can hardly see how you can persist in entering your child
under such unwelcome conditions and thus set up such a trying
situation for us," Miss Illman wrote. She conceded she had no
"legal right to refuse to admit your child," but she hoped Mary
Elizabeth's application would be withdrawn.

However, it was already the beginning of September and
school was starting. The Alexanders wanted their daughter to have
a superior education, better than public school. The Illman School
at Penn was their last and only hope. So they enrolled Mary Elizabeth and began courting her teachers, inviting them to dinner so
they could see how well the family lived, with a cook, butler, and
chauffeur.

All of this eventually convinced Alexander that his future
did not lie with Philadelphia's elite Republican-dominated estab-

lishment. So he left the Republican Party and joined the wave of blacks whose ardor for the New Deal overcame their traditional antipathy to Democrats. But his dreams of a judgeship were undiminished. It was important for him to maintain his standing with persons of influence on the bench and belonging to the bar, especially open-minded Republicans like Judge Alessandroni.

Besides, there was the allure of being first—the first Negro lawyer appointed to defend a white in a capital case. And there was the legal challenge of it.

Alexander acceded to the request of Stella and Judge Alessandroni. He would represent Stella Alfonsi.

22

A MODERN PORTIA

It was now late on Saturday, October 14, 1939. Stella's trial was set to begin a week from Monday. Prosecutor Gordon was well prepared, with an array of cooperating witnesses who were singing for their lives and a team of experts, medical and chemical, who had already testified in several of the cases. Gordon's pioneering colleague, Vince McDevitt, had coached him well in the effective trial strategy that had by now become almost routine.

Raymond Pace Alexander, however, knew nothing of the case except what he had read in the newspapers. He spent the rest of the weekend meeting with Stella in prison. She was persuasive. She was charming. Every lawyer wants to believe in his client's innocence. No matter how much he is a hired gun, he is still a man. The more deeply he believes, or can convince himself that he believes, the more passionate he can be, the more able he is to spur himself on to make the commitment of time and energy needed to win a major criminal trial. Raymond Pace Alexander wanted Stella to be innocent, and with her sad, dark eyes, she gave him all the convincing he needed.

Judge Alessandroni ordered that complete transcripts of the records from the Herman Petrillo and Paul Petrillo trials, relevant coroner's notes, and medical, pathological, and expert physicians' reports be furnished immediately to Stella's new lawyer. It was more than four thousand pages of reading material. Together with Frank Marolla (Stella's previous lawyer, who had agreed to stay on as cocounsel), Alexander reviewed this material during the week. For the final weekend before the trial, he went off to a friend's house in Atlantic City, where he could hole up free of distraction and steep himself in the coming task.

One point that Marolla made clear to Alexander was that their client was not a submissive woman. On several occasions when she had fought with Ferdinando, she had walked out on him and stayed away for months. Unlike so many of her predecessor defendants, she had not been willing to throw in the towel and plead guilty. She had not accepted the first lawyer assigned to her. She would not be willing simply to sit back and let the lawyers handle her case however they wished. This was very different from the clients to whom Alexander had become accustomed. Within the community where he worked, Alexander was a demigod. His clients held him in awe, and they did what he said. With Stella, he would have a headstrong client who came from a culture that, to put it mildly, did not exactly revere Negroes.

MONDAY, OCTOBER 23

Stella's personality quickly manifested itself when the trial opened. She was an actress, and this was to be the performance

of her life. "Despite nearly a year in prison, she looked fresh and
perfectly at ease," the *Philadelphia Record* observed with admira-
tion. "She was smartly arrayed in new and natty widow's weeds,
a long black coat with a frilly lace handkerchief protruding from
the left pocket, a black dress, black patent-leather shoes and purse,
and a jaunty black toque perched on one side of her head, showing
her recently waved black hair." The press quickly saw her as an
alert and dominant figure, dubbing Stella "the modern Portia,"
after the lawyer-imitating heroine of *The Merchant of Venice.* The
nickname was more accurate than they realized. Stella wasn't in
charge. She was onstage.

She told her lawyers she wanted an all-male jury. She felt,
as a woman whose feminine allure had gotten her through life,
that she had a power over the opposite sex, and they were her
preferred audience. All through the morning, the *Record* reported,
"each time a member of her sex was called for questioning, Mrs.
Alfonsi leaned toward her counsel with a peremptory gesture of
her head and the woman was challenged by the defense." They
used thirteen of their twenty-one absolute challenges on the first
panel of forty-five potential jurors. At this point, ten men had been
selected for what the press was now calling "a stag jury."

The prosecution, on the other hand, was wary of black jurors. The third man selected was a twenty-three-year-old Negro
waiter. But someone must have alerted Charles Gordon to the potential problem. From then on, he made sure that no one else who
might have a racial affinity to the defense lawyer was approved.

By late afternoon, three panels of talesmen had been ex-
hausted and no more jurors had been added. The defense was out
of peremptory challenges. They would have to take some women.
But the final choice was Stella's. She listened carefully as each was
examined, reported the *Record,* and she "fixed the woman's face

with a steady regard for several moments before nodding her acceptance to her attorney." Two were chosen, a forty-four-year-old housewife and an unemployed single woman.

The jury was a blue-ribbon group, with seven of the ten men having professional or managerial occupations, ranging from engineer to "theatrical instructor." They were on the young side, with an average age in the mid-thirties; only one was over fifty. No one, oddly, was of Italian extraction. Alexander was pleased. Other defense lawyers had simply accepted a more or less random jury, or, like Lemuel Schofield, had struggled to mitigate the effects of death qualification. Alexander had focused his efforts in another way. He needed a thinking jury, one that might stop to consider the evidence rather than rush to judgment based on press-fomented hysteria, and he had gotten one. Stella had her way, too. The two women were weak, unlikely to resist the will of the ten men.

TUESDAY, OCTOBER 24

Stella was confident on Tuesday as the actual trial opened. Still dressed all in black, she waved gaily to her friends in the courtroom. She smiled at her children who were there with their grandmother to offer support and, just in case it might help, to put a little moral pressure on the jurors. The *Inquirer* thought she was enjoying herself.

Alexander smiled also, but wanly. He was an intense man, and though he loved the spotlight, he felt the pressure of it. He had not had time to prepare with his usual thoroughness. The preparation he had done, including reading the past record, made him wary. His stomach was churning.

There were no surprises at the beginning. Secret Service

agents told the by-now-familiar story of being alerted to Ferdinando Alfonsi's condition by the informer Myer and finding Alfonsi sick and dying. The victim's brother Vittorio added some
family background. "They was separated a couple of times," Vittorio told the jury. "In 1932, around June, he comes home one
day, and finds her writing to a man, and they had a fight. She
takes the children home—over to Bristol—to her mother. How
long she stay? Four years. Until 1936—1932 to 1936." When she
came back, Ferdinando was in hard times. They had to move away
from Passyunk, up to Ann Street in Northeast Philadelphia.

A Home Life Insurance agent named Achilles Tedesco testified that he had gone to the Alfonsi home on Ann Street. Stella
had answered the door. "Who sent you here?" she demanded.

"Paul Petrillo," he replied.

She invited him in. "I want to buy some insurance on my
husband," she told Tedesco, "but this must be a quiet case, because
my husband does not believe in insurance."

She wanted the maximum that could be obtained without
medical examination.

"Well, he'll have to sign the application," Tedesco warned
her.

"I can take care of that much," Stella assured him. "He will
sign it."

So Tedesco filled out the application, with information provided by Stella. "Can't I see him?" he asked her.

"No, because he is a hard man to catch. Leave it here and I
will have it signed for you and you can call back for it."

Tedesco returned the next day and collected the signed application. There was a place on the form where he had to attest
that he had personally seen the insured. Tedesco checked it off
even though, as he admitted, "it wasn't exactly the truth." You

couldn't be too particular when you were hustling business. He also filled in the block that asked if the insured appeared to be a "First Class, Fair or Poor Risk," by checking "First Class." And he agreed to skip coming around to collect the weekly premiums on the policy because Stella told him she would come into the office and pay there.

All of this sounded suspicious, but Alexander mitigated its impact. He brought out that the application had been refused and the policy never issued. The testimony certainly didn't seem to bother Stella.

But then Dr. Henry D'Alonzo took the stand. He was the doctor favored by Paradise Club members, who had treated Ferdinando just before he went to the hospital. D'Alonzo had been summoned to the house after midnight by Stella. He painted a ghastly picture of the scene at the Alfonsi home.

"I went upstairs and found her husband lying in bed," Dr. D'Alonzo testified. 'How long have you been sick?' I asked him.

" 'I've been sick very bad for three or four days,' Alfonsi told me. 'It started with vomiting. The last time was an hour ago.'

" 'What color was it?' I asked him.

" 'Well, to tell you the truth,' he answered, 'I was too sick to look at the color.'

" 'How do you feel otherwise?' I asked.

" 'I have a burning sensation right over here,' he told me. He pointed to the left side of his stomach and the lower part of his heart. 'It seems to me as though the stomach wants to come right out just like a volcanic eruption,' he said. 'It is burning in there, and I have a terrific lot of pain.'

"I found he had a temperature of one hundred and two degrees Fahrenheit. His pulse was one twenty. His tongue was heavily coated, very coated. The soft palate was all swollen and red, his tongue swollen. He could hardly swallow. His stomach was quite distended, a symptom of profound toxemia. I examined his eyes and found his pupillary reflexes were exaggerated. The whites of his eyes were red. His capillaries were standing out vividly red. His upper and lower eyelids were puffed out, and his appearance was that of a person who had a severe toxic condition."

The doctor, seemingly unembarrassed, conceded his prescription for this grim condition had been a can of stomach powders, "bismuth subcarbonas, sodium bicarbonas, magnesium oxidum"— in layman's terms, Pepto-Bismol and Rolaids. He also prescribed castor oil and a soapsuds enema, deciding to launch his medical attack through all feasible orifices.

D'Alonzo was surprised when, on his return two days later, Ferdinando said he was vomiting from the powders. "Every time I take it, I vomit it," he said. The powders were meant to calm the stomach. D'Alonzo asked Stella to show him the can she had been using, but she said it was empty and she had thrown it out. So the doctor gave Ferdinando a dose himself from another can he had brought.

"I put a teaspoon of powder in a half a glass of water and I stirred it up and I made him take it, and I purposely remained there, I would say, thirty-five or forty-five minutes, and the patient never vomited. But he told me, 'Every time my wife gives me that powder, it makes me vomit.'"

At this, Dr. D'Alonzo told Stella he wanted to take Ferdinando to the hospital. "The patient was eager to come," he testified, "but Mrs. Alfonsi insisted, 'No, no, no, I don't want him to go to the hospital. I will pay you whatever it costs. I want him to stay home.'"

Stella leapt to her feet. "Lies, lies," she shouted to the witness. "I can't stand this pack of lies any longer." She turned to the stunned throng in the courtroom and sobbed. "I can't help it. Why doesn't he tell the truth?"

Her twelve-year-old son, Ralph, seated in the back of the room, cried out, "Oh, Momma, Momma," before his grandmother could quiet him. The judge declared a ten-minute recess.

But Dr. D'Alonzo was not through. He thought it odd, he told the jury when court resumed, that Stella had called him, because his office at 806 West Wingohocking, up in North Philadelphia, was more than six miles away. So when he went downstairs on the first night after seeing the patient, "I stood there in the first-floor parlor with Mrs. Alfonsi and I asked her, 'How did you happen to call me in this case? You have so many doctors in the neighborhood.'

" 'A friend of mine who knows you very well recommended you to me,' she said.

" 'Who is he?' I asked.

" 'Oh, he is a patient of yours,' she said.

" 'Well,' I said, 'I would like to know who this is.'

"So she came close to me and whispered in my ear, 'Herman Petrillo.' "

Prosecutor Gordon was pleased. He had desperately wanted to establish this Petrillo linkage. There was still more to come.

Dr. D'Alonzo testified that he finally got Ferdinando to the hospital a few days later on the pretext of just taking him in for an X ray. When they saw his condition, hospital officials would not release him.

"The next time I saw Mrs. Alfonsi was about two weeks later," Dr. D'Alonzo continued. Ferdinando was still in the hospital. I was sitting on the porch with my wife, sister-in-law, and brother-in-law and I noticed a greenish or grayish green sedan go by, and Mrs. Alfonsi was in it, and Herman Petrillo was in it. It was Mr. Petrillo's car, because I have seen him in that car before. They parked about four doors away, and she came up to me at the porch. 'Doctor, I want to see you,' she said. She was pretty nervous and fidgety. She asked about her husband, when he was coming home from the hospital, and everything. I told her I didn't know. It wasn't the first time I had seen them together. Back in June or July, a few months before she called me for her husband, I saw them pass my office on Wingohocking Street. One day they stopped and spoke to me."

Stella was rightly concerned. She was now firmly tied in with the notorious Herman Petrillo. The situation looked even worse when George Myer, the Secret Service informer, told his story of being recruited for the murder by Herman.

Myer had not actually met Stella himself, he conceded, but he accompanied Herman to the Alfonsi house one afternoon and sat in the Dodge while Herman went in for fifteen minutes. When he emerged, Petrillo told Myer that arrangements had been made. Mrs. Alfonsi would go to the eight o'clock show at the movies with her children, leaving the back door open for Myer to sneak in on her husband, who would be snoozing on the settee in the parlor. "Well," Myer told the jury, "I went around there at eight o'clock to see whether Mrs. Alfonsi was really going to the show, and whether she was really connected with this in any way. She went out at eight o'clock and came back a quarter to eleven.

"The next day," Myer continued, "I gave Petrillo a story. I told him the husband hadn't been there at the house. So Petrillo called a telephone number from the drugstore on Ontario Street and Kensington Avenue, and he asked for Stella Alfonsi. Somebody answered the phone—who it was, I don't know—and Herman said, 'Stella, the fellow is here and he said he was around there last night and nobody was home.' Whoever was on the other end of the phone told him I was wrong and that the man had been there. Herman must have figured I had the wrong place, because he then told me to go back again that night. He said I would know the place because the back fence was newly painted and a towel would be placed on it so I could not make a mistake. I went to the rear of the house that night and the towel was there."

Stella jumped up again. "He is lying, Your Honor. There was no towel on the fence. I never put a towel on the fence." Alexander and Marolla had difficulty restraining her.

WEDNESDAY, OCTOBER 25

The pressure was mounting on Alexander as the case against his client built. He was so focused on the trial, he could hardly remember to eat. "My only lunch each day was a chocolate bar," he later told reporters. (Not that he had much choice—the only restaurant near the courthouse that would serve Negroes was Horn and Hardart—the Automat.) Alexander had tried to shake the witnesses' stories, but with little success. They had been saying the same thing for a year.

The state was putting on the case that they had successfully presented against Herman Petrillo seven months earlier. On Wednesday morning, the pattern continued with the testimonies of an expert medical witness, who ascribed Alfonsi's death to arsenic poisoning, and of the Secret Service agents who had seen Alfonsi suffering in bed.

One of the agents told the jury, "I suggested that we try to get him into the hospital. But Mrs. Alfonsi spoke up and said, 'No. I think he will be better off here.' On three different occasions while we were there, Mrs. Alfonsi asked if we were going to take Mr. Alfonsi to the hospital. She was very much interested in that subject, that point. She appeared nervous, very nervous."

Alexander had this last conclusory observation struck, and he had the witness admit, "Mrs. Alfonsi stood beside her husband the whole time. She stroked his forehead, and put the hair back out of his face, and patted the pillow. She seemed very anxious to make him as comfortable as she could." But Stella's lawyer could not stop the bulk of the district attorney's case, which was a damning parade of facts.

With these final witnesses, Alexander expected the state to rest. They had presented their case, and they had completed the list of witnesses stated on the bill of indictment. The situation was not good, but it was just as Alexander had expected. He was prepared, as well as he might be under the circumstances, to go forward with his defense. No one had actually seen Stella do anything amiss. Alexander thought he had a chance.

But the prosecutor was not finished. "Your Honor, the Commonwealth would like to call one additional witness, Maria Favato." Alexander and Marolla were stunned—Maria Favato, the "Wicked Witch" of North Philadelphia. The defense lawyers objected, and with the jury sent out of the room, Alexander hammered away at the judge, reminding him of the burden of short preparation under which the defense was already laboring. To add a surprise witness to the advantage the Commonwealth already had was fundamentally unjust, Alexander protested. But Judge Alessandroni was unwilling to block such key testimony.

The hefty forty-three-year-old Favato trudged to the stand. First off, she admitted she had pleaded guilty to murdering three

Left: Jumbo Valenti and Raphael Polselli. "'Tro him down the stairs and go back to New York."

Above: The "Witch" Favato with police detective Tony Franchetti. "Why don't you just make it pneumonia?"

Left: Favato/Ingrao home. "Let's take in the kids."

Valenti chases reporters, with Herman Petrillo in tow.
"This is a good country to murder people."

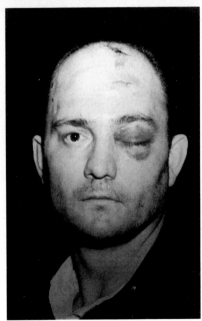

Emedio Muscelli and his shiner.
"I'm the boss of the house now."

Gretta Mancino, mother of Philip
Ingrao, at the grave of her son.
"The boy is going green."

Above: Paul Petrillo.
A candidate for life insurance?

Top left: Official escort for Morris Bolber.
"I am the brains of the arresting bureau."

Major Lemuel B. Schofield.
"That adds up to eighteen hundred dollars."

Taking the jury for an outing.
"Why can't we see *The Wizard of Oz*?"

Raymond Pace Alexander.
"If you believe…you must acquit."

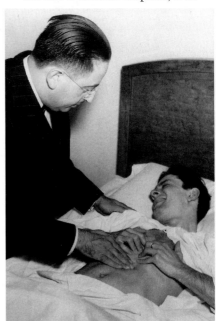

Dr. D'Alonzo poses for the press.
"It's like a volcanic eruption, Doc."

Stella and her lawyers. "The Modern Portia."

Left: The new Rose.
"He was too good a man to kill."

Below: Rose goes to jail. "Kill a couple of chickens and have a celebration."

Above: Rose and Rita under arrest.
"I must be an awfully important woman."

Left: Johnny Cacopardo.
"You know it's the truth, Rose."

Right: DA's scoreboard. Prosecutors 24, Defendants 2.

Above: Herman Petrillo chats with reporter Frank Toughill. "I got a formula for hair restorer."

Above: "Hanging Harry" McDevitt. "Let's let him rave."

Left: Agnes testifies.
"I knew it was no good."

Below: Sortino performs for the jury.
"We gave him the cold bath."

Left:
Agnes
and
Romaine
Mandiuk.
Waiting
for
Norman
Rockwell.

Stella with her sons Leo and Ralph. "Oh, Momma."

Rose Carina (in doorway) with daughters Grace
and Rita and grandson Joey. "She was a great cook."

men—her husband, her stepson, and the husband of a neighbor. Charles Gordon wanted to draw the sting of that fact by bringing it up first. He asked if she was currently married. "Oh, no, I'm a widow." She laughed.

Then she folded her arms and in a flat, unemotional voice, speaking through an interpreter, told the jury, "I first met Mrs. Alfonsi in August 1938. It was about the first or second of August. Herman Petrillo came to my house at 4546 North Bouvier Street about seven-thirty P.M. He asked me to do him a favor, and since I was afraid of him, I agreed. We walked to the park on Eighteenth Street, near Stenton Avenue. It was only a block from my house. On the way, he handed me a small bottle, about three inches high, with a white fluid. It was dark when we got to the park.

"Herman said, 'My car is stopped on the other side of the park. There is a woman in it, Mrs. Alfonsi. Give her the bottle. When she gets out of the car, you give it to her.'

"I walked up to the car and Mrs. Alfonsi got out of it and silently walked up to me. Without a word, I gave her the bottle and I walked back home. Herman got in the car with her and they drove away."

"Did Petrillo tell you what was in the bottle?" the DA asked.

"Sure, he said it was *la fattura*. He said I should give it to her and she was to give it to her husband. He told me not to say anything, because she knew all about it."

The smoking gun. Alexander fought again to have the testimony stricken, but without success. For a moment he seemed to have panicked. With other witnesses, he had been the cautious lawyer, avoiding questions on cross-examination that might backfire. It is better to let damaging testimony pass than ask a question that might let the witness reinforce it. But with Favato, he threw caution to the winds, and paid the price.

"Isn't *fattura* really a love potion?" Alexander asked the Witch.

"Yes, it is," she conceded, "but it gives death. All those who took it died."

THURSDAY, OCTOBER 26

Being a good defense lawyer is like being a good cardplayer. Anyone can win if he holds all the high ones. The real test comes in being able to win with the weaker hand. That was the test that Alexander faced. He saw that Stella had two things going for her.

First, unlike most of the other widows, who were at least nominally the beneficiaries of substantial amounts of life insurance, Stella had received nothing. Shortly after she had returned to Ferdinando following their four-year separation, she had attempted to obtain insurance on him from several companies, but only John Hancock would approve the insurance, for a limit of two thousand dollars. Ferdinando himself added an examination-free $250 burial policy from the Tribune Association in October of the same year. However, on August 13, 1938, while her husband was in the hospital in the throes of his final agony, Stella missed the $15.36 quarterly premium on the John Hancock policy, and no one kept up the twenty-one-cent weekly payment on the Tribune Association policy. Both lapsed.

Why would anyone let a life-insurance policy lapse while the insured person was dying in a hospital? Maybe it was sheer ineptitude, a possibility not to be discounted with Herman on the scene. Maybe Herman and Stella were so confident of the massive arsenic dose given Ferdinando that they were certain he would die before the premium was finally due. Herman always was cheap in that way. Or maybe Stella was truly distraught at her husband's condition and just forgot. Whatever the reason, all that anyone stood to collect on Ferdinando's demise was the four-hundred-dollar death benefit that came along with his membership in the Paradise Club. His funeral had cost more than that. *Where was the motive?* Alexander could ask.

Second, also unlike most of the other widows, Stella had never talked to the police. She had not said, as had Josephine Romualdo, Grace Pirolli, and others, that she had been duped by the arsenic murder ring. In making this plea, these women had indicated at least some complicity, ignorant as it may have been. Stella had just kept her mouth shut. She had admitted nothing, and denied everything. Now, if she had to talk to the jury, she had a story that could explain everything, and she had her big brown eyes. She had convinced Alexander, a tough-minded and skeptical lawyer, of her innocence. He saw that her only chance was to sell it to ten more men, and two women.

"A picture of poise, ebony-haired, olive-skinned Stella Alfonsi took the witness stand yesterday and gave the lie to those who accuse her of the poison murder of her husband," reported the *Record.* "In a voice of utmost calm, her tones so low they could be heard only a few feet, she recited her denial and withstood a two-hour-and-twenty-minute cross-examination. She left the stand in the late afternoon without having lost her composure. Calmly she declared the State's whole case against her was a tissue of lies—that every prosecution witness, including physicians, detectives, insurance agents, Secret Service agents, and other arsenic ring figures, had lied.

" 'Did you cause the death of your husband?' her lawyer

asked her. The youthful widow raised herself partly from her seat.
Her calm deserted her momentarily.

" 'No!' she shouted defiantly, in a voice that rang through
the courtroom. 'No! Positively no. Never! Never! Never!' "

Alexander walked Stella through her story carefully. She had
been a loving wife and mother struggling against Herman Petrillo's
sinister influence on her husband. Herman, she said, was Ferdinando's buddy. They were lodge brothers, fellow members of the
Paradise Club. Ferdinando was sickly, Stella said; he had been
gassed during the war, and always had trouble getting insurance.
He wanted to obtain some policies and relied upon his friend Herman, who had contacts, to help him. That is how Herman came
to send over the agents.

Herman had enticed her husband into shady activities. The
two *cospiratori* frequently took mysterious trips together, bringing
back things such as furs and men's suits. Stella ordered them taken
away. One time, she insisted on going along on one of these trips.
They went all the way to Hoboken, New Jersey, almost to New
York, where they met six or seven other men who talked with
them in low tones that she could not make out. She repeatedly
objected to these dealings and tried to keep Petrillo away from
their home. She didn't trust Herman, who had a fearsome reputation, and she was afraid for her husband. But Herman began
talking to her, explaining how he was only providing opportunity
for Ferdinando, how he was helping out their family. Herman invited her out for drives so they could talk at length.

It was not true, she repeated, that she had fought Dr.
D'Alonzo over taking Ferdinando to the hospital. On the con-
trary, she had pushed for the hospital, but had been vetoed by
D'Alonzo and Ferdinando. Now the doctor was trying to shift
the blame to her because he had been wrong. Nor was it true

that she had chosen him. Rather, it was Ferdinando who had selected the doctor and told her to call him because he was the
"lodge doctor," and it was Ferdinando—not Stella—who had
told the doctor that Herman Petrillo had recommended him. For
her part, she had cooperated fully with the doctor and had done
everything he had requested. When he eventually recommended
the hospital, she had gone along and had visited her sick husband there every day.

It was not true, Stella said, that she had been given poison
by Mrs. Favato. That was all a lie concocted by the Witch, who
was seeking vengeance. "I know this for a fact," Stella testified,
"because another girl at Moyamensing told me so. She told me
Maria blamed me for all the trouble, because Ferdinando's death
opened up the whole investigation." Turning her shapely body so
she could look directly at the male-dominated jury, Stella added,
"I told this girl, 'You tell Maria Favato that I never knew her. I
had nothing to do with her arrest. Why should she hold a grudge
against me?' "

FRIDAY, OCTOBER 27

The tides of any trial ebb and flow. Stella had done her work
the previous day, not merely convincing the jury of her story but
winning them over to her side at least for the moment. But still
there were the facts, the ugly facts. Was everyone lying except
Stella? Everyone?

Prosecutor Gordon, in his rebuttal and summation, pounced
on the inconsistencies in Stella's story. She was a woman "eager
for money," a woman who "painted everyone else black, who in-
vented will-o'-the-wisps" to save herself. Stella buried her face in
a handkerchief and sat sobbing as he reviewed the details of Fer-

dinando's horrible death. Gordon was supremely confident, demanding no less than a conviction of first-degree murder. "Death by poison is a relic of the Dark Ages," he said. "Herman Petrillo was Caesar Borgia. This woman [pointing to Stella Alfonsi] was Lucretia. He directed how the poison should be administered and she administered it. This is purely a case of murder in the first degree. It cannot be second-degree murder or manslaughter."

It was now after five P.M. "Do you wish to put your summation over until Monday morning?" the judge asked Alexander. The defense lawyer thought for only a moment.

"No, Your Honor, we'd prefer to proceed this evening." He did not want the jurors to spend long hours with the prosecution's argument fresh in their minds. The judge acceded and ordered a short dinner break.

The state had made a strong presentation. Far less had convinced other juries. But Alexander understood the weakness in the state's case as other lawyers had not. He thought he saw an opening. During the dinner break, Alexander walked back to his office. Avoiding any lingering clients who might be in the reception room, he used the back stairs, which led to a private dressing room. He showered, put on a freshly laundered shirt, and selected one of his elegantly tailored suits. Alexander was notorious with his secretaries for his insistence on perfect appearance. Every piece of correspondence that emanated from the office had to be flawlessly typed, without so much as a period struck too hard. So, too, for his summation. It would have to be perfect. He had to make the jury believe in him, so they would believe what he was going to say.

Alexander was a tall man—six foot three—with a slender runner's build. He stood erect and spoke in a firm manner that inspired confidence. When this impeccably groomed Negro lawyer addressed the jurors that evening, they saw a man they could trust.

He focused their attention, as if by contrast, on the manifold credibility problems of the prosecution's key witnesses. Was the jury going to take the word of Maria Favato, a confessed triple murderer—a murderer of husbands and children—and the word of the informer Myer, a notorious liar who had been "convicted of forgery in Delaware, counterfeiting in New Jersey and nonsupport in Pennsylvania," over that of an innocent and bereft widow? "Are you going to let those two hang this woman?" he pleaded.

Stella Alfonsi had not gained anything from the death, he reminded the jury, going over the insurance and detailing for them how Ferdinando himself had signed and approved all the applications, how he had even obtained the final Tribune Association policy wholly on his own, without telling Stella. The state's case was "purely circumstantial." The DA had not produced "a single shred of evidence to show that Mrs. Alfonsi killed her husband, wanted to kill him, or could kill him."

The prosecution's case made no sense, Alexander argued. Could this sweet woman have so wantonly and horribly killed the father of her children for nothing? Why? If she had wanted to get rid of him, she would have had no trouble just moving away, as she had done in the past. It just made no sense. For three hours, Raymond Pace Alexander slowly, carefully laid out his case, doing everything possible to shape it as that of a simple, guileless woman trapped by a prosecutor who would stoop to anything to gain a conviction.

As the jurors filed out at 9:36 P.M. to deliberate, one other message rang in their ears. It was the words of Stella's mother, Christina Liberti, who shouted at their consciences as they left the room, "Give my child a break! She's not guilty." At 10:45 P.M., when they had not yet reached a verdict, Judge Alessandroni adjourned court for the night and ordered the jury sequestered in its private quarters on the sixth floor of City Hall. They were free to sleep or ponder through the night.

Stella was escorted back to Moyamensing Prison, where she had to spend at least one more night, and maybe thousands more.

SATURDAY, OCTOBER 28

The jury had stayed up until three in the morning arguing over the case. The division was very close. When they took their last vote before going to sleep, it was five votes for acquittal, four for death, and three undecided. With that kind of balance, a compromise on conviction with life imprisonment seemed most likely.

But when they resumed deliberations early the next morning over breakfast, the night's tossing and turning had modified several opinions. The jury quickly reached a unanimous verdict by eight A.M. The bailiff had to wait for the judge to come in at ten to give him the news. Judge Alessandroni quickly reconvened court and by 10:36 A.M. all were gathered to hear the verdict.

As the courtroom filled with interested spectators, bailiffs escorted Christina Liberti, Stella's sobbing mother, out of the way, for fear of another outburst. This was an ominous sign. Stella was the thirteenth defendant to be tried; she had gotten her lawyer on Friday the 13th; she had been in jail for exactly thirteen months; and the jury had been out thirteen hours to the minute before reaching its verdict. Was this a spell worked by Witch Favato?

"Prisoner, face the jury." Stella rose to her feet, her nerves steeled against the verdict. "Jury, face the prisoner. How find ye, guilty or not guilty?"

Peter Carlin, the jury foreman, pronounced the verdict. "Not guilty."

FLINT STILL IN SOVIET PORT

STORY ON PAGE 2

PHILADELPHIA DAILY NEWS

THE PEOPLE'S PICTORIAL

VOL. XV—No. 181

2 Cents IN CITY 3 CENTS LIMITS 3 Elsewhere 10c a Month by Mail in U. S. A.

RITtenhouse 5700—Bell
Race 2111—Keystone

★

Entered as Second-Class Matter, Daily, Except Sunday, at the Postoffice at Philadelphia, Pa., Under the Act of March 3, 1879

Philadelphia, Saturday, October 28, 1939

POISON WIDOW FREED!

STORY ON PAGE 2

NOT GUILTY was the surprising verdict returned by a jury of ten men and two women in the case of Mrs. Stella Alfonsi, attractive 30-year-old arsenic widow and the mother of two children, charged with the arsenic murder of her husband, Frederick, who died one year ago today. "The testimony was too fantastic for us to believe," declared one juror.

23
THE KISS OF DEATH

Judge Alessandroni commended the jury on Stella's acquittal. "There was a very strong suspicion of guilt," he conceded, but the failure to prove motive left a "reasonable doubt." He faulted the prosecution. The jurors told the press that they had been impressed by defense arguments about the lapse of insurance, and that they had been persuaded that some of the testimony by prosecution witnesses was "too fantastic to be credible."

So there was some luck and some skill involved in Stella's acquittal. For the black press, however, there was no question where the credit lay. HISTORY IS MADE IN THE COURTS, they proclaimed. NEGRO LAWYER WINS WHITE GIRL'S FREEDOM, headlined New York's *Amsterdam News.* "Alexander makes us proud we are Negroes," editorialized the black *Christian Review.* Even the mainstream white papers, which largely ignored Alexander's race, conceded that it was a "fine victory" for him, while featuring the victory in banner headlines. POISON WIDOW FREED, screamed the tabloid *Philadelphia Daily News* on its front page, filled with pictures of the sultry Stella.

It was an amazing story and a marvelous feather in the cap of a skilled lawyer. That was his only reward. As a court-appointed lawyer, he received only token compensation. He had enhanced the status of black lawyers everywhere. He was, in the phrase of the time, a credit to his race. Now was the time to get back to work, to return to his practice and to the clients who supported it. But he began receiving entreaties from other poison widows. Donald Romualdo, Josephine's son, asked him to take her appeal. The children of Agnes Mandiuk sought him to handle their mother's forthcoming trial. And, not least, Rose Carina, the Kiss of Death, implored that he take over her case, scheduled for trial in less than a month.

X X X

Commonly known as Rose Carina, her full name was Rose Carbonato Carina Lisi Stea Tropea, née Ruggieri. Born in Hammonton, New Jersey, on July 25, 1897, and raised on a small farm by her father after her mother's death three years later, Rose became pregnant when she was fourteen. The impregnator was a twenty-six-year-old farm laborer, Antonino Carbonato. Rose went to live with Carbonato and claimed to have married him exactly nine months before the child, a son, John, was born. The couple did not actually wed, however, until two years later, by which time a second child, a daughter, Grace, had joined the family. A year later, Anthony was born, making Rose, who was dropping children at the rate of one per year, the mother of three before she turned eighteen.

As might have been expected, she was not much of a mother,

leaving more memories of disregard and abuse than of nurturing. Within a year or two, however, it didn't matter. Rose tired of Carbonato and decided she wanted to see more of the world. She took off one day, leaving little John, Grace, and Anthony on the sofa and a pot of beans on the stove, saying she had to get some macaroni. At least that is how her children remember it. They would not see her again for years. Carbonato eventually obtained a divorce. He continued to live in New Sharon, New Jersey, where he wound up working in a piggery, a fate better than that which befell Rose's next three spouses.

After leaving Hammonton, Rose at first went to visit a cousin in California, but she soon moved back East to live with a sister in Philadelphia, where she worked as a waitress and sometimes packed cigars at the nearby Consolidated Cigar plants at Eleventh and Wharton or Sixth and Morris Streets. She did not relish this kind of labor. Men were a better source of support, and she always had one around. In 1926, after several years with no fixed attachment, she took on husband number two, Dominic Carina, a lumberyard worker and sometime carpenter. The couple had one child, Rita, born in 1928. This birth may have aroused some maternal instinct in Rose, because she went to New Jersey soon thereafter and fetched her older daughter, Grace, now fifteen, whom she had hardly seen since deserting the family a decade earlier.

One afternoon, as teenage Grace was leaving school, a strange man motioned her over to a car. "Your mother wants to see you," he said. Grace recognized the woman from a few brief visits over the years.

"Get in and get down," said Rose.

The girl, excited at the idea of it, did as told. She stayed scrunched down in the backseat until they got out of the state, via the ferry crossing the Delaware River. All the while, Rose chatted happily about the new life Grace was going to have with her family in the big city of Philadelphia. Back in Hammonton, newspapers carried the story of the "kidnapped" Carbonato girl. But Grace would never be returned.

Rose sent her daughter off to work immediately, finding a job for her in a sweatshop sewing buttonholes on trousers. Rose took the whole paycheck, doling out only an occasional allotment for her daughter to go to a movie at the Alahambra or over on Broad Street. Most evenings, Grace was busy helping out with little Rita.

The Carina family, husband, wife, and two girls, moved into a newly purchased little row house at 919 Cross Street, a typical South Philly residence. It was only a block and a half east of Passyunk Avenue, where Rose did her shopping. Rose was a lively figure in the community. She was friendly to her neighbors, like Stella Alfonsi.

Rose was always busy with the men who hung around the house during the day while Dominic Carina was off at work. They played cards and drank Rose's homemade beer. She was a wonderful cook and flagrant flirt. Rose was not above fooling around a little, but she was always clever about covering her tracks. One time, it is said, while Rose was busy in the bedroom with a gentleman, she got a call from her father, who told her he was in the neighborhood and would be coming right over. While the man quickly pulled on his clothes, Rose, who noted that it was raining, stuck an umbrella outside the door to get it wet, then brought it in and placed it in a obvious spot by the door. When her father arrived a few moments later, she made sure that he noticed her caller's umbrella was still wet.

If he was aware of any of this, Dominic Carina did not seem

to mind. He was kind to Rose and accepting of his stepdaughter, Grace, who got along well with him. Grace was shocked when Dominic suddenly took ill and died in 1931. Several months prior to his death, he had been hospitalized for stomach ulcers, but his health was otherwise good. Then one day, he wasn't feeling well. He went to bed sick and Rose told Grace to take four-year-old Rita out to the movies. When they came back, Dominic was dead, his demise attributed to a heart condition.

R.I.P.
DOMINIC CARINA

Whether *la fattura* played a role in Dominic's death, no one knows. But it was around the time he died that Rose made the acquaintance of Paul Petrillo. Her marital home on Cross Street was only a few blocks from Paul's tailor shop on Passyunk Avenue. Rose often walked past Paul's establishment on her way to market. She had been a beautiful girl when she caught Carbonato's eye twenty years earlier, and she was still an attractive thirty-five-year-old woman, somewhat more plump, but with a pretty face and a vivacity that caught men's eyes. On warm summer afternoons, when Paul sat on a chair outside his stuffy shop, he teased Rose as she strolled by, and she shot back, giving as good as she got. Eventually he invited her in for some lemonade, then to come over in the evening to share a vermouth and some private moments. By mid-1932, Rose and Paul had become more than just good neighbors.

Paul appreciated that Rose did not crumble under pressure. She thrived on it. She loved plotting and manipulation. She loved having money without working. She became Paul's secretary, help-

ing him keep tabs on his *cassaforte* full of policies on "good bets."
He was very busy keeping track of these speculations, and arranging for judicious applications of *la fattura* when necessary to help
move things along.

It was not long before the widowed Rose decided to do more
than just serve as Paul Petrillo's passive assistant. Paul was busy
seducing Millie Giacobbe, a neighboring Passyunk shop owner,
and setting up the demise of Millie's husband. With no role to play
in that arrangement, Rose packed up daughter Rita, leaving
nineteen-year-old Grace to fend for herself, and returned to her
Hammonton birthplace, ostensibly to live with her brother. But
she had other plans. On February 23, 1933, only a year and a half
after Dominic Carina's death, Rose married husband number
three—Prospero Lisi, a Hammonton widower with substantial
property and three children all under age five.

Four months later, Mr. Lisi, an apparently healthy man of
thirty-eight, died of a "heart ailment." Rose refused permission for
an autopsy. She turned Lisi's children over to his family and hired
a lawyer, who negotiated a handsome property settlement of five
thousand dollars from her short-time husband's estate.

Taking her sizable inheritance, Rose moved back to Passyunk, and to Paul Petrillo.

R.I.P.
PROSPERO LISI

The next amour to be graced with Rose's kiss of death was
Peter Stea. He operated a grocery at Ninth and Tasker, only a
block away from the Cross Street home that Rose had shared with
her second husband. She had known Stea well as her corner grocer

and was aware he had substantial assets. She also knew he was in need of a helping hand to fend off his estranged wife, Mary, who was pursuing him for alimony.

Stea was flattered when Rose began dropping by the store, hanging around longer than was necessary to make purchases. When she offered the hexing services of Paul Petrillo to drive away Mary, he willingly accepted. A few days later, his store-home was surrounded by piles of brown dirt that Paul claimed possessed magical properties. Amazingly, the harassing Mary seemed to disappear from Stea's life. A private visit by cousin Herman Petrillo to Mary, with warnings of dire consequences if she did not back off, may have had something to do with this, but Stea knew only about the piles of dirt.

Stea was enchanted by Rose Carina, this woman who could arrange potent magic. Before long, Rose had installed herself in the Stea household, moving in as Peter's de facto wife. The couple occupied the second-floor apartment in his house at 1539 South Ninth Street, along with Rose's daughter Rita and four of Stea's children (two teenage daughters and two small sons). Stea's married daughter and son-in-law lived on the third floor. During 1934 and early 1935, Rose lived with Stea, keeping house for him and working by his side in the store downstairs, along with his daughters.

By January 1936, Mr. Stea felt close enough to her to name "Rose Lisi, friend" as beneficiary of a five-hundred-dollar life-insurance policy formerly payable to his children. Two months later, on March 2, 1936, he leased the entire store to her for several years, at a bargain rent of twenty-five dollars per month.

Three months later, the symptoms began. Stea had terrible vomiting attacks and coughing fits. He complained of an "intense burning in his throat" and "a severe pulling sensation in his throat and upper abdomen." The first doctor they called prescribed cough medicine. The next, Dr. Frank Didio, who was a fellow member of the Order of Brotherly Love with Stea, diagnosed the problem as "globus hystericus," which, he explained to the family, "is a nervous lump in the throat." He gave Stea a shot of morphine. Nothing worked. The wretched man died in the hospital on June 29, vomiting and "foaming at the mouth." The doctors attributed the death to diabetes.

Paul Petrillo would come by the store during the weeks of Stea's suffering, even though it was blocks out of his way. He would make a small purchase and casually ask Rose, "How's Pete tonight?" All during the month of June, every few days, Paul would stop by. At the time, it seemed to Stea's daughters, who overheard this while working behind the counter, that Paul was just being neighborly.

That was not Paul's only involvement in Stea's affairs. He arranged a clever manipulation to milk maximum value from Rose's interest in the grocery store. Right after Stea died, Rose signed a promissory "judgment" note to Paul for five hundred dollars, giving him the power to seize any of her property and sell it without need to bring legal proceedings first. A cooperative notary backdated the note to March, so it would appear to have been signed before the death. Rose and Paul moved all the nonperishable stock, hundreds of dollars' worth, maybe more, of canned goods, beer, and such, out of the Stea grocery store and into Paul's basement. (Rose had had several months to build up the stock using Stea's well-established credit.) Paul then turned the judgment note over to his lawyer, advising him to collect it by levying on the grocery store that had been leased to Rose.

A public auction was held on August 11, at which the high bidder for the leased store and its bare shelves offered only $476, all of which was paid to Paul. When added to the five-hundred-dollar life-insurance benefit received by Rose, the collaborators cleared $976 cash and a stockpile of goods from the death of her de facto fourth husband.

Three men in little over four years. In her youth, Rose had dropped three babies in three years. Now grown men were falling around her at almost the same rate.

R.I.P.
PETER STEA

24

RAKISH ROSE

When she had first been arrested, back in May, Rose had seemed frantic. She broke her eyeglasses and swallowed the shards in a botched suicide attempt. When that failed, she tried to starve herself to death. After four days, the police transferred her to Hahneman Hospital for forced feeding. Finally, she relented and was returned to her cell. Giving up on her efforts to cheat the chair, she began focusing on how to beat it. She later told her family that had been her game all along. The business with the eyeglasses and fasting had only been tactics to get the police to stop questioning her.

After she settled down, her stay in jail seemed to work wonders on her. Freed of the pressure and tension of being on the run, she slimmed down and, with the aid of her older daughter, Grace, acquired a handsome wardrobe. Those who saw her in court at the end of August, when she appeared for a preliminary hearing, hardly recognized the formerly pudgy, matronly woman of three months earlier. Rose wore a rakish broad-brimmed straw hat and a lovely silk dress short enough to show some attractive calf as she crossed her legs for the photographer. Her face, now free of the eyeglasses that she had munched, showed a look of aplomb that belied her precarious legal situation.

Rose's counsel was thirty-five-year-old Louis Lipschitz, a diligent and skilled practitioner who was preparing a traditional defense for her. As an experienced criminal lawyer, he had acquired the ability to believe in his client, including the ability to suspend disbelief when required. As he listened to Rose sweetly protest her innocence and deny any involvement in any poison murder ring, he thought she had a credible story. He embraced it and was planning to try to convince the jury likewise. Rose seemed to be an amiable and accepting client and to have confidence in him. Lipschitz was therefore a bit surprised when she called him in only a month before trial and said she wanted to get Raymond Pace Alexander for her lawyer. But he understood. Word of the Negro lawyer's success, when all else had failed, had flowed like wine through the jail cells where Stella and Rose were being held. Stella spread the story herself. She had been returned to jail, rather than released following her acquittal, while the district attorney decided about the possibility of bringing other charges against her.

Rose had written to Alexander, soliciting his help. Alexander wrestled with the problem. Part of him wanted to be rid of these nasty cases that seemed to lead nowhere. "I did not want to start any wholesale cutting in on other lawyers' cases," Alexander wrote, "and frankly, I could not hope to have such favorable results in the other cases, so I was very reluctant to accept any of them." But part of him reveled in the glory that had followed the Alfonsi acquittal. Only he, among all the lawyers in Philadelphia, seemed to understand how to win justice for these poor women.

Alexander discussed the case with Lipschitz, who was his friend. Lipschitz, having already convinced himself of Rose's innocence, painted a picture of the case that won Alexander to the same view. The black lawyer visited Rose in her jail cell, and this woman who had been enticing men all her life appealed deeply to him. She told him she was raising five children, apparently adopting Peter Stea's four younger children momentarily for purposes of her pitch.

"I really felt sorry for this woman," Alexander later reported, "because I felt that the other defendants, especially the male defendants, had a gigantic frame-up against her. She did not present as pretty a picture as Stella Alfonsi, but the fact that she had all those children made up for what her appearance lacked. Sympathy and the feeling that this woman, with the attorney whom she had, a very fine fellow, but weak in presenting a case, would have gone to the electric chair caused me to accept the case." Rose's son-in-law, Joseph Buttacavoli, Grace's husband, went to Alexander and promised to raise the money to pay his fee if he would take on the case. Alexander could not resist.

On Monday, November 27, 1939, a month after Stella Alfonsi's startling acquittal, the next two poison widow trials opened in the Quarter Sessions Court, those of Camella (Millie) Giacobbe and Rose Carina. The contrasts in the cases could not have been greater. In Room 653, Millie was charged with the poison murder of her sole husband, Antonio. In Room 443, Rose was charged with the poison murder of her third successive husband, Peter Stea. Millie was appearing before one of the most lenient judges on the bench, Louis Levinthal. The judge in Rose's case, Francis Shunk Brown, Jr., was an unfamiliar judge brought in from another county, whose proclivities were not well known. Millie's case was being prosecuted by Charles Gordon, the lawyer whose

ineptness had already contributed to the blown victory string in
Stella Alfonsi's case. Rose's prosecutor was James Tracy, a
scrappy, experienced old-timer. Anyone laying odds might have
given Millie a much better chance of acquittal than the notorious
"Kiss of Death" Carina, who had earned a place in the evil pan-
theon with the Petrillos, Morris Bolber, and Maria Favato. Rose
had only one thing going for her. While Millie was defended by
an experienced, well-regarded lawyer, Claude Lanciano, Rose had
The Man—Raymond Pace Alexander.

The difference in defense strategies was evident at the outset.
Alexander, the lawyer who had prevailed for hopeless clients like
Louise Thomas, the policeman's mistress, and Stella Alfonsi,
seemed to have an instinct for jurors who might see things his
way. He understood something that lawyers today take for
granted—that a case is largely won or lost on voir dire. No matter
how strong a lawyer's presentation is at trial, it will be for naught
if it falls on deaf ears. You need a jury that will respond to your
persuasion. So Alexander was very focused and deliberate in se-
lecting jurors. While Claude Lanciano over in Room 653 had approved ten of Millie's jurors by the end of the first day, only two
of Rose's had been selected. Judge Brown ordered a special night
session in Rose's case to speed things along. By the next day, Alexander had run through all the available veniremen. Judge Brown
had to send marshals out on the streets to collar citizens for another panel and order another night session before a full jury could
finally be picked.

x x x

The case against Millie Giacobbe presented in Room 653 was almost routine. She was the owner of the dress and lingerie shop at

1816 East Passyunk, just three doors down from Paul Petrillo's tailoring establishment. The amiable Paul would frequently stroll over to visit his fellow *commerciante*. The forty-year-old Millie dressed with style, favoring bright prints over the plain dresses commonly worn by old-world women. She had a net worth of thirteen thousand dollars, she bragged. Paul admired her business success, and he admired the way she made good use of her wares on her own hefty figure. With a sickly wife who was apparently not satisfying his manly needs, Paul actively worked the female population, seeking substitutes. In Millie, he found an opportunity to combine business and pleasure.

Millie's husband, Antonio, a hatmaker at the sprawling Stetson factory at Fourth and Montgomery, was in poor health. He had diabetes and high blood pressure and constantly complained of pains in his chest. He regularly went to the clinic at the University of Pennsylvania Hospital, where they gave him shots of insulin and monitored his heart. Millie was tired of her boring, sickly spouse. She went down to work every day from their apartment upstairs and plied her trade, shaping buxom figures into appealing packages with girdles and D-cup bras and draping them in the latest fashions. She was privy to the personal secrets of her clients, whose purchase of *biancheria intima* seemed to encourage familiarity, and she dealt with the salesmen pushing their lines of dresses and Formmold corsets. Antonio did nothing but go to the factory, where he processed felt in vats of vitriol, breathed in the foul air, and learned nothing of the world.

How much more charming was the elegant tailor at number 1822. Millie could talk to Paul. She shared his belief in witchcraft, often going to spiritualists and psychics herself for guidance on life and affairs. She was impressed by Paul's knowledge of the occult. She understood him when he groused about his invalid wife. "All the time, it's doctors," Paul complained to Millie. Some prescribed medicines. Some said it was in her head. But nothing did any good. It was depressing living with such a woman, Paul told his lady friend, not the way it would be with her. Paul seemed to be genuinely attracted to Millie. "She's just the type I like," Paul told his partner Bolber. "She's short and I'm short; she's rich and I'm rich; she's smart and I'm smart. We're a nice pair."

After a while, Paul and Millie were doing more than just talking. Millie would later claim that she had been bewitched by Paul. But whether it was bewitched or charmed, she and Paul began making use of the couch in the back room of the dress shop, with provocatively clad mannequins standing by as witnesses.

Paul befriended Antonio and invited him over to his shop. Antonio sat around in the evening with Paul and his insurance-agent buddies, discussing many things. "I'm going to ask you some questions," said the agent Alphonse Cirillo one night, "just like I ask my customers." He took down the hatmaker's date and place of birth and other vital statistics and wrote them on a Metropolitan Life application for the no-examination maximum of five hundred dollars. Cirillo put down Antonio's address as the third-floor apartment over Paul's shop. In the space for beneficiary, though the two men were unrelated, he entered "Paul Petrillo, nephew." "Just put your mark here," he told Antonio, "it won't cost you nothing," and Antonio obliged. The always-reliable Gaetano Cicinato added another five-hundred-dollar policy.

There was ample opportunity to lace the victim's vermouth during evening socializing. Antonio also took many medications, some in little capsules that could be broken open and modified. Paul had little difficulty gaining access to the Giacobbe medical supplies while tarrying with Millie. With Bolber's help in obtaining supplies and calculating dosage, Paul decided to exploit these opportunities.

Millie and the doctors were so accustomed to Antonio's complaints that neither they nor he paid much attention when he had worsening stomach and chest pains in March 1933, nor was there any cause to comment upon the odor of garlic on his breath. But on Thursday, March 30, the situation became acute. Millie summoned Dr. J. A. Pescatore, a physician who had been treating her for a woman's problem. The doctor found Antonio "lying on his bed in shock, suffering from epigastric pain, vomiting, and nausea." He gave Antonio a shot of morphine "to calm his nerves." The next day, the ailing man felt better and went to his regular appointment at the hospital clinic.

By Sunday, April 2, however, Antonio's condition was much worse. He went with Millie to Mass in the morning, but as they sat down to lunch, he began breathing heavily and rushed for the toilet in the yard. When he collapsed after a few steps and lay moaning on the kitchen floor, Millie screamed out the back door for her neighbors. Several came and helped Antonio up to the bedroom. Millie called Dr. Pescatore. Two of the neighbors called other doctors. The medical men all came about the same time, Drs. Pescatore, Bove, and Pelosi, converging on 1816 East Passyunk Avenue like a task force. But Antonio died just before they arrived. He lay there in a foul mess on his bed, never having made it to the toilet. Pescatore, the most experienced man on the case, signed the death certificate "myocardial degeneration," or heart failure.

R.I.P.
ANTONIO GIACOBBE

Paul was gleeful. But the superstitious Millie began hearing sounds in her basement at night, sounds that she thought were the spirit of Antonio come back to avenge his death. "I can't sleep. I see my husband coming all the time," she said, sobbing.

Morris Bolber came to call on Millie. The rabbi listened carefully to her story and offered his perceptive insight. "Your conscience bothers you. Your husband is not coming back. He is dead. The problem is your conscience is bothering you. But I can fix."

That evening Bolber snuck a frog into Millie's basement. Returning at midnight a few days later, he led a quivering Millie into the darkened basement, the only light a small candle flickering in his hand. The two tiptoed along, listening to the ever-louder croaking voice of the late Antonio. When Millie could stand it no more and fled screaming up the stairs, Bolber calmly squashed his little green prop, exorcising the evil spirit forever.

Cured by this Bolber magic, Millie relaxed and began enjoying her newfound freedom.

x x x

The state quickly put on witnesses who testified as to the level of arsenic found in Antonio's body and to the many life-insurance policies taken out by Millie and by Paul Petrillo on the man's life. Millie had admitted to having an intimate relationship with Paul, police detectives testified. And Johnny Cacopardo, the serenader from Sing Sing imported to help the Philadelphia DA, told of the night they had met Millie outside the Alahambra Theater, when Paul bragged about killing her husband.

In her defense, Millie called on Paul, who had by now confessed to the murder of Antonio and was awaiting determination of his punishment. In his hour of utmost desperation, with the threat of a death sentence hanging heavy over his head, knowing well that cooperation with the prosecutor was the surest course to clemency, Paul had nonetheless agreed to testify in his ex-lover's defense.

"Sure, I had two policies on Giacobbe, for one thousand and eight dollars," Paul said. "His Mrs. knew nothing about them. She had nothin' to do with any of it." And, oh, yes: "She never had any improper relations with me." Somewhere within the heart of the worst of us lies a hint of the gentleman. But Paul's testimony didn't count for much. When the jury in Millie's case retired to deliberate on Thursday, it took only a couple of hours to reach a verdict. Guilty, but with a recommendation of life imprisonment. Lanciano, her lawyer, was proud that he had at least saved his client from a death sentence, gotten her a better fate than that which had befallen most of the other widows.

x x x

Down in Room 443, even though Judge Brown had the court running on triple sessions, resuming each evening for a few hours after a dinner break, Rose Cavina's trial continued. She must have decided that Stella's à la mode dress was good luck, because she, too, wore a smart fur-trimmed black coat and a black toque, to which she added a dark veil. Rose was calm, looked unconcerned, and smiled amiably at friends in the courtroom. It was a bravura performance in light of the evidence against her. In addition to the now-routine evidence of poison (antimony in this case), plus insurance manipulation and the looting of the grocery store, Rose had to confront the personal accusations of Peter Stea's daughters, who had lived in the house with them, and the damning tale spun by Johnny Cacopardo, now a prosecution pet.

"When I refused to poison the old man Zambino," said Johnny, "Rose told me, 'What are you afraid of? I gave poison to my husband and they never found out.' "

Rose leapt to her feet. "Liar!" she shouted at Johnny.

He gave her a measured look. "You know it's the truth, Rose."

Judge Brown had to gavel the courtroom quiet. It broke out in an uproar again as Rose was being led out for the midday break. One of Peter Stea's daughters, seated at the aisle, thrust out her foot at Rose, kicking her in the shin. Rose reared back as if to level the girl with a right cross, but detectives grabbed her and pulled her away.

The attacking daughter, Lena Stea, got in more than just a kick when she took the stand. "On the morning of June twenty-ninth," she told the jury, "we were downstairs in the store, and Rose took a cup of black coffee up to my sick father. He began vomiting and complaining of the burning in his throat. Only this time, the pains were much more severe, and he did not recognize anyone. He just stared and threw up." By noon that day, he was dead.

The pressure on Alexander had grown as word came down of the conviction verdict in Millie Giacobbe's courtroom up on the sixth floor. The state's record was now thirteen and one. Alexander remained alone, the only lawyer to have gained an acquittal for any of the poison murder defendants. He probed every detail of the prosecution's case, looking for an opening, drawing on the extensive technical research that Louis Lipschitz had done in preparation.

There was no doubt in Alexander's mind that Rose would have to testify in her own defense. She would have to persuade the jury that the witnesses against her were lying. The courtroom was quiet on Thursday afternoon as Rose took the stand, looking and acting every bit the victimized widow as she daubed her tear-soaked eyes.

"I didn't kill Peter," she said. "He was too good a man to kill."

She admitted that two of her other husbands had also died, but on that score, she told the jury the same thing that she had told husband number five, Isadore Tropea. She had suffered all her life from bad fortune, from the time her mother died when she was a child and she was sent to live with a cruel aunt to the three terrible times she lost beloved mates to tragic illnesses. She was a victim. That was the image she and Alexander were building.

When the police arrested her, she said, they kept "pounding" at her, trying to get her to confess. They even gave her something to drink that made her unconscious. But she held firm, she told the jury, because she had nothing to confess. The real scoundrels were trying to put the blame on her, an innocent victim. Every bit of evidence against her was just more proof of it. That was the beauty of her "I'm being framed" defense. The stronger the prosecution's case got, the more evidence there was of the breadth of the frame-up.

For the conclusion of Rose's case, Alexander called character witnesses, friends who attested to her upright behavior and honesty. In rebuttal, the police officer who had arrested her said she had been having an affair with Paul Petrillo. Will the real Rose Carina stand up? the jury must have thought.

Rose's chances did not appear any better by the end of the trial on Saturday then they had at the beginning. Her only remaining hope was Raymond Pace Alexander's final word, his summation. Could he again rise to the occasion, as he had in Stella's case? He had succeeded in getting the thinking-man's jury he

sought, made up of seven men and five women. It was, he would
say, "one of the most intelligent juries that ever sat in the box.
One of the women was the mother of a senior at Bryn Mawr
College. Three were students; two were retired manufacturers, and
all were of a high level of intelligence."

Alexander spoke to this blue-ribbon group masterfully, bringing even his client to tears as he laid out her story: a pathetic
motherless child who had endured the death of a beloved husband
three times over. She had taken care of Stea's whole family, not
only Peter but his four younger children, as well as her own
daughter Rita. She had cooked and cleaned and helped out in the
store, doing all that could be expected of a wife and more. Now
she had to suffer the ultimate indignity of being blamed for the
death of this man for whom she had labored so mightily, accused
by a gang of vicious hoodlums. Was it not enough that she had
borne such grievous personal losses? Sixty-three-year-old David
Sinn, juror number four, broke into open tears of sympathy for
the pitiable defendant.

Having warmed the jury to his side, Alexander cleverly
turned to the medical testimony, reminding the jury as he had
many times before of the state's burden of proof, *beyond a reasonable doubt.* "There are five possible causes of death," Alexander
said, "natural causes, accident, mistake, suicide, and intentional
crime. The state must prove beyond a reasonable doubt that it
was not any of the first four," as if to suggest the odds were already four to one in her favor. Pursuing this point, Alexander
went through the medical testimony. The attending physician,
Dr. D'Emilio, the man closest to the death, said Stea had influenza.

"If you believe Dr. D'Emilio, you must acquit," said Alexander.

Dr. Didio said he had globus hystericus. "If you believe Dr. Didio, you must acquit," repeated Alexander.

The hospital records and all the attending doctors in the emergency room and in the ward who treated Stea agreed with Dr. D'Emilio or Dr. Didio. "If you believe the hospital and its doctors, you must acquit," intoned Alexander.

The death certificate said that the final death was from complications of diabetes. "If you believe the doctors who prepared the death certificate, you must acquit" went Alexander's refrain.

Alexander mocked "the amazing autopsy findings." The amounts of poison found were quite small compared with those in the other cases—only .164 milligrams of antimony in the liver and .0056 milligrams in the kidneys—which gave Alexander a break that he exploited with a vengeance. Setting up a blackboard before the jury, he put the findings in terms they could understand.

"We know what an ounce of flour is, that is, one-sixteenth of a pound. So what is this in ounces, how much of an ounce?" Alexander carefully did the calculations in front of them. The answer was, of course, minuscule: one 170,731th of an ounce in the liver and one 5,121,930th of an ounce in both kidneys combined. Alexander held up a pin. "It was a mere speck. The amount of antimony in the dead man would be lost on this pinhead. Can we believe this was a fatal dose? Did anyone testify that this could be a fatal dose?" It could have come from anywhere, he said, rattling off a list of possibilities: "rosary beads, the inside of the coffin, the tacks in the coffin, the nails, the metal covering and metallic casket, the soil, religious medals, metal buttons, bolts, welding, paint or varnish on casket. . . ."

And again, the refrain: "If you believe that it could have come from any of these sources, if there is a reasonable doubt, you must acquit."

Of course no one had said that this was all the antimony given to Stea. It was only the reside found on autopsy. But Alexander pressed on, mocking the amount. Anyone could have slipped this speck to him. It could have been in a dose of a medicine, maybe the cough medicine he was known to take. *Emphasize that he took proprietary cough medicines,* Alexander wrote in his summation notes. There is no basis for thinking it was given as poison. There was no basis for thinking his wife gave it to him. No one saw her do it. There was no evidence of her acquiring antimony.

Alexander attacked the work of the Homicide Bureau and the district attorney's office with a new refrain. *"Argue loudly,"* he wrote at this point in his summation notes. Alexander was renowned as a performer in the courtroom, and now he rose to the top of his form.

"Do you approve of detectives working as Captain Kelly and his men did, pounding away at this poor widow in interrogations, forcing her into hunger strikes to protect herself?" Alexander bellowed at the Bryn Mawr mother and her colleagues. *"Do you approve of the district attorney making deals with the worst kind of convicted murderers, felons, rapists, and perjurers trying to vent their spleen and hate against this innocent woman?"* he shouted, alluding to Johnny Cacopardo's record.

The only real evidence against Rose was that she was too friendly, too open with men like Paul Petrillo who could use and abuse her, who could exploit their friendship to gain access to her house and husband. That may have been a mistake, but it was no crime. "This is a ring," Alexander exhorted the jury. "Get the ringleaders, not the innocent victims."

The jury went out at four on Saturday afternoon. They were back before dinner.

"Not guilty," said foreman Charles L. Press, Jr.

"Thank you, thank you," said Rose Carina as she collapsed into the arms of Raymond Pace Alexander.

Juror number four, David Sinn, was still crying, now joined by several of his jury colleagues.

"God bless you all," Rose cried to the jury as she was led from the courtroom. Three times she shouted it, "God bless you," until she disappeared through the door.

Judge Brown was a little taken aback. He admonished the jury, "Because of the verdicts in other cases of this sort, there are going to be many persons who will be inquiring how you came to your decision. It would be best if you did not discuss it."

And they never did. This was the end of the matter for them.

But not for the district attorney: McDevitt immediately announced that Rose would be tried again, this time for the murder of Pietro Pirolli, the man to whom Rose and *sorella* Josephine Sedita had ministered in his final days. Pirolli's wife, Grace, had already been sentenced to the chair for merely aiding Rose in that killing.

25
THE TIDE TURNS

Rose basked in the glory of her acquittal as she was returned to the Moyamensing Prison. The prison was in her familiar Passyunk neighborhood, only a few blocks from Paul's tailor shop and Peter Stea's store. Now, for the first time, the stone walls of the place they called the "Moko" had the warmth of home. "Her fellow inmates gave her an ovation," the *Bulletin* reported. "They banged cups against the walls and bars and showered her with hugs and kisses." Maybe they thought some of her luck might rub off on them.

To those who knew the evidence and understood the case, the acquittal of "Kiss of Death" Carina was even more stunning than that of Stella Alfonsi. By all rights, Raymond Pace Alexander should have been gathering kudos that outshone those of a month earlier. But the press was largely silent. The verdict was reported, but without headlines.

The downward spiral of world affairs was creating a news

whirlpool, sucking up all interest. In Europe, Hitler and Stalin had signed their cynical pact of nonaggression, carving up Poland. Russia began moving against the Baltic countries and launched a brutal invasion of Finland. The world watched in awe as the tiny Nordic nation held out against its massive adversary. No petty, essentially repetitive events in a local courtroom could compete with this true-life David and Goliath saga. So there was another conviction, or maybe it was an acquittal. Who cared?

Even Vincent McDevitt, who had built a reputation on these poison murder cases, seemed to have lost interest. Ever since his magnificent triumphs in the two Petrillo cases, work had been flooding into his private law practice. This was where his future lay, the means of feeding his growing family. The murder ring was increasingly a distraction. Worse than that, it was becoming an embarrassment as a single Negro lawyer seemed able to turn the tables on the prosecutors, making them the villains because of their aggressive interrogations and use of tarnished witnesses. Maybe if the prosecution had continued to roll on unvanquished, maybe if they could have maintained an unbroken victory string, there might have been a point to pressing on. But the verdict of reality was now in. The glory days were over. It was time to mop up.

McDevitt reviewed the outstanding cases. Next on tap was Susie DiMartino, whose husband, Guisepi, had succumbed under the care of Maria Favato and Raphael Polselli. Both Favato and Polselli had already pleaded guilty to first-degree murder in this case. A third coconspirator, Susie's boyfriend and husband-impersonator, Emedio Muscelli, had also been found guilty of first-degree murder in a jury trial. If Susie's case were pursued, she, like several other witless widows, might also be found guilty of murder one. But there was no longer any certainty. She might be wholly acquitted, like Stella Alfonsi and Rose Carina.

The tide had turned. Only a few weeks earlier, each conviction had seemed to support the next. Each jury was made up of people who read about the work of prior juries (or even, like the repeat juror, James Magee, had served on them) and could not help but be influenced by the findings of their predecessors. McDevitt had had the momentum. But no more. Now the pools of veniremen would have heard that poison widows could be victims as well as villains. Each case would have to be won on its merits, without the dominating aura of guilt by association that had paved the way earlier.

McDevitt himself may have begun to have doubts. It was now December 1939, with Christmas looming. That may have affected his feelings. In any event, he did what he had adamantly refused to do before. He accepted a plea bargain to a reduced charge of second-degree murder from Susie DiMartino. There would be no trial. But there would be no electrocution or life sentence, either. A panel of judges would determine Susie's punishment, which could be up to twenty years' imprisonment, but could involve little or no jail time. He made the same deal with Christine Cerrone, David Brandt, and Sophie LaVecchio.

The evidence against each of these defendants was no weaker and probably stronger than that against Josephine Romualdo, Emedio Muscelli, Grace Pirolli, and Millie Giacobbe, all of whom had been convicted of first-degree murder. But the wisdom of McDevitt's bargaining was confirmed a few days later when Rose Carilli, a Delaware poison widow who admitted using some *fattura* supplied by Paul Petrillo "to get my husband to stop drinking," was tried down in Wilmington. It "looked like baking powder," she said, but as a result, her husband not only stopped drinking; he stopped eating and breathing, as well. She was convicted, but only of manslaughter.

One widow fared even better. Marie Woloshyn was the woman who collected thousands of dollars in life insurance when her husband had an unfortunate run-in with Jumbo Valenti's lead pipe and Herman Petrillo's car. Herman, who was still appealing his conviction, refused to testify against her, and the erratic, unpredictable Jumbo had gone mute again. Without these witnesses, McDevitt had to drop all charges against Marie.

Joseph Swartz was the defendant different. He was the only Jew (other than Rabbi Bolber, of course). He was accused of murdering his mother-in-law, rather than his spouse. And he refused to accept McDevitt's deal.

As his trial commenced on December 12, 1939, Swartz seemed confident, "dressed snappily in a blue pinch back suit and suede shoes, and sporting a purple flower in his buttonhole." But, after listening to pathologists tell of finding arsenic in the victim's flesh and bones, and hearing Morris Bolber accuse him of arranging the "job" on her, Swartz was a changed man.

Called to testify on his own behalf, he faced the jury unshaven, disheveled, and mumbling. Whatever suit he was wearing was hidden beneath an overcoat that he refused to remove, even though the courtroom was well heated. At first he answered his lawyer's routine opening questions, giving his name and address, his age and place of occupation.

But then Swartz suddenly lost it. "This has been going on too long. I can't stand it!" he shouted, jumping up from his seat in the witness box. "They want me to die. What can I do? They want to put all these charges against me." He moaned, emitting a profoundly pained sigh from deep within. "Ooh, God help me! Be with me, please."

Two court officers had to pull him away. His long overcoat dragged across several jurors as the officers carried him out of the courtroom, back to his holding cell beyond the jury box. When the report came back from the "psychopathic division" of the hospital, the judge ended the proceedings. Joseph Swartz was no longer sane enough to stand trial. He was instead clapped into a mental hospital.

x x x

The new decade of the 1940s began a few weeks later. Most Americans, despite growing concern about Europe, welcomed the end of the thirties. They were a generation that had lived through a war universally known as the Great War, and a period of economic misery that would become known as the Great Depression, with the foolhardy, frantic time of the Great Drought in between. What more could they fear? As the Finns continued to resist Stalin with elan, even humiliating their vaunted adversary in winter battles between ski-mounted troops, Americans cheered. There was reason to hope.

Vincent McDevitt, his professional star now rising, was also optimistic. He had spent fifteen months on the set of cases sometimes called the "Great Arsenic Murder Ring." It was wearing him down. But there were only a few cases remaining. At the top of the list was the disposition of the two acquitted widows, Stella Alfonsi and Rose Carina, both of whom were still being held. It seemed to McDevitt a gross miscarriage of justice that these women might go free while some of their seemingly less guilty peers were strapped into the electric chair or rotted their lives away in jail.

Stella and Rose saw things differently, of course. They began to pepper Alexander with letters, demanding that he do something to get them released. "Dear Sir," wrote Rose Carina, "I have heard that you have been ill. Very sorry of the sad news, hoping that this letter will find you in the best of health. Please, Mr. Alexander, I beg of you to inform me of when I am gong to get out. I wish it will be some time this week. Hoping to hear from you soon. Please don't disappoint me."

In answering her letter, Alexander acknowledged that he was speaking with her sisters about further representation. He also reminded her that they had to "make some arrangements" for payment. "All of my work for you has been done without any compensation whatsoever."

Despite this grumbling about fees, Alexander and Lipschitz kept up the pressure on the DA's office, filing petitions for habeas corpus to have the women set free. McDevitt, temporizing, agreed to their release on bail, hoping they might slip up while free and lead him to more evidence.

Rose went back home to Hammonton and began stiffing Alexander on his bill. "I am a little disappointed that I have not heard from you since your discharge on bail on the 2nd of January," Alexander wrote to her on January 18, 1940. "You realize you have to prepare for the other trial and that I have just as much confidence in your innocence of this as I had concerning the past one. Won't you please call to see me and make some payment of my fees. I need not tell you of the amount of energy, time, labor and study that I put into your case and the personal interest I exhibited in the same. I leave this matter entirely up to you now to do the proper thing regarding payment of my fee for services."

"I was glad to hear from you," Rose wrote back. "At the present time I can't make any arrangements when to see you. But at my first opportunity I will stop in." She was waiting to see what

McDevitt was going to do. There was no point bothering with her lawyer if she didn't need his services anymore. She sensed, perhaps better than Alexander, how the tide had turned.

After a few months, McDevitt eventually had to face reality. As much as he might wish otherwise, he had nothing else on Stella. And without the cooperation of Grace Pirolli (who was appealing her conviction) and Josephine Sedita (who was still on the lam), he had no case against Rose, either. He dropped all further charges against both women. Raymond Pace Alexander's triumphs on their behalf were absolute.

Now there was only Agnes Mandiuk.

26
THE LAST WIDOW

Among the poison widows, there were dupes, like Josephine Romualdo; duds, like Grace Pirolli; and dames, like Stella Alfonsi. Agnes Mandiuk was a dweeb. Tall, bespectacled, and plain, the forty-six-year-old Agnes did not come from the Passyunk milieu of most of the other widows. She and her husband, Romaine, a baker, were of Austrian-Slavic descent and lived at 3043 North Twenty-sixth Street in North Philadelphia. A contemporary picture shows the couple seated on the stoop of their home, dressed in their Sunday finery, with Agnes's hair neatly set in finger waves, her hand lovingly resting on Romaine's shoulder, and a perky little white dog between them. They had two devoted children, a daughter, Anna, twenty-two, and a son, William, twenty-four. The Mandiuks were a poster family for *The Saturday Evening Post.* A less likely user of *la fattura* than Agnes Mandiuk was hard to imagine.

Agnes, however, had been a client of Morris Bolber, a be-

liever in his mystical powers of healing. Bolber had pleaded guilty
to the murder of Romaine, who was found to have a cocktail of
arsenic, antimony, bismuth, and mercury distributed throughout
his internal organs. These facts alone were enough to put it in the
classic poison widow pattern. But with responsibility for this killing firmly pinned on Bolber, one of the ringleaders, it would have
seemed that the case of Agnes Mandiuk was in line for the same
deal that the other widows were now receiving, a negotiated plea
of second-degree murder. Four other defense lawyers, confronted
with similar circumstances, had welcomed this arrangement as a
good bargain for their clients. With any luck, the women would
be free in a few years at most.

But Agnes's lawyer wanted a better deal. Why shouldn't he?
He was Raymond Pace Alexander, the one lawyer who knew how
to win these cases. At first Agnes had retained a lawyer named
Frank Carano, recommended to her by a friend of her son, William. Carano was a young man, only a few years out of the University of Pennsylvania Law School, just building a small practice
for himself in West Philadelphia. He was bright enough, but he
had little criminal or trial experience. With his urging, the family
managed to enlist the services of Alexander as cocounsel. It had
not been easy. Alexander had been compensated only with glory
in the Alfonsi case, which he did as a court-appointed public service. He was paid only in tribulations for the trial of Rose Carina,
who turned a deaf ear to his requests for cash once she no longer
needed his services. Both cases had been hard-fought and had been
a tremendous strain on him. But the Mandiuks were willing to
pay a fee up front. Alexander must have thought that if he could
gain an acquittal for the "Kiss of Death," how difficult would it
be to prevail for a picture of domestic felicity like Agnes Mandiuk?

Here, finally, was a poison widow case it made sense for him to take.

Agnes, an accused murderer without bail, remained locked away in Moko as Alexander and McDevitt fenced over the terms of a possible plea.

x x x

For several months, in the spring of 1940, negotiations stalled as McDevitt was distracted by new developments in the case of Herman Petrillo. The Pennsylvania Supreme Court, outraged by Judge Harry McDevitt's overbearing conduct at Herman's trial, reversed his conviction. The possibility loomed that this cock of the North Philadelphia walk might again thumb his nose at prosecutors.

Vince McDevitt never doubted he would retry Herman, but the odds in his favor had now been drastically reduced. Herman had a new lawyer, the brilliant Tom McBride, later to become state attorney general and a justice of the Pennsylvania Supreme Court. There would be a new judge, presumably neutral and wary of repeating Judge "Hanging Harry" McDevitt's foolish errors. And the appellate court ruling made it clear that Herman could no longer be smeared with evidence about unrelated cases under the abstruse theory of "system." He could not even be charged with conspiracy, because his putative coconspirator Stella Alfonsi had been found innocent. A conspiracy charge required at least two guilty persons.

But Vincent McDevitt was up to the occasion. His strategy was as brilliant as it was simple. Forget Alfonsi. Forget Favato. Forget Paul Petrillo. Forget widows. Forget arsenic and antimony. Get back to basics. Prosecute Herman for the murder of Ralph

Caruso, the pathetic cripple whom he drowned in the Schuylkill River. For proof of this crime, the state had the testimony of Christine Cerrone, the hot-pillow landlady, who had already pled guilty. They had the testimony of insurance agents from whom Herman had procured life insurance by falsely representing himself as Caruso's brother and nephew. They had the testimony of Salvatore Sortino, the disciple of Bolber and shover of Caruso, who had already pled guilty. They had the testimony of marvelous Morris Bolber, who knew all and told all.

It was indeed an overwhelming case. McDevitt led the jury out to the banks of the Schuylkill in Fairmount Park, accompanied by a phalanx of reporters, and had Sortino stage a dramatic reenactment of the drowning. Bolber, who had been offstage for months, exploded with histrionics when returned to his beloved arena. Bolber, said the *Bulletin,* "supplied the trial's fireworks." Shouting and waving his arms, he told defense counsel McBride to be more careful in framing his questions.

"He's just trying to look smart," Bolber confided to the jury.

"Remember, I'm trying to defend a man for his life," complained the shocked lawyer.

"Maybe if you knew the defendant like I do, you wouldn't represent him," chuckled Bolber.

The jurors, to no one's surprise, again opted for the maximum punishment. The no-longer-cocky Herman was returned to death row.

x x x

With Herman Petrillo's scalp again firmly attached to his belt, Vincent McDevitt was in no mood to let Agnes Mandiuk off easily. Raymond Pace Alexander might have gained unjustified triumphs in two cases, but McDevitt's own record in these cases was un-blemished, with a verdict of first-degree murder in every case he tried. He might have begun these cases as a relatively inexperi-enced young prosecutor, but he had grown in skill and confidence over the previous fifteen months as he matched wits with men like Lemuel Schofield and Tom McBride, the best the Philadelphia criminal-defense bar could offer. McDevitt had no fear of Ray-mond Pace Alexander. He welcomed the chance to match his night law school–honed street smarts and native Irish charm against the cosmopolitan Harvard-educated black man who had become his nemesis. It was, as McDevitt saw it, an opportunity to right the scales of justice that had been knocked so awry by Alexander.

As the two lawyers negotiated, the tide of history rolled on in Europe. On May 10, 1940, a week after Herman Petrillo's sec-ond conviction, the Third Reich's panzer divisions rumbled to-ward the Low Countries, which, only a few months before, Goebbels had promised they "had no intention of attacking." Hol-land fell, then Belgium, Norway, and France. In six weeks, Hitler was the master of Europe. Great Britain cowered in fear behind its English Channel moat. Even Japan was wary. Authoritative sources in the Far East reported that the Asian power was seeking to mend relations with the United States to gain an ally against the German juggernaut. The lesson of England's failed appease-ment strategy was clear to all who read the news. Excessive com-promise was a fatally flawed approach to human affairs.

The proud lawyers on each side of the Agnes Mandiuk case understood this too well. Though they discussed a plea bargain, they were destined never to agree. On January 20, 1941, the trial of Agnes Mandiuk began in Quarter Sessions Court, her fate the prize in a clash of legal egos. It had a been over a year since the last poison widow trial, in December 1939. The public, looking for some distraction from the appalling war news about the bombardment of Britain, showed a renewed interest in the what they all called the "Arsenic Murder Ring." The trial of Agnes received prime coverage.

As the trial began, Alexander and Carano had reason to be hopeful. McDevitt was not able to handle the case himself. He would supervise the prosecution as the established master strategist of the arsenic murder cases, but the actual trial work would be done by another assistant, Franklin Barr. The weakness in Barr's preparation showed on the very first day.

The prosecution had opened with testimony from Dr. Thomas Nock, the doctor who had cared for Romaine Mandiuk in his final days. Nock had attributed the death to ptomaine poisoning, a diagnosis that was much closer to the mark than the cardiac misperceptions of quick-buck artists like the busy, hundred-patient-a-day Dr. Boccella. They added some damning evidence regarding insurance. Agnes had thirteen thousand dollars of life insurance on her husband, taken out under three separate names, Agnes Mandiuk, Catherine Mandiuk, and Kayerta Mandiuk. Several of these policies had been purchased in April 1934, ten months before his death. So far so good. But then prosecutor Barr called the infamous Dr. Horace Perlman to the stand.

Perlman, who had pleaded guilty to second-degree murder in the case of Jennifer Pino after being tricked into a confession by Vince McDevitt, was serving a sentence of ten to twenty years. Prosecutors expected him to testify, consistent with an earlier statement, that he and David Brandt (the ex–veterinary student and Bolber disciple) had arranged to supply Agnes Mandiuk with *la fattura*. Barr had relied on this in his opening statement, promising to show that Agnes had paid seven hundred dollars to purchase "a mysterious package from two men on a street corner," which contained poison.

The prosecutors felt that they had some leverage over Perlman because his cooperation with the state would be a positive factor in any future parole application. But when the time came to take the stand, Perlman decided he wasn't taking any chances implicating himself in another murder. Instead he refused to say anything about Agnes Mandiuk, even repudiating his earlier statement. When asked about the statement, Dr. Perlman now said he had been under duress and hadn't understood the document when he signed it.

"Why don't you remember?" an annoyed Judge Otto R. Heiligman asked him.

"I just don't" was all Perlman would say.

Things got worse for the state when they tried to establish the actual cause of death. Dr. Martin Crane, the coroner's physician who performed the autopsy, was bedridden with a severe case of influenza. Barr requested that court proceedings be moved to Crane's bedside for this critical testimony. But Judge Heiligman, remembering the deadly influenza pandemic of 1918, refused to expose the jurors (and himself) to that risk. The trial, with sequestered jurors, could not be continued indefinitely while Crane recovered. Without Perlman and Crane, ARSENIC CASE FACES COLLAPSE, reported the *Inquirer.*

Dr. Crane managed to drag himself to court the next day, testifying that the victim's liver, stomach, and kidneys contained 43.7 milligrams of arsenic, 1.86 milligrams of antimony, and more than 13.5 milligrams of bismuth, another metallic poison, all of which had killed him. But the witness was too sick to give his testimony much vigor.

As if in some reaction to Crane's sickly pallor or the subject of his testimony, two jurors suddenly fell ill. Juror number twelve, Albert Kessler, had terrible indigestion. Juror number eleven, Dante Cimini, crumpled in his seat with something diagnosed as "hysteriod complex." On advice of the police surgeon, Judge Heiligman dismissed them both. The two alternates were sworn in. The loss of one more juror would require a mistrial.

The prosecutors seemed to be on the ropes when they called on the ever-reliable Morris Bolber, the self-styled savior of the Homicide Bureau, who had consistently delivered whatever evidence the state needed. His testimony would be especially relevant here because the Mandiuk death was the one to which Bolber had pled guilty. Barr asked Bolber about the seven hundred dollars Agnes Mandiuk had paid him, money that Barr wanted to prove was for the purchase of poison.

"Yes, she gave me seven hundred dollars," Bolber admitted. But then he shocked Barr. "It was for curing her back. She had a bad back and I fixed it for her. I only told her to have faith and pray, old-fashioned stuff like that."

That was one story from Bolber. Another story he told was that seven hundred dollars—maybe the same, maybe a different seven hundred dollars—was paid to him by Herman Petrillo, who was the real killer of Mandiuk. "I accepted seven hundred dollars for keeping quiet, and I feel myself guilty; that's why I pleaded guilty." As for Agnes, the only thing he would say about her was, "I think she was going out with Herman Petrillo or someone. She used to come to my place while she had a lover. She had a loving place in my place. Maybe that's why she gave me the seven hundred dollars—she didn't want me talking about that." That didn't make Agnes an angel, but it didn't make her a killer, either.

The district attorney's case was a shambles. Alexander and

Carano had hardly done a thing. They were wondering whether they would ever have to. Meanwhile, Barr and McDevitt met with their final witnesses, the homicide detectives who had interrogated Agnes Mandiuk. She had made some incriminating statements to them. She had never signed any confession or statement. But she had *said* some things. The prosecutors made the situation clear to the detectives. The case would stand or fall on their testimony. They had better tell their stories well.

They tried. Lt. James Kelly said, "The defendant told me she obtained a bottle of poison from David Brandt. She got it in a school yard at Twenty-sixth and Clearfield Streets. She said she tasted it herself and gave the rest of it to her husband." Detective Michael Schwartz said, "The defendant pointed out David Brandt in a cell room. She said it was him that supplied her with the poison." But on cross-examination, Lieutenant Kelly admitted that none of these statements were in writing. He also said that when he accompanied Agnes to her home to retrieve the bottle of "poison," she gave him a bottle that contained only harmless patent medicine, saying it was all that Brandt had given her.

The defense lawyers were in high spirits as they put Agnes Mandiuk on the stand. She was a big woman, and she spoke in harsh, clipped tones, but her testimony was compelling. "It's a lie," she had cried out at Lieutenant Kelly when he had testified about the school-yard rendezvous with Brandt. Now she elaborated her version of the story. It was not a simon-pure account, but it was consistent with all the evidence. "I went to see Bolber," she said, "because we had a boarder in the house. I was in love with him."

She as much as admitted there was some hanky-panky with this boarder. Tales about this Stanley Pilcinski, described as Agnes's "young lover," had circulated in the press months earlier.

The *Record* even claimed she had used her insurance loot to get a face-lift to hold young Stanley's affection. Alexander had tried tactfully to screen out jurors who might be aware of these old, unsubstantiated rumors, but he apparently thought it best to let Agnes concede and justify this troublesome matter, rather than ignore it. "I knew it was no good," she explained. "I wanted Bolber to help me get free."

Agnes told the fascinated jury, "Bolber took me upstairs to a room, where he had me stand against a wall. He took out a long knife. He waved it over my head and mumbled strange words. When he was done, he asked me if I felt any better. 'I don't know,' I told him, 'I'm too scared.' "

But she paid him five dollars and came back.

"The next time, Bolber told me to hang a fish in the moonlight for four days. After that I was supposed to take it down and eat it. Another time he came to my house with a dead bird. He told me to burn it in the stove and inhale the fumes. He said this would cure me of love."

No doubt.

As Bolber treated Agnes, he probed for information on her financial status. He volunteered the psychic insight to her that her husband was going to die, and that she had best take out insurance on him, as much as she could. She did it. "I believed Bolber. I did everything he told me," she said. "The only thing I wouldn't do was when he told me to go down in the basement with him at midnight and take off all my clothes. He said we were going to stand in the middle of the floor and pray."

As Bolber's mastery over her grew, he introduced Agnes to his disciple, David Brandt. Brandt gave her a ride home from Bolber's office in South Philadelphia on several occasions. One time she did meet Brandt in a school yard, according to Bolber's instructions, and got a package. But it contained only the bottle of patent medicine she gave to Lieutenant Kelly. Then Agnes came to the key point of her story, implying that David Brandt himself administered the poison.

"I introduced Brandt to my husband. Bolber told me to introduce them. Brandt gave my husband a ride to work. He got sick while he was at work that day and came home. I called Dr. Nock right away."

That was February 21, 1935. Romaine died on February 22, and Nock signed off with his "ptomaine" diagnosis.

It looked good for the defense. But Alexander knew that emotion was as important as facts in winning a case. He called Agnes's two children as the final witnesses, in the hope that they could blot out any remaining stain from their mother's dalliance. They poured out their hearts for her, telling how loving she was and how much she and their father had loved each other. They always ate together as a family, sharing the same food, helping themselves from the same serving dishes, the children said pointedly.

That was it. The jury went out to deliberate at 6:30 P.M. on Thursday evening, the fourth day of the trial. They decided to have dinner first and did not convene to deliberate until 7:30. An hour and half later, after brief deliberations, they were ready with their verdict. It was a shocker.

"Guilty," said Charles Dickinson, foremen of the nine-man, three-woman jury.

Agnes stood stoically as her women friends wept. Her sister fainted. Their only solace was that the jury sentenced Agnes to life imprisonment. She would, pronounced Judge Heiligman, spend the rest of her natural life in the State Industrial Home for Women, in Muncy, Pennsylvania.

x x x

Raymond Pace Alexander took it hard. When he had agreed to represent Agnes, she had written a touching letter, saying she put her "whole faith and soul" in him. Alexander, a man who lived for his clients and became emotionally invested in them, berated himself. What had gone wrong? The evidence against Agnes seemed trivial compared with that against Stella and Rose Carina. Was it that Agnes had collected thirteen thousand dollars' worth of life insurance, while Stella and Rose had collected little or none? Was it that Agnes had admitted to an affair, while Stella and Rose—who surely could have taught Agnes a thing or two about men—had claimed to be as pure as the San Pellegrino spring? Or was it that Agnes was tall; she was strong; she was cold as ice; she had a native Germanic demeanor? Did that, in 1941, lead a jury to see her as a woman who could kill?

Whatever the reason, her conviction marked the end of the poison murder trials. The fount of justice had dispensed all that it would to this strange set of conspirators. Now, their debts to society having been writ in the great book, they would begin to pay.

PART III

Le Conseguenze

> "IT'S SO MUCH OF A MYSTERY TO ME, AND ALWAYS WILL BE."
>
> —RALPH ALFONSI, SON OF STELLA AND FERDINANDO

27
THE DEBT TO SOCIETY

Just after midnight on the morning of March 31, 1941, Paul Petrillo was aroused from a deep sleep by prison guards at Rockview Prison in Bellefonte, Pennsylvania. The condemned man was calm and seemingly resigned to his fate, mumbling the litany as they shaved his head and slit his trousers for attachment of electrodes. "He sat nonchalantly in the death chamber, much as a man trying out a new desk chair in his office," reported the *Bulletin*. "His glance wandered from one part of the chair to another. Obligingly, he lifted his head to enable guards to slip the heavy leather mask over it." The mask quieted his prayer, but a clergyman standing by kept the refrain going, *in nome del Padre, del Figlio, e dello Spirito Santo,* as the executioner threw the switch that sent a lethal two thousand volts at fourteen amperes through his body. Paul's last recorded words were a final personal appeal for clemency. "I am innocent," he said, "an unwitting tool in the hands of a man well versed in magic."

The magician, Morris Bolber, remained awaiting the determination whether he, too, would be strapped into that chair. He
would still be waiting seven months later, on October 20, 1941,
when the second Petrillo was marched into the death chamber at
Rockview.

All that summer and fall, Herman Petrillo had been firing off
letters to his lawyer, to the press, and to officials. An *Inquirer*
reporter, Frank Toughill, became the conduit by which Herman
smuggled out long, rambling letters that the newspaper agreeably
splashed across its pages with reassuring headlines such as AR-
SENIC MURDER RING WORLD-WIDE IN SCOPE.

"My conscience is clear; it does not bother me," Herman told
the public. "I didn't kill anyone. I hate to rat. I never did in my
life. For this reason everybody trusts me. But what can I do if
others accuse me? Naturally I got to defend myself and come out
with the truth. I don't lie like the chief Bolber. He has been the
originator of this so-called Phila. arsenic ring. But will be better if
you will change the name to the International Poison Murder Syn-
dicate, Morris Bolber President and General Manager in the
United States." Herman was terrified of dying himself. But if he
went, he, like his cousin Paul, wanted to take Bolber down with
him.

When his time came, Herman did not go quietly into the
night. The warden at Rockview called him the "most unruly
death-house inmate in the prison's history." He was calm enough
as guards led him into the death chamber, but he froze when he
saw the heavy oaken chair. Herman began moaning loudly, struggling so hard that they had to haul his body across the room. It
took all their efforts to strap him in. Still he cried out, "I'm innocent! I want to see the governor!"

Through it all, Willie Jones, a condemned man who occupied

the cell adjoining Herman's, chanted Negro spirituals that could be plainly heard in the death chamber. Jones, the *Record* reported, "was to have walked the last mile with Petrillo, but was given a last-minute respite for a mental examination."

Paul and Herman both died without knowing the fate of their nemesis, Morris Bolber. McDevitt had held off Bolber's sentencing to ensure his continuing testimonial cooperation. It was not until January 1942 that a sentencing hearing would be convened for this egomaniacal Russian Jew whom Herman Petrillo called "President and General Manager" of the murder ring. Captain James Kelly, recently promoted head of the Homicide Bureau, testified on behalf of Bolber, describing him as a "man who worked day and night locating evidence in seventeen murders that never would have been discovered without him." For this yeoman service, Bolber was rewarded with a life sentence.

"The day cometh, and all the proud, and all those who do evil will be straw, and they will be burned to ashes," said the prophet Malachi. Portentous words for the Petrillos, but not for Louie the Rabbi. The natural instinct of any criminal is to stand mute and deny all. It takes skill, wit, and savvy to know when to cut your losses, confess, and cooperate, realizing that a negotiated deal is your last, best hope. When the ultimate test came, Bolber proved that he was the true mastermind of the arsenic murder ring, outmaneuvering even the slick Petrillos. However, he met his match in the corrections system, for Morris "Louie the Rabbi" Bolber never again saw the unbarred light of day.

Once in jail, Bolber did not cease his incessant maneuvering. He served as a model prisoner, working hard on scholarly articles that he published in obscure journals. He began filing petitions for parole as soon as he could. In 1951, his lawyer, Bernard Cohn, wrote Vincent McDevitt, seeking a supportive letter from the

famed prosecutor. "Bolber is a sick man, having had several operations while in prison," Cohn told Vince McDevitt. "His wife
divorced him. He is now 68 years of age." Even Judge Harry
McDevitt "sent a fine letter recommending commutation," Cohn
added. But Prosecutor McDevitt refused to help, more or less echoing the sentiments of a parole-board member, who snapped, "He's
lucky he didn't get the chair."

Three times Bolber filed, promising to go to Israel and start
a new life as a Hebrew teacher. He died on February 15, 1954,
while his third parole petition was pending, having spent his final
fifteen years in prison. Only the rabbi knows whether it was a real
triumph to have gained those years.

The Petrillos and Morris Bolber undoubtedly deserved what
they got (putting aside the question of whether capital punishment
is ever deserved). But what of the other defendants? McDevitt and
his team identified thirty persons who were believed to have participated in one or more murders. No one other than the Petrillos
was executed, the other death sentences being reversed on appeal
or commuted. Instead, the other participants in the Great Arsenic
Murder Ring received a widely disparate collection of punishments, ranging from decades of imprisonment to nothing at all.

Thirteen men and women besides Bolber and the Petrillos
were convicted of or pled guilty to first-degree murder. All these
convicted "murderers" suffered long sentences, including not only
such dreadful characters as Maria "the Witch" Favato, Raphael
Polselli, and Caesar Valenti but also lesser lights like Emedio Muscelli, Providenza Miccichi, Dominick Rodio, and Salvatore Sortino,
as well as relative innocents like Dominick Cassetti and Millie
Giacobbe. Several served full life terms. Even those eventually released spent not less than fourteen years in prison, gaining release
only when old or sickly. The fate of Agnes Mandiuk, the Slavic

woman whose conviction seemed to owe as much to her demeanor as to the evidence against her, was typical. She did not leave prison until December 24, 1954. The twist of fortune that dealt her a guilty verdict, rather than the acquittal won by Raymond Pace Alexander's other two clients, was a vicious one indeed. It cost her almost sixteen years of her life, from her mid-forties until she was over sixty.

Prison did not much crimp Jumbo Valenti's style, as he pursued a vendetta against Raphael Polselli, the perceived cause of his downfall. In March 1941, the *Bulletin* reported, "The lumbering, 250-pound, 6-foot, 3-inch Valenti, snarling in rage, leaped at the undersized Polselli with a prison-made knife and ripped his left eye and ear, his head, side and shoulder, as he jabbed with the blade in an attempt to reach a vital spot." Polselli recovered, but he lost an eye.

Jumbo was a model prisoner after that, jovial and good-natured. He was said to greet everyone with "Merry Christmas," no matter what the time of year. Jumbo sought parole several times, promising to return to Italy, but with no apparent success. He was destined to die in America, the land of his dreams.

The record for length of imprisonment went to the pathetic Josephine Romualdo, "the slowest," who was convicted after a summary two-day trial. Her death sentence was commuted to life imprisonment, but she was not freed until December 1958, almost twenty years after she was first arrested and jailed in April 1939.

Compared to the lengthy terms meted out to those persons sentenced for first-degree murder, the men and women who managed to cop pleas to reduced charges fared very well indeed. Grace Pirolli, who pleaded guilty to second-degree murder after her death sentence was overturned on appeal, was given credit for the two years she had already served and was immediately released on probation. Bolber's henchman, David Brandt, who had helped the master arrange multiple murders, served only two years. Most of the others in this category—Susie DiMartino, Christine Cerrone, Sophie LaVecchio, Rose Carilli—probably served short terms, though no confirmed date of release is on record. (Among this group, only Dr. Horace Perlman is known to have served an extended sentence, remaining in prison for ten years and gaining release only as a broken and disgraced man.)

Sorella Josephine Sedita, the diminutive mystic who did the job on Pietro Pirolli with the help of Rose Carina, got away with murder. She, alone among the suspects, evaded capture for years. It was not until 1945 that she walked voluntarily into Raymond Pace Alexander's office, saying she wanted to turn herself in. Because all the witnesses had dispersed (or been exterminated by the Commonwealth), and enthusiasm for her case had waned, Alexander was able to work out a favorable deal. Josephine pleaded guilty to a minor charge and spent only a year in prison. The charge—ironic in light of the circumstances—was practicing medicine without a license.

Anna Arena, widow of a Petrillo/Bolber drowning victim, and Marie Woloshyn, whose husband had been clubbed by Jumbo Valenti and then run over by Herman Petrillo, did better yet. Marie, as previously noted, went scot-free because of evidentiary problems. Charges against Anna were likewise dropped when prosecutors in Philadelphia and Cape May, New Jersey, could not decide who should handle the case. She walked, along with two other coconspirators in the case, Steve Crispino (the thug who helped pound Arena over the head with an oar) and the insurance agent Gaetano Cicinato (who had split the proceeds of the policy on Arena).

The good fortune of escaping punishment was shared, of

course, by Stella Alfonsi and Rose Carina, who were acquitted. But the participants in the cases who fared best were not the clients, but the lawyers.

Raymond Pace Alexander continued his impressive career, never losing his taste for representing the underdog. In 1948, in the midst of a busy and lucrative practice, he took on the cause of several young black men charged with murder—the so-called Trenton Six. All had been sentenced to death, but the New Jersey Supreme Court had reversed the convictions and ordered a new trial. The second trial ran for almost half a year—at the time, the longest murder trial on record. When it was over, the famed winner of lost causes had obtained an acquittal for four of the boys and life sentences for the other two.

A few years later, in 1951, Alexander was elected to the Philadelphia City Council, part of a reform movement that threw out the entrenched political machine that had dominated Philadelphia life for most of the twentieth century, and which had so rudely refused to allow him to run for judge in 1936.

Vincent McDevitt also built a solid and successful career. He left formal public service in 1947, becoming general counsel and later vice president of the Philadelphia Electric Company. He also became active in bar association work, acting as the Philadelphia Bar Association's delegate to the American Bar Association and being elected vice-chancellor in 1957.

These former adversaries, both active in Philadelphia legal circles, developed a professional friendship. When the Barristers Law Club gave a testimonial banquet for Alexander in 1951, McDevitt was there along with the other honoring guests. Despite the differences in their backgrounds, the two men had much in common. Both had risen from poverty to become prosperous and prestigious members of their community. Both were social animals who relished the company of their fellowmen, and were famed for hosting grand parties. Both were master networkers, skilled in building relationships through charm and politesse.

Neither man could entirely forget the historic arsenic murder cases, which had brought them such fame. Throughout the 1950s, while he was serving as city councilman, Alexander filed a series of parole petitions for Salvatore Sortino, characterizing him as "a drawn, tiny little man, at the end of his nearly ebbed out life." Alexander had not represented Sortino in earlier proceedings, and he had no obligation to him. The petitions were simply a good deed, something Alexander did because he felt the pathetic man had been imprisoned too long.

For several years, Alexander had worked his contacts to gather support for Sortino's parole. He had won the endorsement of Tom McBride, now the state attorney general (and formerly Herman Petrillo's lawyer). However, Alexander had not bothered to pursue Vince McDevitt, because McDevitt had adamantly refused all pleas to aid in obtaining clemency. The black lawyer was reluctant to demean himself by begging for help that he knew would not be forthcoming. But when he filed his fifth petition for Sortino in July 1957, Alexander, for some reason, changed his mind. He sent a note to McDevitt, entreating the former prosecutor to write a letter to the parole board endorsing Sortino's position.

The request sat on McDevitt's desk for seven months. He did not respond to it until February 17, 1958. But when he did, his letter said all that Alexander wished. Within weeks, Sortino was released.

"Your great letter was the turning point," Alexander wrote McDevitt with characteristic effusiveness. "My sincere thanks to you, Vince. It never would have happened until it was given the final push by that great former Assistant District Attorney, that courageous, marvelous, wonderful fellow, the Vice-Chancellor of our Bar Association. I hope I may have the great opportunity to place your name in nomination for the Chancellor of our Bar Association when that occasion presents itself."

What Alexander did not say, but everyone knew, was that he was still trying to gain appointment as a judge. He had broad support but had failed to win the endorsement of the Philadelphia Bar Association. He wanted the backing of bar leaders. Sure enough, the next year McDevitt was elected chancellor, and Alexander received his judgeship.

Alexander had a distinguished career on the bench, serving until his death in 1974, and rendering notable decisions on behalf of the poor and the oppressed. The underdog was always assured of justice in Judge Alexander's courtroom.

Philadelphia. Go along to get along. It works better than arsenic.

28
(IN)JUSTICE

I would like to report that the disparity
of results reached in the various poison widow cases was somehow
justified—by the degree of complicity of the defendant, by the hei-
nousness of the crime, or by some other measure of justice. But I
can find no basis for any such conclusion.

Reviewing the cases against the two widows—Anna Arena
and Marie Woloshyn—who were released without even a trial, it
seems that the potential proof against them was not noticeably
different from that against their peers who were convicted. Certainly there was ample evidence that both women were involved
with Bolber or the Petrillos, that they purchased extensive life insurance on their husbands in anticipation of the unblessed event,
and that their husbands were murdered in Petrillo-organized plots.

The only real distinction about the Arena and Woloshyn
cases is that the killings were by force and violence—drowning
and automobile crushing—rather than by the subtlety of poison.

This offered the widows an important legal protection, because it removed them from any suspicion of involvement in the ultimate deed. It also eliminated the one kind of evidence that no stone-walling could obscure—the damning proof of those accumulated, nondecomposing metallic deposits in vital organs. Had the cases of Anna or Marie gone to trial in Philadelphia in September or October of 1939, and had the bodies been saturated with poison, there is little doubt that these two women would have found themselves in the State Industrial Home at Muncy, if not in the big oaken chair at Rockview.

What of the eight widows and one widower who were convicted? Is there any rationale that might justify the radically different punishments—ranging from a mild two-year term to a life-destroying twenty years—given to these unfortunates? Not on the available evidence. If I had to rank these nine individuals in terms of apparent complicity, three would be at the bottom of the list, the women who seem most likely to have been the stupes and stooges whose superstitions and naïveté were exploited by the ring—Josephine Romualdo, Grace Pirolli, and Susie DiMartino. These were, by all indications, the least likely to have been guilty. Yet both Josephine and Grace were initially sent to the electric chair by juries, and all indications are that Susie probably would have fared the same had she been tried before Vince McDevitt began accepting plea bargains.

Or consider the case of Paul's shopkeeper girlfriend, Millie Giacobbe. She was probably more competent than Josephine, Grace, and Susie, but nonetheless, she seems to have been at most a passive bystander to her husband's demise. There was never any evidence that she actually administered poison or even that she made helpful arrangements (such as tying a towel on a fence to guide hit men). At most, she was somewhat aware of what might have been happening and did nothing to stop it. If true, this did not make her a nice person. But as a legal matter, a passive bystander is not a guilty conspirator. Yet Millie received a life sentence that was fully affirmed on appeal.

At the other extreme, the two widows against whom the evidence seems most overwhelming, whose *witting* involvement was attested to by multiple witnesses—Stella Alfonsi and Rose Carina—were acquitted by their peers. Anyone taking an overview of these cases would be hard-pressed to defend the jury system as a rational process for determining guilt. Rather, the cases of Stella and Rose offer valuable pointers to anyone with a mariticidal bent.

One, get a good trial lawyer. Of all the men who represented poison widows, Raymond Pace Alexander was the one who best understood how to massage the evidence for the jury so that it seemed less than entirely damning. He was a brilliant lawyer, learned in the law. But far more important, he was a commanding presence in the courtroom, able to understand the jury and to win its confidence so that his spin on the facts could be accepted as plausible (or at least within the bounds of *reasonable doubt*). There is no doubt that Alexander's skillful summations were the capstones of his trial triumphs.

Two, don't be an immigrant, at least not a swarthy, foreign-speaking one. Both Stella and Rose were native Americans who spoke perfect English and could use it to persuade the jury. The jurors were *their* peers, not those of illiterate, ill-spoken aliens like Josephine Romualdo.

Three, learn how to bat your eyes. Stella and Rose were, by all indications, the two most alluring of all the widows. Even Alexander could not save the charmless Agnes Mandiuk.

Four, don't act too forlorn. Women like Josephine Romualdo,

Grace Pirolli, and Susie DiMartino were a lot more pathetic than Stella and Rose. But pathos was not nearly as winning with the jury as the "Who me, little old me?" innocence projected by the two acquitted women. If we can deduce anything from the verdicts, it is that the juries felt the simplest women were just stupid enough to have done it, while the more enchanting ones were too smart to, or needn't have bothered.

Factors such as these, more than the evidence presented, appear to have determined the outcomes of the poison widow cases.

But is this too cynical a view? I seem to be assuming that Stella and Rose were in fact guilty, a conclusion that is difficult to resist on the basis of the archival record. And yet there never was any *absolute* proof against either one. The prosecution's case was made up of circumstantial facts, suspicious conduct, and finger-pointing by witnesses who had something to gain from cooperating. A bothersome doubt remains, which Raymond Pace Alexander so brilliantly exploited.

Was there something more to the situation, something that the printed record does not capture, that might fortify this doubt and convince us that justice was truly done? In search of the answer to this question, I tried to track down persons who were present at the trials or who knew the defendants.

None of the key participants are still alive, not Alexander or McDevitt or any of the defendants. I did, however, succeed in locating several other lawyers who worked on the cases, including one lawyer who represented the ringleader, Herman Petrillo; one who represented one of the naive dupes, Grace Pirolli; and two lawyers who worked as cocounsel with Alexander, one from the Mandiuk case and one from the case of Rose Carina. To each of them, I put the question "Do you think your client was guilty or not?" The clients were all long dead and forgotten, so the answer could do no harm. No legal ethic precluded a forthright response, particularly because I made it clear that the answer would be, if they wished, off the record, to be used only as unattributed background.

x x x

Milton Leidner, the lawyer for Herman Petrillo in the very first trial, is no longer actively practicing, but he still maintains an office, to which he goes most mornings. He is alert and friendly when I meet him there, ready to tell whatever he remembers. Without prompting, he digs out his old files on the matter and gives them to me to keep. Maybe, he implies, they can do me more good than they did him.

Leidner has no affection for his opponent in the case, Vince McDevitt, who he believes treated him badly. "It was always, 'You Jews want this, and you Jews want that,'" Leidner says with a sneer to match the one he recalls. But Herman's old lawyer has no hesitancy in admitting that McDevitt was on the right side of the case.

"Petrillo was guilty," Leidner concedes. "At first I thought he was innocent. He told me the wife, Stella, did it, and I believed it. But there were too many fingers pointing to him. The evidence was overwhelming."

x x x

The lawyers who represented the widows, however, had different views.

The outer office of Michael Marchesano, lawyer for Grace Pirolli, is cluttered, looking more like a set for a newspaper city room than a law office. As I give my name to the receptionist, a lively man in the background calls out, "Mr. Cooper? Come back here." He leads me into his equally cluttered office. I have barely sat down when he leaps to the subject. I have to hold him back while I fish out my tape recorder. Then he is off, telling his story. All the time, he is smiling, jumping up to walk around the room or to shift his seat from a chair to the couch and back again. He is very informal, very friendly, not at all the eighty-year-old man, but a boy relishing the story of his first triumph, not the least intimidated by his age, of which he seems only barely aware.

"There is absolutely not the slightest doubt in my mind that my woman was one hundred percent innocent," Marchesano says, "one hundred percent—no, not the slightest doubt. Grace was an immigrant peasant woman. Imagine, she had a chance to have John Patrick Walsh and Harry Polish. They were appointed to defend her. They were known as top lawyers. Instead, she chooses me, a twenty-eight-year-old, three years out of law school, because I was her countryman. I could speak Italian; I could talk to her.

"My mother was an 'educated woman' Italian-style. In the Italian community in the area, she was sort of like a leader, a wise person. People like Grace would come to our home and she would write letters for them to the old country, because the people couldn't write. When they came in, they would kneel down and kiss my mother's hand. They had that mentality. I'm sure that was one of the reasons she wanted me; she figured I was the son of *Julia,* my mother. As my mother would say, they believe in *fatturas;* they believe in this kind of business, that someone could put the evil eye on you.

"We were up against terrible prejudice because of all the publicity about these 'arsenic widows.' To give you an idea, on the voir dire I asked the jurors, 'Assuming that a man died of arsenic poisoning, is it possible that his wife could be innocent, not know anything about it?' The judge said it was a crazy question. Anyway, along comes a juror and says, 'No way, she's got to know something—she's the wife.' Three separate jurors said that the wife could not be innocent if her husband died of arsenic poisoning; that's the way the hysteria was.

"The case they put on was so outrageous. They had a witness who testified that, at her husband's bedside, Grace said, 'I swear on the grave of my mother.' Grace's mother was still alive then! It couldn't have been true.

"Grace didn't really understand what was going on. She spent eleven hundred dollars for a funeral, to buy the best casket, a very airtight box, and when they did the autopsy, they had a body that was perfectly preserved. Does that make sense?

"Later, when I took the appeal, somebody got to Grace and said that they could fix it. He wanted some money from her, I think seventy-five or a hundred dollars. This guy was going to straighten up with the state supreme court judge, Maxey, and so forth, and get the case fixed. She paid him. He guaranteed he would get the case thrown out. After we won, Grace said to me, 'You know, I really appreciate what you did for me and everything, but it cost me seventy-five dollars to get the case fixed up.'

"By the time the case came back from appeal, Grace had been sitting in jail a year and a half. The district attorney says to me, 'We're going ahead with a new trial.' I said, 'You have nothing. How can you possibly retry her case?' But the DA, a fellow named Ephraim Lipshutz, said if I pled her guilty to second-degree murder, he'd let her go right away. The sentence would be for time served. I was all for waiting for a trial. But Grace said to me, 'If they want me to confess I killed Jesus Christ, and I'll get out of here now, I'll do it.' I said, 'I personally feel you should try to vindicate yourself; you know you didn't do it.' But she said she couldn't stand another day. So I pled her guilty to second-degree murder and she walked out the next day. She walked home."

Marchesano's grin and his spirit are infectious. "If you write a book, and there is a movie, I want to be played by Woody Allen," he says, suggesting he was a bewildered little schlemiel, not a young Robert Redford. If you believe him, and it's difficult not to, the initial conviction of Grace Pirolli was a gross miscarriage of justice. But if you believe him, you also have to wonder about Josephine Romualdo. She was tried only a week apart from Grace, also in a two-day trial and with similar evidence, and initially received the same death sentence. But no one fought on for Josephine. Her lawyer did not even pursue an appeal in her case, substituting instead a clemency petition that gave her the privilege of living in the State Industrial Home for twenty years.

You have to wonder not only about Josephine but about almost all the poison widows.

x x x

Louis Lipschitz, cocounsel for Rose Carina, is also pleased to speak with me. His office is in the same building as Michael Marchesano's. Both men have been feisty, antiestablishment criminal-defense lawyers all their careers. Both are still active in their practices, if somewhat slowed down.* But Lipschitz is more soft-spoken, more courtly, slightly older at eighty-seven. He insists on having our interview over lunch at his lawyers' club—a club where, he notes, Raymond Pace Alexander would not have been admitted back then.

*Mr. Lipschitz has since died.

"Alexander and his wife, Sadie, became my good friends. I liked him very much. Raymond was very smart and articulate. He was a handsome light-skinned man. He was also very charming and knew how to work his charm—the type who was always coming up to you, putting his arm around you, and saying what a great job you were doing for your clients. In the courtroom, he was an exhibitionist. If he made an objection, he did not just interpose it; he made a speech about how opposing counsel was abusing the system or him, something like 'I don't know why counsel has made that objection, when he knows it is improper and unfounded.'

"He worked to get appointments for blacks in capital cases, in part because of the publicity. He always had his eye on publicity and knew the value of it. In the *Carina* case, I did most of the law, wrote memos, planned examinations, prepared voir dire, watched the courtroom, and kept an eye on the prosecutor, but Alexander tried the case. I did some witnesses, but only the ones whose testimony would not be attractive to the newspapers.

"Rose Carina was quiet, unassuming. The 'Kiss of Death' label was concocted by some newspaper reporter or some half-assed policeman who was not Italian. She made a good appearance and won the sympathy of the jury. The Petrillos were obnoxious know-it-alls who made a bad impression. Rose was very different from them. She was very articulate, much nicer than my average client.

"I never pressed her regarding her previous husbands because that might have caused her to lose confidence in me, make her think that I did not believe her. No, I have learned you don't call attention to the weaknesses or mortal sins of your clients. Now whose side is he on? would be the first thought.

"But I find out what I need to. When I have a fellow who

says to me, 'Why do you ask me all these questions?' I say, 'I want to know more about you.' If he says, 'You have no right to know any more,' I say, 'Do me a favor, get yourself another lawyer.'

"I said to Rose, 'You tell me the truth. Once I get the feeling you are not telling me the truth, I'll tell you.' She insisted on her innocence, said she was being framed. She never wavered.

"I asked her if she was guilty. She said, 'No.'

"I pushed her: 'Are you going to stick to it?' She said, 'Yes, I'm not going to make any deals.'

"I did not doubt her. I thought she was innocent. My wife thought so, too."

If you believe Louis Lipschitz, you can believe a fair measure of justice was handed out in the Rose Carina case.

x x x

Frank Carano was the lawyer to whom Agnes Mandiuk first went, on the recommendation of a law school classmate who knew Agnes's son. A stocky, mild-mannered eighty-three-year-old who still goes to his office daily, Carano seems happy to talk with me and reminisce about his "considerable recollections of the case." His place is well furnished, sedate, prosperous-looking. It is not the office of a plucky criminal practitioner, but of a successful civil lawyer with a specialty in estates and wills, a man of whom a colleague comments, "He represents every cautious Italian in Philadelphia." Carano is not now and never was a criminal lawyer or even a trial lawyer. He is the first to admit that the courtroom was not his milieu and that he welcomed it when the family brought in Raymond Pace Alexander.

"I did a lot of the investigative part. We picked the jury together, of course. But Alexander carried the ball. I questioned some of our witnesses. He did all the cross-examining of the prosecution witnesses.

"Agnes Mandiuk was a very heavyset woman, wore very thick glasses, as I recall. And she had a lot of growth—hair—on her face. When she was in prison, she was always asking for a razor to shave off the growth of her beard. She had two children, a son and a daughter. The daughter was very cooperative, spent a lot of time with the mother and with us. We got most of our information from her."

I show Carano the picture of the Mandiuks sitting on the stoop with their dog. It does not seem familiar to him.

"She gave the impression of being extremely strong. I have a mental picture of her face now, and her body. She was built sturdily and on the heavy side. I would guess she was at least one eighty, one ninety pounds. When I met her, she was at least thirty pounds heavier than that picture. She was, as I recall, not a native-born American, and I think she had an accent, too. I think she was Polish. She had the features of a Slav, heavyset.

"But she was a dupe of these leaders. They ingratiated themselves. I think this was all for life insurance; they collected on the life insurance of their husbands.

"My only explanation why Alexander lost this case when he won the others is that it was a tougher jury. I think the evidence was pretty much the same. It was a pattern. These leaders would get these women; I think they furnished the arsenic, too."

I ask Carano, "Was she the kind of woman, in terms of her personality, who would fall for the Morris Bolbers and Herman Petrillos of this world?"

His answer is firm. "Definitely."

"So she was a patsy?"

"Yes."

"Did she actually feed *la fattura* to her husband?"

Carano becomes ambivalent. When I point out that the state's witnesses said she admitted doing so, he offers no denial, preferring not to comment. "Okay, assuming she administered the stuff, did she know it was poison?" Carano has no new insight to offer on that ultimate question and, again, no comment. He offers none of the exculpatory excuses or protestations of innocence that characterized Marchesano's and Lipschitz's statements.

Listening to this cautious, measured civil lawyer, you can believe the Mandiuk verdict not unreasonable. It was a tough call, but the jury was there, so to speak.

x x x

Interviewing these lawyers, a not-unsurprising pattern emerges. Those who won acquittals believe in the validity of their victories, while those who lost believe their clients were guilty. No revelation there. How much finer the world is for Louis Lipschitz when he can believe his client was truly innocent, rather than that he had tricked the system to free a spousal scourge. How could Frank Carano, knowing Agnes Mandiuk suffered in prison for almost two decades, think of her as innocent all that time? It would be too heavy a cross to bear.

The same tendency emerges in Raymond Pace Alexander's memoirs. In an autobiographical sketch written when he was being honored by the Philadelphia Bar Association, he speaks proudly of the Stella Alfonsi and Rose Carina cases. There is no mention of Agnes Mandiuk. It is as if her case never happened. Vincent McDevitt's papers show the same self-protective proclivity. He wrote a lengthy memoir on the arsenic murder ring, in which he details the nefarious deeds, including, at length, those of

Stella Alfonsi and Rose Carina. After much talk of prosecution successes, he concludes, "The case is closed. All of the leaders have been convicted and justice has had its sway." The reader would never know that Stella and Rose were acquitted.

Selective memory, it's a wonderful thing. But it doesn't really tell us much about the defendants' actual guilt or innocence. The question remains: Is it possible that Stella Alfonsi and even Rose Carina were innocent dupes of the Petrillo cousins, unaware of the true nature of what was happening? Could they really have been framed?

29

THE INIQUITIES OF THE MOTHERS

Guilty or not guilty? Who might know best?

I sit in the living room of a mild-mannered, slightly over-weight sixty-seven-year-old man. He is Leo Alfonsi, the younger son of Stella. The house is in Bristol, Pennsylvania, only a few blocks from where his mother grew up. Leo seems pleased to see me, happy to talk about his family background. He remembers well the time after his father died, when his mother was arrested and imprisoned for a year.

"The family never talked about the case. The only thing I remember is that my father's funeral was held at my uncle Vittorio's house down the street. My father was laid out in the living room. Ralph and I were sent down to the basement. We were staying and sleeping there, because my mother was in jail. They brought her in handcuffs to see the body at the funeral. She was crying and screaming."

He was ten years old at the time. Shuttled from foster home to foster home for the first months of their mother's imprisonment, Leo and his brother were eventually taken in by their maternal grandmother, Christina Liberti, and moved back to Bristol. It was good to get away from Passyunk. In South Philadelphia, while the boys were in foster care, other children would call them "arsenic kids" and mock them.

Though Leo has tried to put the matter behind him, it persists. Driving back from the country with a friend about ten years ago, the friend volunteered, "You really don't know if your mother did it. You really don't." He remembers being hurt at the time. "I wouldn't have had this discussion with you ten years ago," he admits to me. But he feels he has come to terms with it now. He has managed to build a decent life—good wife, kids, steady job. He is retired now, from a long-term job at U.S. Steel. He is ready to talk.

"After my mother was released from jail, she came to Bristol for a while. She had no idea what to do with her life. She didn't want to go back to Philadelphia, so she moved to New York. She had an apartment on East 103rd Street and found some work doing radio commercials. She spoke perfect high Italian that she learned from the nuns and an excellent English, so she could do commercials on the Italian stations like WBNX. After a while, I went up there to live with her. She took up for a while with an announcer on the station. Then she married a younger man, an elevator mechanic who made a good living."

Leo was sixteen or seventeen at the time. He remained in the small apartment where he had lived with his mother, while she move out to the mechanic's place. He was on his own after that. Stella's second marriage broke up quickly, and she moved back to her parents' home in Bristol.

"This was in 1950–1951. She met another man, an older man named Jimmy Speranza, who lived in the neighborhood, and she married him. They moved into an apartment upstairs from my grandparents. That didn't last too long, either. She took up with many men after that. She moved down to Asbury Park for a year or two with another guy. He ran a bar and bowling alley. But it never lasted.

"She was a prima donna, like a spoiled kid. Always wanted to be the center of attention. She always needed a man to take care of her. Like a wayward child, she would befriend someone, go live with him, and then it would break up. Even in later years, when I was married myself and had a family, she would always call me to come get her if she had a problem. But she was interesting. I always told her, 'I wish I had enough money to bring you here to live with me, so I could watch you all the time, just to see what you would do.'

"She was very high-strung, and a heavy smoker. Sometimes she would call me up from Philadelphia or some other place twenty miles away and say, 'You have to come get me.' I would go, and find that she just wanted me to get her cigarettes. She always needed someone to take care of her, always seemed distraught. Eventually she had a breakdown and was put in the hospital. She was in and out of the hospital for depression many times. I blamed myself for not looking after her better. I got her on SSI, got assistance for her because of mental disability even before she was eligible for Social Security. She died about ten years ago."

I ask gingerly, "What do you think? Could she have done it?"

Leo is not put off by the question. He wants an answer himself. "Knowing her, she couldn't have done anything malicious. She was very friendly, wanted everyone to like her. But she was very suggestible. It's conceivable that she went along with Petrillo, that she was deceived into going along without really realizing what she was doing. Particularly if Petrillo was a charmer, a ladies' man.

"You should talk to my brother, Ralph. I was always the good kid. I never got into any trouble. Ralph was a wild kid. But his wife has shaped him up. He has a nice family now. He was older. He was at the trial. I bet he'd talk to you. There's no one else left who knows anything about it."

Ralph Alfonsi lives in Levittown, Pennsylvania, only a few miles away. The postwar prototype development has aged well, full of established trees and shrubs, making it into a cozy old neighborhood. There is a new Buick and a pickup truck in the driveway. Ralph greets me at the door. We sit down at the table in the clean, modern kitchen. It is a beautiful May morning and sunlight streams into the room. Ralph is as promised—tattooed, bolder, and gruffer in manner than his younger brother. I am wary. But as I prop the tape recorder up on the table in front of him, he starts before I can even ask a question.

"You know, I went to see Raymond Pace Alexander. It was back when I got out of the service, in 1946, when I was nineteen years old. I told him I had heard a lot of rumors about what happened with my mother, and I wanted him to tell me the truth. I knew he had been her lawyer. But he said to me, 'You're too young. Come back in a few years and I'll tell you.' I never got around to going back.

"When we were kids, they never told us anything about what happened. When my mother was in jail, they told us she was being held as a material witness; that's all they ever said. I never knew how my father died; they never told us as kids. I remember visiting my father in the hospital before he died. He was squeezing some balls in his hands. I asked him why he was doing that, but he couldn't explain. I wanted one of the balls, but he wouldn't give it to me. No one told me why he was there. They just said he was sick, that's all. You know *sick—sick* can mean anything. To a ten-year-old, sick is sick. That covers the whole thing. Nobody ever told anybody more than they had to know, anyhow, in those days.

"My parents used to fight all the time. He used to beat on my mother a lot. He'd be pushing and shoving most of the time. She'd be crying, hollering out. I used to try to help her when I was little. I remember I used to bite him on his calves, and he'd kick at me; he'd do it a few times, until I got pretty badly beaten up from him. I was trying to bite him so he would get away from her. Apparently it didn't work out. . . ." His voice trails off for a moment.

"I was very upset about the way we were treated when my mother went to jail. We were turned over to Catholic foster care. They placed Leo and me with families. But the families always had other children. We were outcasts. Often they didn't even let us sit down and eat with the rest of the family. I remember Leo always holding me. We held each other and tried to help each other out. After a while, Leo and me went to my grandmother's. But I was trouble. I cut school all the time. Eventually, they sent me to a *home,* which was really a place for incorrigibles in Phoenixville.

"When my mother came out of jail, she visited me on one visiting day; I think it was the first weekend of the month. Every time she came to see me, she would lie, because I'd say to her, 'Please get me out of this place,' and she'd say she would. She wouldn't come the next month. She would be there a couple of months later, and then she'd say the same thing over to me again, 'It won't be long that I'll be coming home again,' blah, blah, blah.

By that time, I knew that she didn't care whether I was going to go home or not."

Ralph's wife, Connie, who has been out shopping, joins us. She is a lovely woman, but when she makes us coffee and offers me some Italian cookies dusted with white powder, my reaction must tell her something. "It's powdered sugar," she says with a smile. As I eat apprehensively, Connie offers a memory of Stella.

"I first met her in 1951, when I married Ralph. She had just married Jimmy Speranza. She seemed all right then. But in 1956 someone got out of prison and Stella went crazy. She was terrified that he was going to come after her. I was living in Sunnybrook at the time and she was living at my house. It was a Sunday morning; the *Inquirer* came. And it showed someone who'd gotten twenty years to life and he was getting out. I think it maybe was Petrillo. [It was probably Johnny Cacopardo, whose parole period ended about that time.] She went completely berserk. In fact, two days later Ralph's grandmother was so scared Stella had flipped, she hid the knives and everything. After that, Stella was never right again. She was in and out of institutions for the rest of her life, Norristown State Hospital and others."

Ralph resumes: "You talk about Petrillo. The only thing that stuck in my mind about my mother, the thing that kept sticking in my mind, was that I followed her one time up Belgrade to Allegheny. We lived on Ann Street, and if you walked up Belgrade to Allegheny, that was the big street where you didn't go without your parents or someone. That was a no-no. I followed her there and she got into Herman Petrillo's car. I was about ten years old, eleven, I remember. I told my father the story, and my mother denied it happened. In fact, she said I was making it up, so my father came down on me. [He laughs.] I remember he used to beat the heck out of me. Sometimes there was a reason, but this time it stuck in my mind, because I thought, Why am I getting hit for telling the truth?

"She was dressed like she was going to somebody's wedding or somebody's . . . a gala event. That's what made me follow her to begin with. You know, she was a pretty woman. She never got dressed up that I can remember, going out anywhere. That is what gave me the curiosity, even as a ten-year-old, to find out what she was doing, where she was going. Not that I was thinking she might be going out with somebody, but I was thinking, Hey, she's going somewhere nice that I want to be going to. I'm wondering why she's not taking me with her.

"I can see her now. She had a wide-brim hat, like an Easter bonnet. I think there was some kind of a fur involved. It wasn't cold out then. It had to be sometime in the spring or the summer. I wasn't wearing a coat or anything myself. But she was wearing like a fox stole, a colorful print dress. I guess I was having the same kind of a feeling toward her as a jealous husband might have toward his wife.

"Petrillo's car was a new model, because I saw some older models on the street and this was a more fashionable car, a newer car than you would usually see on the street. I remember that. It was black, or it could have been dark green. I'm pretty sure it was black. Because of the shine. It was a square-built job. It was a wide avenue. She walked across the street, walked around the car to the passenger side. There was hardly any traffic that time of day. She got in the front with him. I remember distinctly, as they were pulling away, I can remember his head and her head in the same line."

I don't even have to ask Ralph the critical question. He segues right to it.

"You know I'm her son. But I'm sitting here thinking about

it, and I think she did it. I have thought that for years. And now
I believe that I was right all the time. She was running on my
father, and that makes her guilty in my mind."

"You mean the time she got in his car when you were a kid?"
Connie asks.

"Yeah, that's what happened."

"He told me that years ago," Connie confirms.

"Let me tell you something," Ralph continues. "Your eyes
never lie. One thing your eyes never do, they never lie. They can
be tricked, but they never lie. It was afternoon, early afternoon,
and I remember her. I couldn't cross Allegheny Avenue, but I can
remember her going across Allegheny Avenue into his car. He
came around and opened the door for her in fact."

"You knew him because he was at your house?" offers Connie.

"Yeah, I knew him because I had seen him at the club and
he was at the house. I mean, he was 'Mr. Petrillo' to us when we
were kids."

"How do you feel about what we were just talking about,
about your mother?" I ask.

"How do I feel? What's done is done. There's no possible
way you can bring it back. So why even think about it at all? Go
on with your life. I'm sorry I didn't have the education or the
wherefore of having an idol to look up to when I was young. I'm
sorry about that. But what I had and the way I am is what it is.
And I can do as much apologizing as I want. I can't bring any of
that back. I can't apologize for anyone else. I can't tell my mother
and father that they were wrong. I don't know the circumstances.

"The one thing that I do know is what my eyes saw. And I
told you. From the point I saw that man, and then after my father
died and I started listening to different stories, things kept coming

back to me about her going into that car. It might have been, you
know, an innocent thing, but no, it wasn't. Me, I got in my mind
that my father died because of that man.

"I been thinking that for quite a number of years. From the
first time I heard the story about how my father died. You ask me
now when that was, I don't know. It's been bits and pieces all my
life. A bit here, a piece there. And it isn't that it was being told
exactly to me. It was what I was picking up from background,
from people around me. You know what I'm saying? And when I
remembered something, I didn't come out then and tell anybody,
'I know this and I know that.' I didn't say any of that. Not until
now."

x x x

Grace Buttacavoli and her son Joe sit in the living room of her
garden apartment in suburban New Jersey. She is the older daughter of Rose "Kiss of Death" Carina, the girl who was abandoned
by Rose in Hammonton as a child and then kidnapped and brought
back to Philadelphia when she was fifteen. Grace lived in South
Philadelphia, near Passyunk, all through the 1930s and was in
touch with her mother. Unlike Leo and Ralph Alfonsi, who were
only boys of ten and eleven when their father died, Grace was a
young married woman during the time of her mother's saga.

At first Grace did not want to speak with me. "No one did,"
son Joe tells me. I had sent out letters to dozens of Carinas and
Steas and related people in Pennsylvania, New Jersey, and elsewhere, but none to Buttacavolis, because I had no leads with that
name. One recipient of my letter, a woman coincidently named
Rose Carina, knew Grace and passed it on to her, and she asked
Joe for advice. Joe knew all about it. He had talked to some other

relatives in Hammonton. "They all said, 'Let a sleeping dog lie,' "
Joe says. But he was interested and prevailed upon his mother to
cooperate.

Grace is a small, thin, attractive gray-haired woman of
eighty-one. She smiles as I give her the bunch of flowers I have
brought, and she offers me a piece of homemade pineapple cheesecake. "This is just cheesecake, nothing in it," she says with a
knowing laugh before I can say anything.

We talk a bit of the recent death of Rita, the younger daughter of Rose, who was dragged around with her mother for those
months in the spring of 1939 when Rose was evading arrest. Rita
married an engineer and moved to California, where she raised
her family of three children. Grace shows me a picture of a handsome well-dressed couple.

Grace launches into her story without any prodding. We go
over her Cinderella childhood. "I was just a kid when she left us.
I don't remember much. My brother John tells me she used to tie
us up in the cellar when she had to go somewhere. My father
couldn't handle the three of us. He sent me to live with his aunt.
She made me work for everything. I worked in the fields picking.
I had a hard life. Before I could get something to eat, I had to clean
the boarders' rooms in the house. I even worked across the street
in the candy shop, but I never saw the money. I never saw my
brothers. I didn't even know where they were.

"Rose came back to Hammonton only once or twice. She
came to see her sister. When she came, she had a man with her.
She *always* had a man with her. She was with a man when she
was picked up by the FBI. She went from man to man all her life.

"Dominic Carina was her husband when I came to Philadelphia. He was a nice-looking man. He treated me good. I don't
know what he thought of the way Rose always had men in the

house, serving them beer, carrying on. She never had any girl-friends around. Just guys. She was always home entertaining, cooking. She was a great cook. You'd come to the house, and just like nothing, she'd have a tremendous dinner for everyone. Later on, when she was called the 'Kiss of Death,' my friends were surprised. 'She was a good woman,' they said. 'She would do anything for you.' That's the way they saw her.

"But she was always ready to move out. One time, after the war, I remember she was living with a nice guy. But she left. 'Where you going?' I used to say.

"When I got married, I didn't invite her to the wedding. Stea, who she was living with, was a nice guy. He picked me up in a limousine and drove me and my fiancé to the wedding. It was in 1936. Her sisters were invited but not her. Rose was burned up.

"I didn't invite her because I didn't have any love for her, because of the life she gave me. One time she came after me with a knife. I had been hiding some of my pay in a hollowed-out powder puff that I kept in an old Whitman's Sampler candy box, the kind with a little key that you could save for use as a jewelry box. When I came home one day, I saw Rose sitting in the window staring out, waiting for me.

" 'You've been holding out, stealing money from me,' she yelled, and she pulled out a knife. 'Don't you ever do that again,' she said. Rose called up the factory after that, so she would know the exact amount of my pay and get it all.

"That's when I moved out of her house. But she wouldn't let me take my clothes. I had to take her to court. The judge gave me a guy to go with me, and I went and got the clothes. She wasn't like a mother to me. She never did anything for me. She ruined my whole life."

Joe adds, "I always heard you didn't invite her because she

had such a bad reputation. Even back then, before there was talk about the 'Kiss of Death,' there were apparently rumors around."

"After the trial," Grace continues, "Rose and Rita went to live in the low-income projects at Twenty-ninth and Snyder. She never got married again. But she was always with a man. She was with a guy named Mr. Schwartz, who made Joe a jacket. She lived with a guy in Baltimore and she left him. Later she had a restaurant out at Sixty-ninth Street, a luncheonette out at the end of the subway. Rita worked as a waitress. Rose either owned the restaurant or was a cook in it. That's where Rita met her husband, Danny. He was completely different from the rest of the family, English, Dutch, Irish, something. He was a good guy. For what she went through, she's lucky his family liked her.

"Rose died in 1954, of cancer. Near the end of her life, she lived with a man and his two children. Rose told him she was twenty years younger than she was. He was a salesman in cars. When she died, they said, 'Don't tell Grace that her mother died, because that man buried her, and he never knew that she had three other children. He would have passed out.'

"Back when she was arrested, Rose sent a message for me. I went to see her. I helped her out. My husband got her that lawyer, the colored lawyer. They had me testify at her trial. They asked me to tell about my relationship with my mother, like 'What did your mother do to you?' I just told them the story about Rose leaving us on the couch and going off to buy macaroni. I remember the Stea girl trying to trip Rose when she walked up the court aisle. But the Steas all said I was a wonderful girl, I had nothing to do with it. Nobody has ever bothered me about it."

It is time for my question. "Do you think your mother was guilty?"

"I don't know. Why would she do such a thing? Why did she get in with so many people? I used to go with her, over on Passyunk Avenue to Petrillo's place, in the back. There was another woman there who was involved; she had a store that sold *maderi,* linens and ladies' stuff. That was on Passyunk Avenue, too, close by the tailor shop. I met some of those other women they say were involved. They were no prize bags, I'll tell you.

"Rose used to go over to Petrillo's place a lot. She used to go there all the time, and they'd talk, you know. This was after Dominic Carina was dead. I think I was married. I used to go there, too. I used to know Petrillo. I'd say hello to him on Passyunk Avenue. He was a little short guy. Looked like a good guy.

"Rose wasn't working at this time. I don't know what she lived on. Maybe she was getting extra money from somebody. I don't know. Maybe she was collecting a lot of money, what do I know?"

I mention my conversation with Louis Lipschitz, telling Grace, "I talked to Rose's other lawyer, a Jewish lawyer. I went over the whole case with him. He told me he thought she was innocent."

This is too much for her. She scoffs. "I don't believe it! You believe it? I don't believe it. If I didn't do anything, why would I want to run away? Uh? Why would I run away? I remember when the story was first in the paper about these poison murders, in 1938. I saw her get the paper; I knew she was nervous about something. She never would tell me. She never would tell me anything. But that's when she left town, right after that."

"Maybe because she was afraid," offers Joe.

"Well, then, after she was acquitted, why didn't she lead a good life? Why did she run around with all those guys? She was not innocent. There's a lot of things that I see, and I can figure things out. If she was innocent, and she never killed anybody, why did she have to do all the things she did?

"Everybody used to kid my husband, joking, about being poisoned. But I told him, 'You got a good one in me. I'm not like my mother; she had every Tom, Dick, and Harry.'

"You say she's innocent? She couldn't be innocent. She had to have something to do with it, a little bit, I don't care what the lawyer told you."

x x x

Such are the views of the descendants of Stella Alfonsi and Rose Carina. No one can lightly dismiss the judgments of children who are willing to conclude that their mother was, indeed, guilty of poisoning their father. Even without evidence that would stand up in a court of law, their overall feeling and sense of the situation is a powerful and telling testament. Still, the nagging doubt remains. The only persons who really knew what happened are the defendants themselves and their victims, all of whose lips have been sealed by the grave.

Guilty or not guilty? The Passyunk Avenue of the Petrillos and the widows is still there, serving a community that has changed far less than one might expect in the more than half a century since the days of the Great Arsenic Murder Ring. Many of the shops that served Rose Carina, Stella Alfonsi, and their peers remain under the same family ownership—Arnold Costantini's men's shop at number 1837 (just across from where Paul's tailor shop was), Pete Monastero's Barber Shop at number 1722, Nick Tascione's Tailoring at number 1614. Many that have changed ownership still cater to the same trade—Fiori's Pizza at number 1651 (now renamed Ozzie's Trattoria), Mancuso's cheese shop at number 1902 ("the only homemade ricotta in the East, except maybe New York"), even the Little Grill (now renamed Scrappy's) on Thirteenth Street, where Johnny Cacopardo refused to "powder" the drink of Tony Zambino. There is no shortage of old-timers, whiling the time away in such hangouts as Uncle Phil's sandwich shop (at number 1824), who were around when these notorious events occurred. One can even find old women sitting around in straight-backed chairs with their stockings rolled down around their ankles—apparitions of Maria Favato.

An aura of *la fattura* and *il mal'occhio* yet lurks. Perhaps someday the powers of this witchcraft will put us in touch with the truth. Until then, we can only wonder about other men of Passyunk who died of heart conditions, with the odor of garlic on their breath.

APPENDIX A:

VICTIMS

Victims are listed chronologically by date of death.

1. *Dominic Carina,* died 9/26/31: Second husband of Rose "Kiss of Death" Carina, he suddenly took ill and died. No other information available. No charges brought.

2. *Joseph Arena,* died 6/30/32: first victim of the Paul Petrillo/ Morris Bolber conspiracy; drowned by Herman Petrillo at the Jersey shore with the assistance of Dominick Rodio and Steve Crispino. Dominick Rodio convicted of first-degree murder in Cape May, New Jersey. The facts of this murder were also raised in the prosecutions of both Petrillos and helped convict them.

3. *Luigi LaVecchio,* died 8/9/32: first poisoning victim; died of arsenic and antimony furnished by Morris Bolber and administered by Paul Petrillo, possibly with the assistance of the victim's wife, Sophie. Paul Petrillo pled guilty to first-degree murder and was executed. Sophie LaVecchio pled guilty to second-degree murder and was sentenced to imprisonment for ten to twenty years.

4. *Antonio Giacobbe,* died 4/2/33: died of arsenic furnished by Morris Bolber and administered by Paul Petrillo, possibly with the assistance or acquiescence of the victim's wife, Camella (Millie).

Millie Giacobbe was convicted of the murder and sentenced to life imprisonment.

5. *Prospero Lisi*, died 6/13/33: Third husband of Rose Carina, he suddenly took ill and died within months after marrying her. No charges brought.

6. *Ralph (Rafael) Caruso*, died 7/1/34: vagrant "befriended" by Herman Petrillo, who then drowned him in the Schuylkill River with the assistance of Salvatore Sortino. Herman was convicted of first-degree murder and executed. Sortino pled guilty to first-degree murder and was sentenced to life. Christine Cerrone, who provided housing for the victim and was named as beneficiary of some of his life insurance, pled guilty to second-degree murder and was sentenced to imprisonment for two to ten years.

7. *John Woloshyn*, died 1/3/35: killed with a lead pipe and hit-and-run assault by Caesar Valenti and Herman Petrillo, possibly assisted by the victim's wife, Marie. No charges brought.

8. *Romaine Mandiuk*, died 2/22/35: died of poison probably obtained by David Brandt from Morris Bolber and possibly administered with the assistance of the victim's wife, Agnes. Bolber pled guilty to first-degree murder and was sentenced to life imprisonment. Agnes was convicted of first-degree murder and also sentenced to life imprisonment.

9. *Pietro Pirolli*, died 4/21/35: died of arsenic administered by Josephine Sedita and Rose Carina, with the possible assistance or acquiescence of the victim's wife, Grace. Grace was found guilty of first-degree murder and sentenced to death, but the conviction was reversed on appeal. She then pled guilty to second-degree murder and was sentenced to imprisonment for two to ten years but

was released immediately for time served. No charges were brought against Rose Carina or Josephine Sedita for Pirolli's death.

10. *Charles Ingrao,* died 8/14/35: common-law husband of Maria Favato; killed with arsenic obtained from Herman Petrillo and administered by Favato, Raphael Polselli, and Caesar Valenti. Favato, Polselli, and Valenti all pled guilty to first-degree murder and were given life imprisonment.

11. *Lena Winkleman,* died 2/9/36: mother-in-law of Joseph Swartz; died of poison obtained from Morris Bolber and probably administered by Swartz. Swartz's first trial was stopped when he was declared temporarily insane. He was later retried and convicted of first-degree murder, but he died in prison before sentence could be imposed.

12. *Peter (Pietro) Stea,* died 6/29/36: fourth husband (de facto) of Rose Carina; apparently died of antimony poisoning. Rose was tried but acquitted. No one else was ever prosecuted in connection with the death.

13. *Jennie Pino,* died 11/11/36: died of poison obtained from Morris Bolber and administered by David Brandt with the assistance of Dr. Horace Perlman and the victim's husband, Thomas, who died before charges could ever be brought. David Brandt and Horace Perlman both pled guilty to second-degree murder. Brandt was sentenced to imprisonment for two to twenty years and Perlman for ten to twenty years.

14. *Antonio Romualdo,* died 11/13/36: died of poison obtained from Herman Petrillo and probably administered by Maria Favato, with the possible assistance of the victim's wife, Josephine. The wife was convicted of first-degree murder and sentenced to death, but the sentence was commuted to life imprisonment.

15. *Molly Starace,* died 12/17/36: girlfriend of John Cacopardo; shot to death in a scuffle involving Paul Petrillo. Cacopardo was convicted of second-degree murder in New York and sentenced to imprisonment for thirty years to life. He failed in his attempts to obtain early release by cooperating in the poison murder prosecutions and eventually served fifteen years before winning parole in 1953.

16. *Guiseppi DiMartino,* died 2/7/37: died of poison obtained from Herman Petrillo and administered by Maria Favato and Raphael Polselli, with the possible assistance of the victim's wife, Susie, and her boyfriend, Emedio Muscelli. Maria Favato pled guilty to this murder, among others. Muscelli was convicted of first-degree murder and sentenced to life imprisonment. Susie pled guilty to second-degree murder and was sentenced to imprisonment for three to twenty years.

17. *Jennie Cassetti,* died 6/11/38: died of poison obtained from Morris Bolber and administered by her husband, Dominick, with the possible assistance of Providenza Miccichi. The husband and Miccichi both pled guilty to first-degree murder and were sentenced to life imprisonment.

18. *Philip Ingrao,* died 6/25/38: stepson of Maria Favato; died of poison obtained from Herman Petrillo and administered by Favato and Raphael Polselli. Favato pled guilty to this murder, among others.

19. *Salvatore Carilli,* died 8/11/38: died of poison probably furnished by Paul Petrillo and administered by him or the victim's wife, Rose. The wife was found guilty of manslaughter in Wilmington, Delaware, and sentenced to imprisonment for five to ten years.

20. *Ferdinando Alfonsi,* died 10/27/38: died of poison provided by Herman Petrillo and administered by him and/or the victim's wife, Stella. Herman was convicted of first-degree murder in this case, but the conviction was reversed on appeal. Stella was acquitted. No other person was ever prosecuted for this death.

APPENDIX B:
DEFENDANTS AND CASE OUTCOMES

Defendants are listed alphabetically.

1. *Alfonsi, Stella:* trial October 23–28, 1939, acquitted.
   Accused of poisoning her husband, Ferdinando.
   Lawyers: R. P. Alexander; Frank J. Marolla

2. *Arena, Anna:* freed June 6, 1939, because of jurisdictional issues.
   Implicated in killing of her husband, Joseph.
   Lawyer: unknown

3. *Bolber, Morris:* pled guilty to first-degree murder, May 25, 1939.
   Pled guilty to murder of Romaine Mandiuk but suspected of complicity in many others.
   Sentenced to life imprisonment; died in prison February 9, 1954.
   Lawyer: Bernard R. Cohn

4. *Brandt, David:* pled guilty to second-degree murder, December 13, 1939.
   Pled guilty to delivering poison in case of Jennie Pino but may have aided in others.

Sentenced to imprisonment for two to twenty years; served minimum and paroled May 26, 1941.

Lawyer: Morton Witkin

5. *John Cacopardo:* trial in New York City in 1938, guilty of second-degree murder.

Accused of shooting and killing Molly Starace in a scuffle.

Sentenced to thirty years to life; Cacopardo obtained no immediate clemency for helping the Philadelphia DA and was not paroled from Sing Sing until August 20, 1953, after serving fifteen years; he went on to become an ordained minister and worked in that profession for many years. His sentence was commuted and parole ended in 1957.

Lawyers: Leo Healy; William B. Moore

6. *Carilli, Rose:* trial in Wilmington, Delaware, December 11–13, 1939, guilty of manslaughter.

Poisoned her husband, Salvatore.

Sentenced to imprisonment for five to ten years; release date unknown.

Lawyer: Joseph A. L. Errigo

7. *Carina, Rose:* trial November 27–December 2, 1939, acquitted.

Accused of poisoning her paramour, Peter Stea, but suspected in murders of two husbands and others. Sometime girlfriend of Paul Petrillo.

Lawyers: R. P. Alexander; Louis Lipschitz

8. *Cassetti, Dominick:* pled guilty to first-degree murder, September 7, 1939.

Poisoned his wife, Jennie.

Sentenced to life imprisonment; commuted January 27, 1953.

Lawyers: Joseph N. Bongiovanni, Jr.; Charles F. G. Smith

9. *Cerrone, Christine:* pled guilty to second-degree murder, December 8, 1939.
   Implicated in killing of Ralph Caruso.
   Sentenced to imprisonment for two to twenty years; release date unknown.
   Lawyer: Robert Hagen

10. *Cicinato, Gaetano:* freed June 6, 1939, because of jurisdictional issues.
    Implicated in killing of Joseph Arena and maybe others.
    Lawyer: unknown

11. *Crispino, Steve:* freed June 6, 1939, because of jurisdictional issues.
    Aided in drowning of Joseph Arena.
    Lawyer: unknown

12. *DiMartino, Susie:* pled guilty to second-degree murder, December 8, 1939.
    Implicated in killing of her husband, Guiseppi.
    Sentenced to imprisonment for three to twenty years; release date unknown.
    Lawyer: William Berkowitz

13. *Favato, Maria*:* pled guilty and stopped trial, April 21, 1939.
    Pled to poison murders of Charles Ingrao, Philip Ingrao, and Guiseppi DiMartino but may also have been implicated in murder of Antonio Romualdo.
    Sentenced to life imprisonment; release or death date unknown.
    Lawyer: Edward A. Kelly

---

*The first name of the woman referred to in this book as Maria Favato was actually Carina. Her name has been changed to avoid reader confusion with Rose Carina.

14. *Giacobbe, Camella (Millie):* trial November 27–30, 1939, guilty of first-degree murder.
    Implicated in murder of her husband, Antonio; sometime girl-friend of Paul Petrillo.
    Sentenced to life imprisonment; commuted March 5, 1956.
    Lawyers: Claude Lanciano; William L. Rubin

15. *LaVecchio (Davis), Sophie*:* pled guilty to second-degree murder, December 16, 1939.
    Implicated in murder of her husband, Luigi.
    Sentenced to imprisonment for ten to twenty years; release date unknown.
    Lawyer: unknown

16. *Mandiuk, Agnes:* trial January 20–23, 1941, guilty of first-degree murder.
    Implicated in killing of her husband, Romaine.
    Sentenced to life imprisonment; commuted December 24, 1954.
    Lawyers: R. P. Alexander; Frank Carano

17. *Miccichi, Providenza:* trial October 2–13, 1939, stopped by plea of guilty to first-degree murder.
    Implicated in the murder of Jennie Cassetti.
    Sentenced to life imprisonment; commuted February 17, 1954.
    Lawyer: Michael A. Spatola

18. *Muscelli, Emedio:* trial September 19–27, 1939, guilty of first-degree murder.
    Implicated in killing of Guiseppi DiMartino.

---

*The first name of the woman referred to in this book as Sophie LaVecchio was actually Rose. Her name has been changed to avoid reader confusion with Rose Carina.

Sentenced to life imprisonment; commuted April 18, 1958.
Lawyer: William Berkowitz

19. *Perlman, Dr. Horace:* pled guilty to second-degree murder,
February 26, 1940.
Pled guilty in case of Jennie Pino but implicated in others.
Sentenced to imprisonment for ten to twenty years; paroled
November 17, 1948.
Lawyer: Lemuel B. Schofield

20. *Petrillo, Herman:* trial March 13–23, 1939, guilty of first-
degree murder, but reversed on appeal. Retried May 2, 1940,
guilty of first-degree murder.
Found guilty of murdering Ferdinando Alfonsi in first trial
and Ralph Caruso in second trial but implicated in many others.
Sentenced to death and executed October 20, 1941.
Lawyers: Milton S. Leidner; Harry M. Berkowitz; Thomas D.
McBride

21. *Petrillo, Paul:* trial September 11–28, 1939, stopped by plea
of guilty to first-degree murder.
Pled to murder of Luigi LaVecchio but implicated in many
others.
Sentenced to death and executed March 31, 1941.
Lawyer: Lemuel B. Schofield

22. *Pirolli (Giovanetti), Grace:* trial September 25–27, 1939,
guilty of first-degree murder, but reversed on appeal; pled
guilty to second-degree murder.
Implicated in killing of husband, Pietro.
Sentenced to imprisonment for two to ten years; released for
time served June 30, 1941.
Lawyer: Michael Marchesano

23. *Polselli, Raphael:* pled guilty to first-degree murder, May 25, 1939; plea withdrawn, but pled to same again, September 6, 1939.

    Pled guilty in killings of Charles Ingrao and Guiseppi Di-Martino but implicated in Philip Ingrao and Romualdo cases as well.

    Sentenced to life imprisonment; died in prison November 27, 1953.

    Lawyer: Thomas Boylan

24. *Rodio, Dominick:* trial in Cape May, New Jersey, October 11–13, 1939, guilty of first-degree murder.

    Murdered Joseph Arena.

    Sentenced to life imprisonment; paroled September 21, 1954.

    Lawyer: John E. Boswell

25. *Romualdo, Josephine:* trial September 19–21, 1939, guilty of first-degree murder.

    Implicated in killing of husband, Antonio.

    Sentenced to death; sentence commuted to life by parole board; paroled December 9, 1958.

    Lawyer: Frank J. Marolla

26. *Sedita, Josephine:* pled guilty to fraud and practicing medicine without a license, December 12, 1945.

    Suspected in killing of Pietro Pirolli, but she evaded arrest until evidence was stale.

    Sentenced to one to two year's imprisonment; served one year.

    Lawyer: R. P. Alexander

27. *Sortino, Salvatore:* pled guilty to first-degree murder, May 25, 1939.

    Participated in killing of Ralph Caruso.

Sentenced to life imprisonment; released March 18, 1958.
Lawyers: William Cohen; R. P. Alexander

28. *Swartz, Joseph:* trial December 1939, stopped because of temporary insanity. Retried June 10–14, 1940, guilty of first-degree murder.
Murdered his mother-in-law, Lena Winkleman.
Died in prison before sentence could be imposed, September 15, 1940.
Lawyer: Marcus I. Hutkin

29. *Valenti, Caesar:* trial September 11–15, 1939, stopped on plea of guilty to first-degree murder.
Pled guilty to murder of Charles Ingrao but suspected in Woloshyn case.
Sentenced to life imprisonment; date of death or release unknown.
Lawyers: John Patrick Walsh; Samuel Weinrott

30. *Woloshyn, Marie:* freed December 11, 1939, because of lack of evidence.
Suspected in killing of her husband, John.
Lawyer: Abraham Koppleman

SOURCE NOTES AND
ACKNOWLEDGMENTS

The principal sources for this book are contemporary newspaper reports and trial records. It all really happened.

The major Philadelphia newspapers of the time, the *Inquirer,* the *Daily News,* the *Bulletin,* the *Ledger,* and the *Record,* all gave extensive coverage to the Great Arsenic Murder Ring from the time the story broke in 1938 until the final trial of Agnes Mandiuk in 1941. The *New York Times* and the *New York Daily News* also provided coverage and background feature stories. In addition to back copies of all these newspapers, which are available on microfilm at various libraries in New York and Philadelphia, I was able to consult the morgues of several now-defunct Philadelphia papers, which are preserved in archives. These newspaper morgues provide an invaluable research clipping service, collecting all the stories about the murders in convenient packets. They also have wonderful collections of original photographs taken by newspaper staff photographers, which are the sources of most of the illustrations in this book. The morgues of the late *Philadelphia Bulletin* and *Ledger,* as well as some older records of the *Inquirer* (which is very much alive and kicking) are preserved in the Urban Archives, Paley Library, Temple University. The morgue of the late *Philadelphia Record* is at the Historical Society of Pennsylvania.

For trial records, I was fortunate to find complete transcripts of testimony from several key trials (most notably those of Paul Petrillo and Herman Petrillo) as well as various legal briefs and pleadings in the archives of the Supreme Court of Pennsylvania. As a consequence of assistant DA Vincent McDevitt's theory of "system," the thousands of pages of transcripts from these trials include detailed testimony about virtually all the multitude of murders described in the book. These printed records were supplemented by interviews with several lawyers who participated in the cases: Frank Carano, Milton Leidner, Louis Lipshitz, and Michael Marchesano.

The case notes and records of Raymond Pace Alexander and a memorandum he wrote of his experience with these cases are marvelously preserved in the voluminous Alexander Collection at the Archives and Records Center of the University of Pennsylvania (a collection crying out to be mined for a full-length biography of this remarkable man and his equally remarkable wife). Vincent McDevitt has left no similar archive, but he did write a lengthy paper on his experiences, which was provided to me. Materials at the Jenkins Law Library of the Philadelphia Bar Association provided background information on these and other lawyers involved in the cases.

I owe a very special thanks to Leo and Ralph Alfonsi and to Grace Frances Buttacavoli, who so willingly offered memories of their mothers to me. My interviews with them were a revelation. The manner in which they have come to terms with and transcended these troubling events in their past is a tribute to the human spirit. I only hope that our meetings, in which we combined and shared the results of my researches and their recollections, were of value to them, as well. Thanks also to Joseph Buttacavoli for arranging the interview with his mother, Grace.

For personal recollections of Messrs. Alexander and Mc-
Devitt, I am indebted to the following persons who freely shared
their time and memories with me: Rae Alexander Minter (daughter of Raymond Pace Alexander), Margaret "Pixie" Biddle (daughter of Vincent McDevitt), David Berger, Louise Boyer Brinkley and
Sally Boyer, Gussella Gelzer, Judge Curtis Carson, Samuel Evans,
Harold Kohn, and Jerome Shestack.

For background on Passyunk, no resource could have been
more valuable than the patrons hanging out at Uncle Phil's, at the
corner of East Passyunk Avenue and Thirteenth Street (right next
to the former site of Paul Petrillo's tailor shop) and the longtime
Passyunk merchants, some of whom (or their parents) served Paul,
Rose, and the gang. They gave me a flavor of the district no written
record has preserved.

Johnny Cacopardo's story is more fully discussed in his book,
Show Me a Miracle, by J. Jerry Cacopardo and Don Weldon.

Thanks also to Ariel Berghash for sharing his knowledge of
matters Judaic, to Michael Meltsner for help with capital punishment legalities, and to Kathy Rose, photo printer *straordinario.*

As any work of history, this book owes its existence to libraries and archives, which would be useless without librarians
and archivists. Among that rare breed of helpful people, I would
like to thank in particular Laura Beardsley of the Historical Society
of Pennsylvania, who braved dirt and dust (and maybe asbestos)
to get photographs for me when I desperately needed them; Brenda
Wright of the Urban Archives at Temple University; and Mark
Lloyd and Martin J. Hackett of the Archives and Records Center
at the University of Pennsylvania.

My gratitude to my agent, Matt Bialer, who believed he could
sell this manuscript even when I didn't, and to my original editor
at St. Martin's Press, Tom Burke, another true believer.